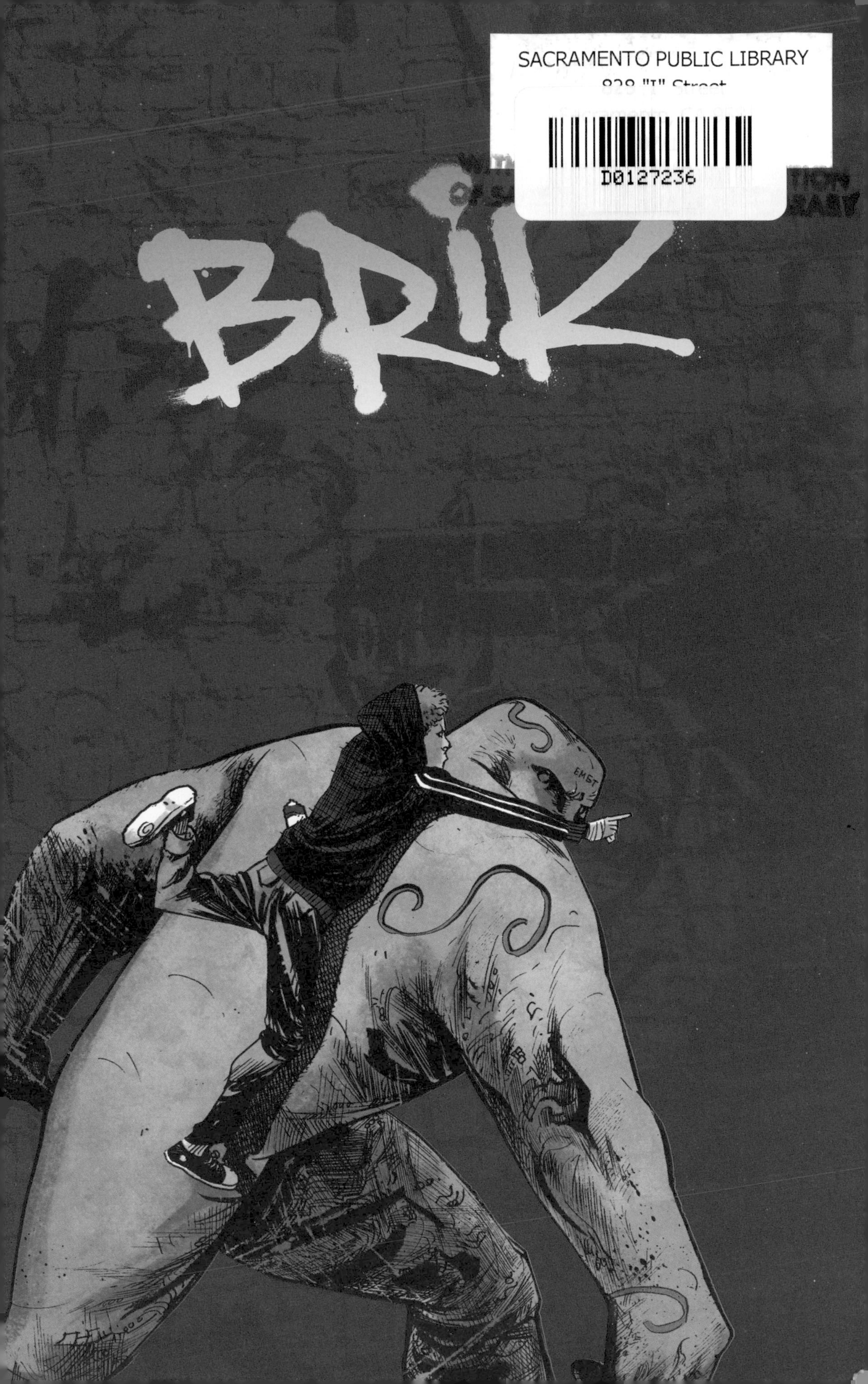
BRIK

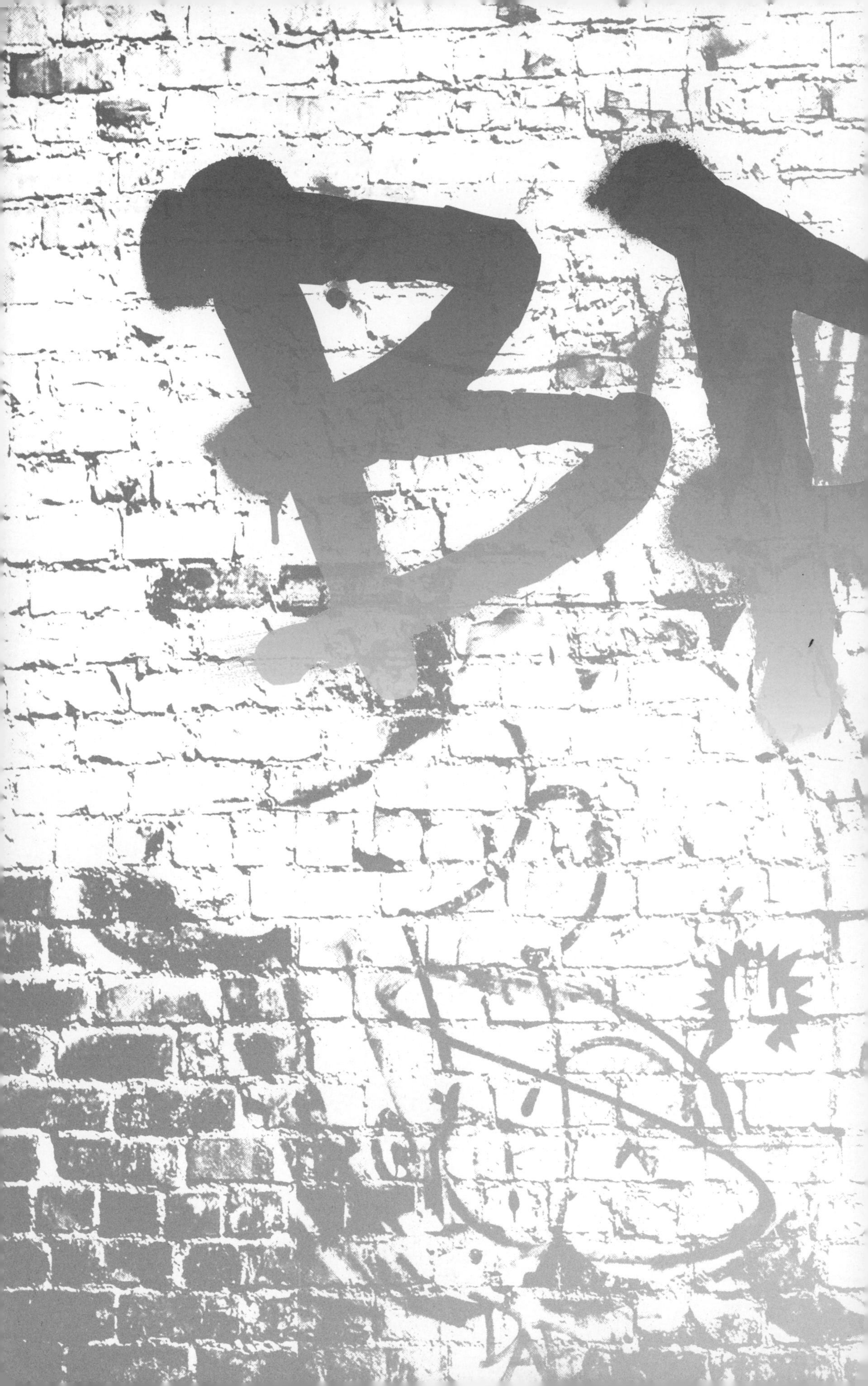

WRITTEN BY

ADAM GLASS AND MICHAEL BENSON

ILLUSTRATED BY

HARWINDER SINGH

COLORED BY

GONZALO DUARTE

DESIGNED BY

DYLAN TODD / BIGREDROBOT

LETTERED BY

MELANIE UJIMORI

EDITED BY

JAMES LUCAS JONES & BESS PALLARES

ONI PRESS

AN ONI PRESS PUBLICATION

PUBLISHED BY ONI PRESS, INC.

JOE NOZEMACK PUBLISHER
JAMES LUCAS JONES EDITOR IN CHIEF
ANDREW MCINTIRE V.P. OF MARKETING & SALES
DAVID DISSANAYAKE SALES MANAGER
RACHEL REED PUBLICITY COORDINATOR
TROY LOOK DIRECTOR OF DESIGN & PRODUCTION
HILARY THOMPSON GRAPHIC DESIGNER
ANGIE DOBSON DIGITAL PREPRESS TECHNICIAN
ARI YARWOOD MANAGING EDITOR
CHARLIE CHU SENIOR EDITOR
ROBIN HERRERA EDITOR
ALISSA SALLAH ADMINISTRATIVE ASSISTANT
BRAD ROOKS DIRECTOR OF LOGISTICS
JUNG LEE LOGISTICS ASSOCIATE

1305 SE MARTIN LUTHER KING, JR. BLVD.
SUITE A
PORTLAND, OR 97214

ONIPRESS.COM
  FACEBOOK.COM/ONIPRESS
  TWITTER.COM/ONIPRESS
  ONIPRESS.TUMBLR.COM
  INSTAGRAM.COM/ONIPRESS

@ADAMGLASS44
@MPBENSON
  GONZALODUARTE.COM
@MERUMORIMARU
  MERUMORI.COM
@BIGREDROBOT
  BIGREDROBOT.NET

ORIGINALLY PUBLISHED AS ISSUES 1-6 OF THE ONI PRESS COMIC SERIES *BRIK*.

FIRST EDITION: JUNE 2017

ISBN 978-1-62010-392-0
EISBN 978-1-62010-393-7

Library of Congress Control Number: 2016960955

1 3 5 7 9 10 8 6 4 2

PRINTED IN SINGAPORE.

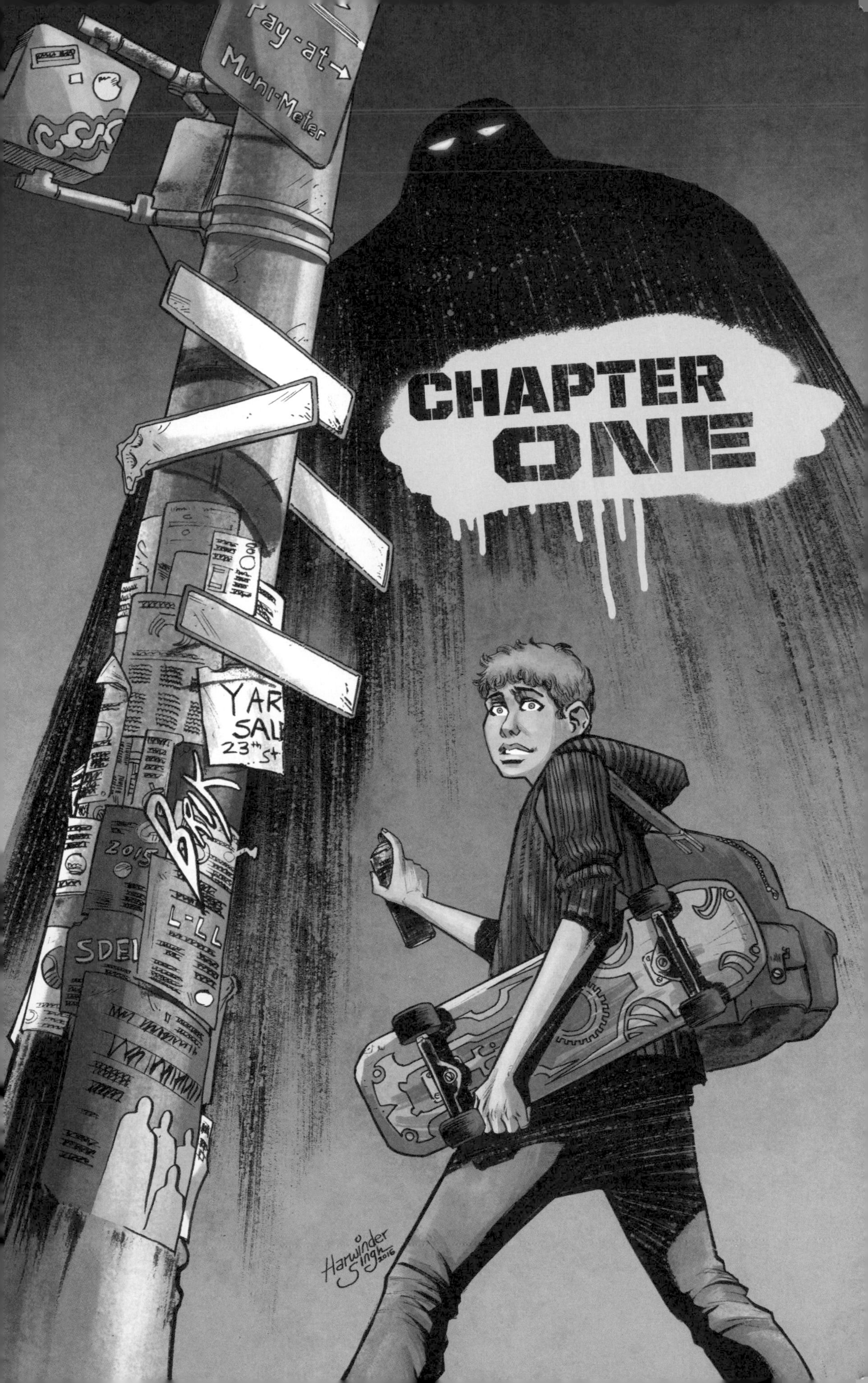
Pay-at-
Muni-Meter
CHAPTER
ONE
YAR
SAL
23th St
2015
L-LL
SDEI
Harwinder Singh 2016

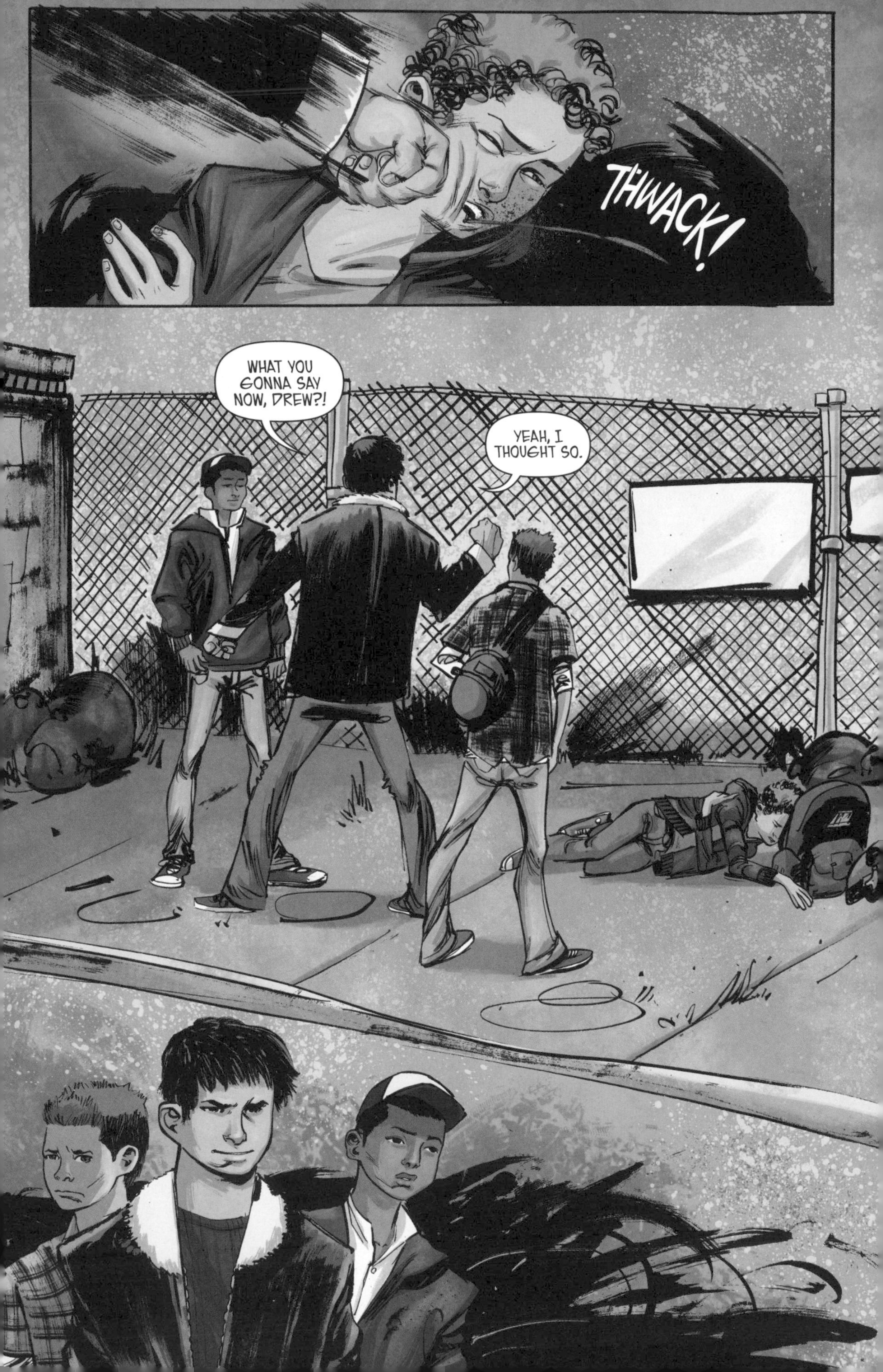
THWACK!
WHAT YOU GONNA SAY NOW, DREW?!
YEAH, I THOUGHT SO.

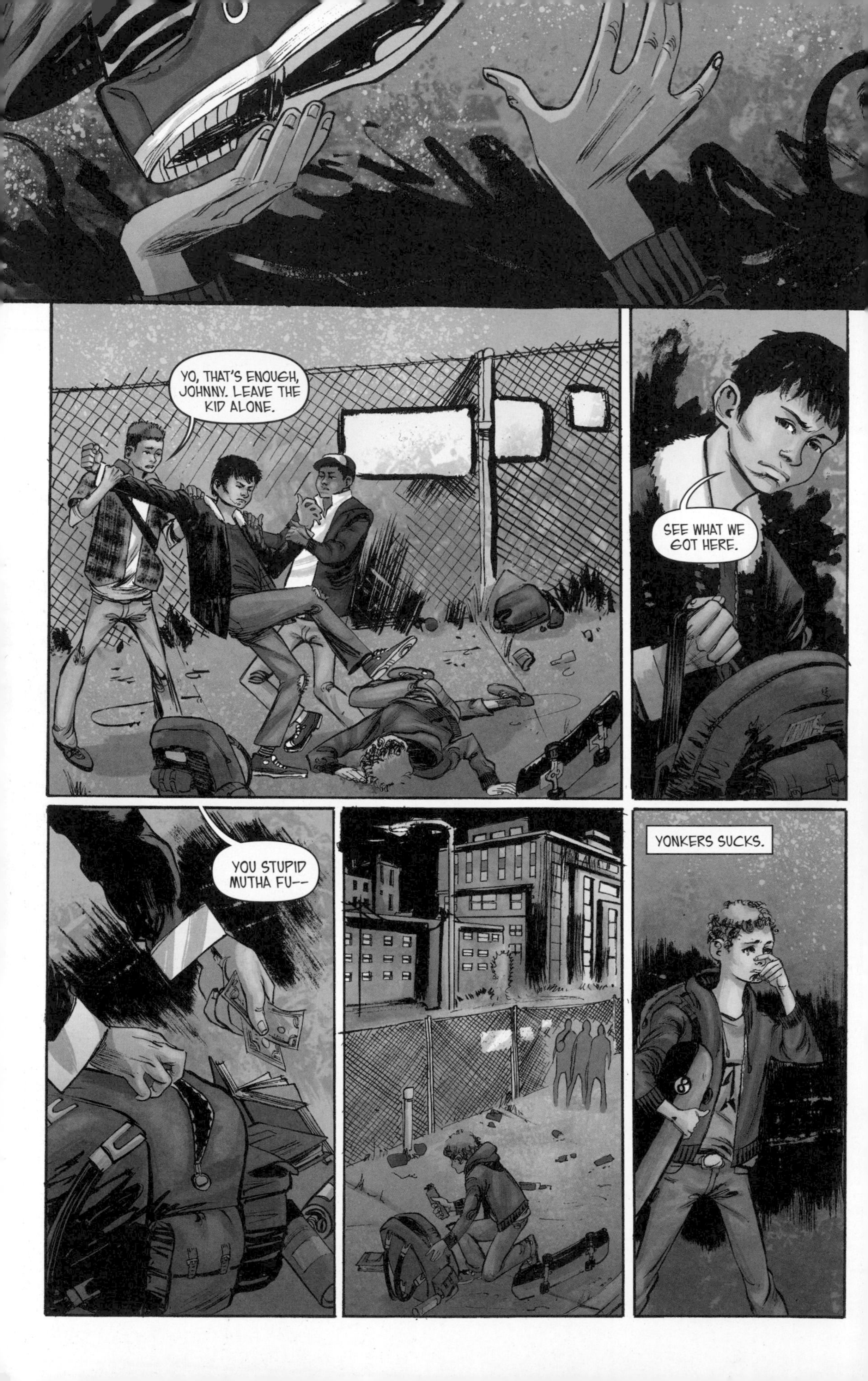
YO, THAT'S ENOUGH, JOHNNY. LEAVE THE KID ALONE.
SEE WHAT WE GOT HERE.
YOU STUPID MUTHA FU--
YONKERS SUCKS.

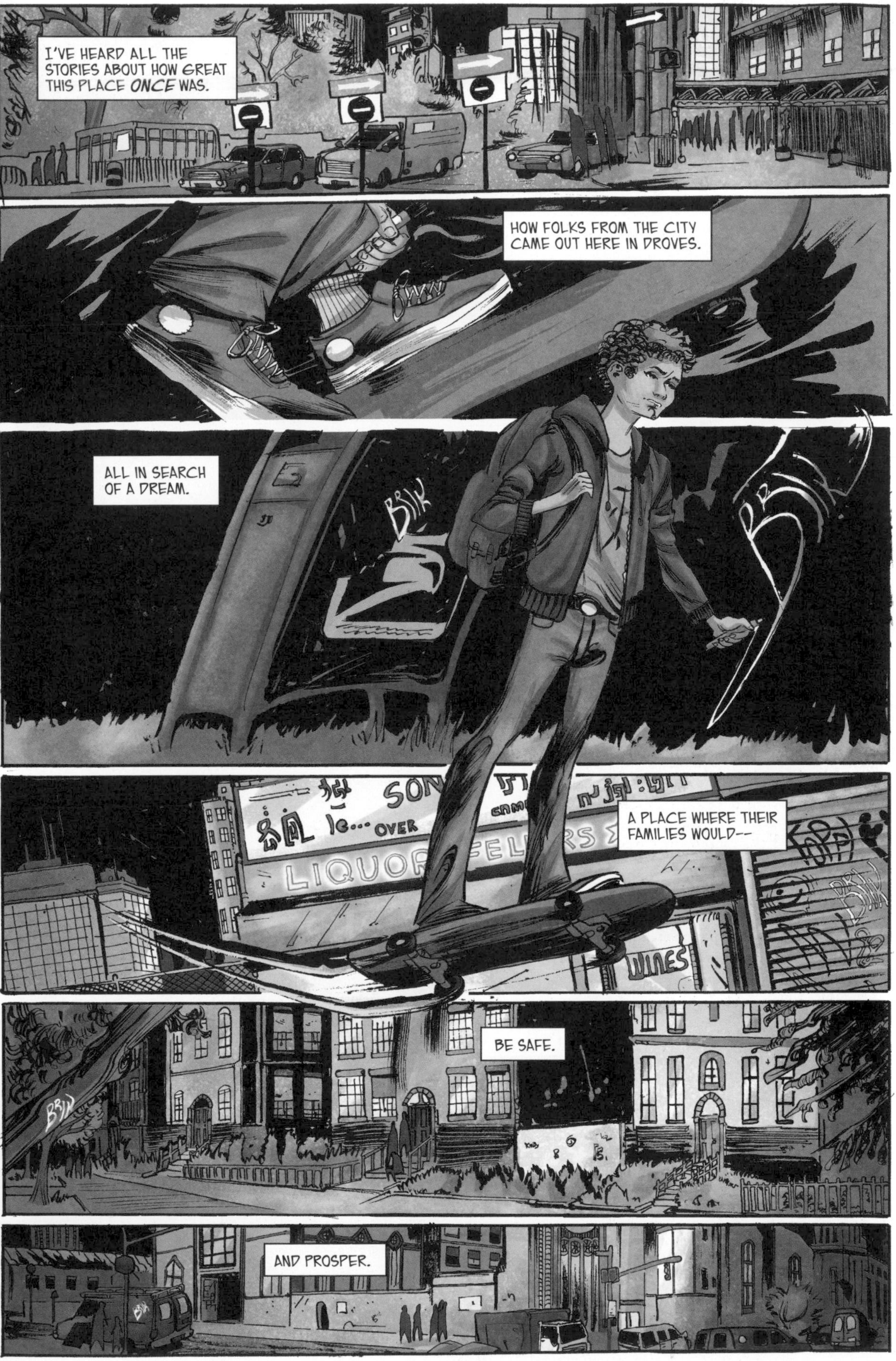
I'VE HEARD ALL THE STORIES ABOUT HOW GREAT THIS PLACE *ONCE* WAS.
HOW FOLKS FROM THE CITY CAME OUT HERE IN DROVES.
ALL IN SEARCH OF A DREAM.
A PLACE WHERE THEIR FAMILIES WOULD--
BE SAFE.
AND PROSPER.
LIQUOR
WINES

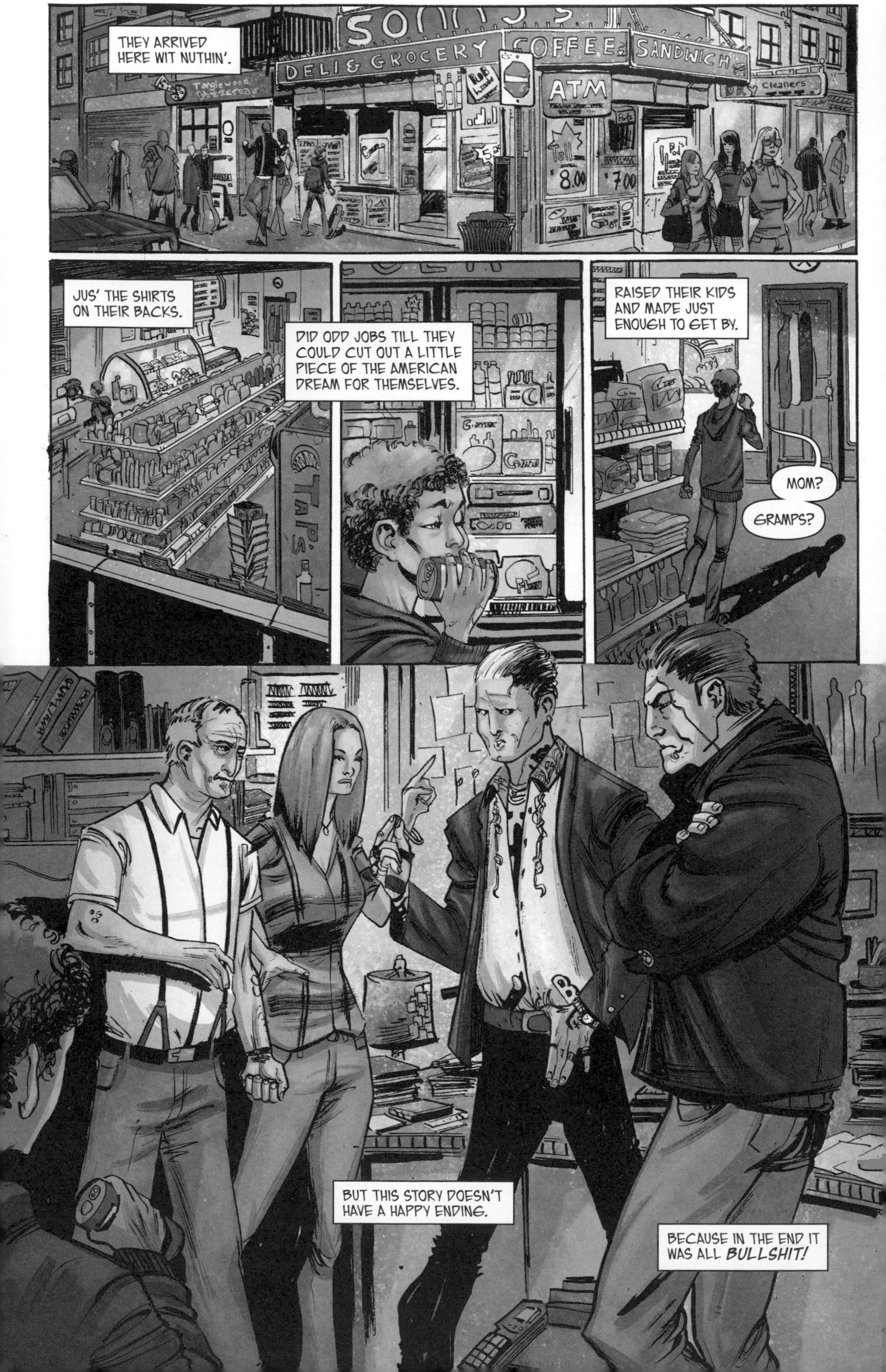
THEY ARRIVED HERE WIT NUTHIN'.
DELI & GROCERY
COFFEE
SANDWICH
ATM
Tanglewood Pozzeria
DRY Cleaners
JUS' THE SHIRTS ON THEIR BACKS.
DID ODD JOBS TILL THEY COULD CUT OUT A LITTLE PIECE OF THE AMERICAN DREAM FOR THEMSELVES.
RAISED THEIR KIDS AND MADE JUST ENOUGH TO GET BY.
MOM?
GRAMPS?
BUT THIS STORY DOESN'T HAVE A HAPPY ENDING.
BECAUSE IN THE END IT WAS ALL *BULLSHIT!*

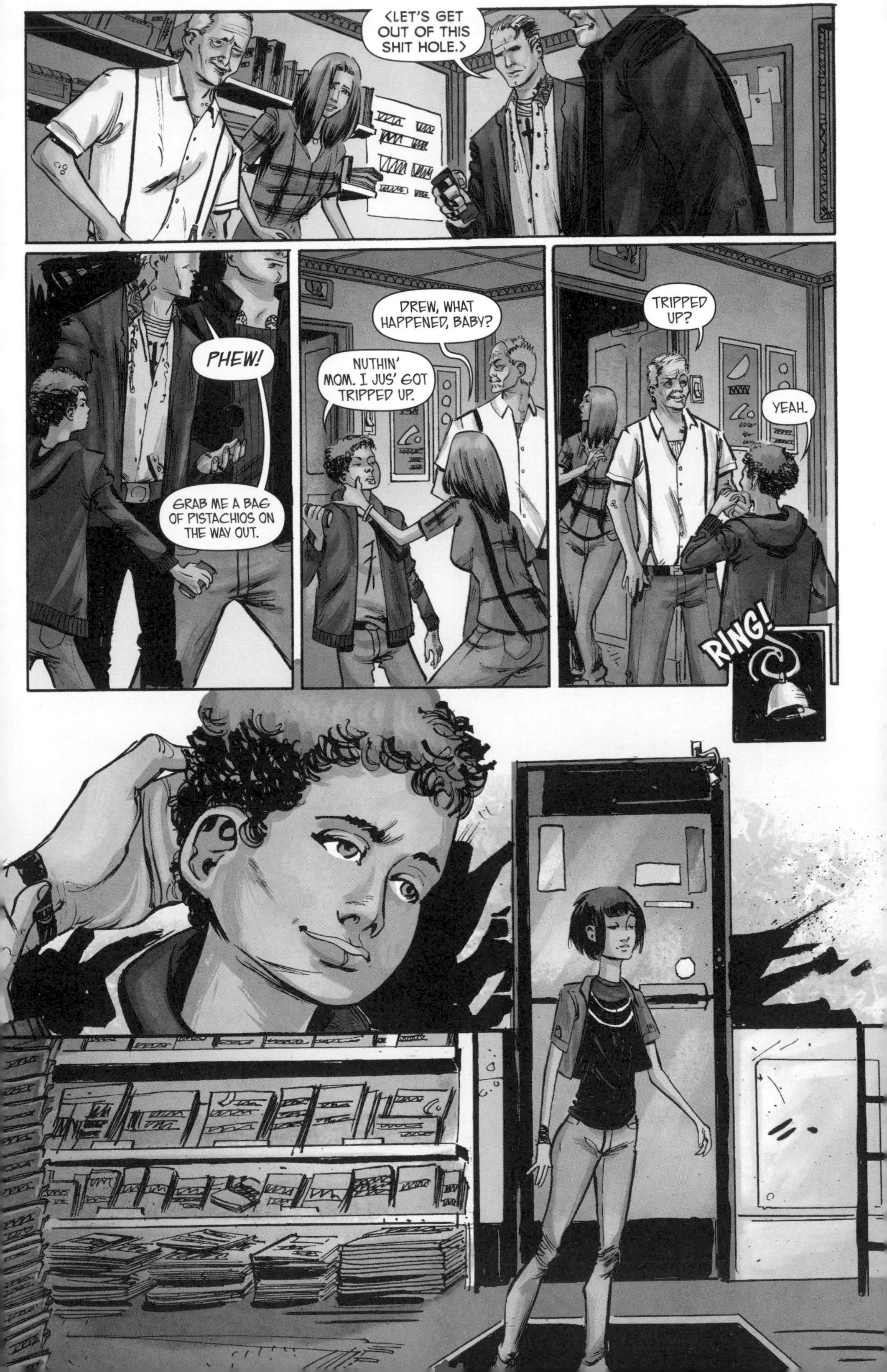

<LET'S GET OUT OF THIS SHIT HOLE.>
PHEW!
GRAB ME A BAG OF PISTACHIOS ON THE WAY OUT.
DREW, WHAT HAPPENED, BABY?
NUTHIN' MOM. I JUS' GOT TRIPPED UP.
TRIPPED UP?
YEAH.
RING!

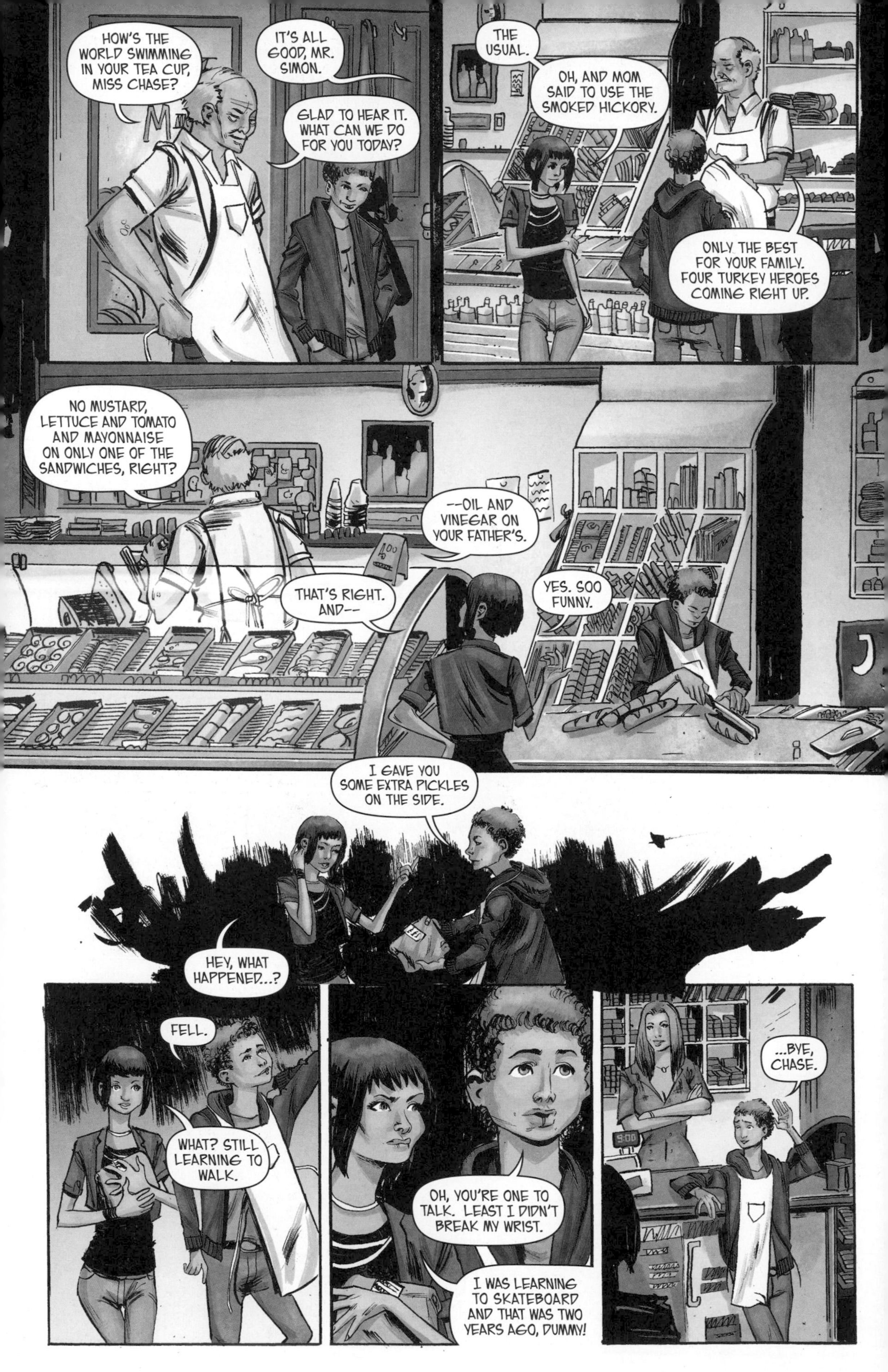
HOW'S THE WORLD SWIMMING IN YOUR TEA CUP, MISS CHASE?
IT'S ALL GOOD, MR. SIMON.
GLAD TO HEAR IT. WHAT CAN WE DO FOR YOU TODAY?
THE USUAL.
OH, AND MOM SAID TO USE THE SMOKED HICKORY.
ONLY THE BEST FOR YOUR FAMILY. FOUR TURKEY HEROES COMING RIGHT UP.
NO MUSTARD, LETTUCE AND TOMATO AND MAYONNAISE ON ONLY ONE OF THE SANDWICHES, RIGHT?
THAT'S RIGHT. AND--
--OIL AND VINEGAR ON YOUR FATHER'S.
YES. SOO FUNNY.
I GAVE YOU SOME EXTRA PICKLES ON THE SIDE.
HEY, WHAT HAPPENED...?
FELL.
WHAT? STILL LEARNING TO WALK.
OH, YOU'RE ONE TO TALK. LEAST I DIDN'T BREAK MY WRIST.
I WAS LEARNING TO SKATEBOARD AND THAT WAS TWO YEARS AGO, DUMMY!
...BYE, CHASE.

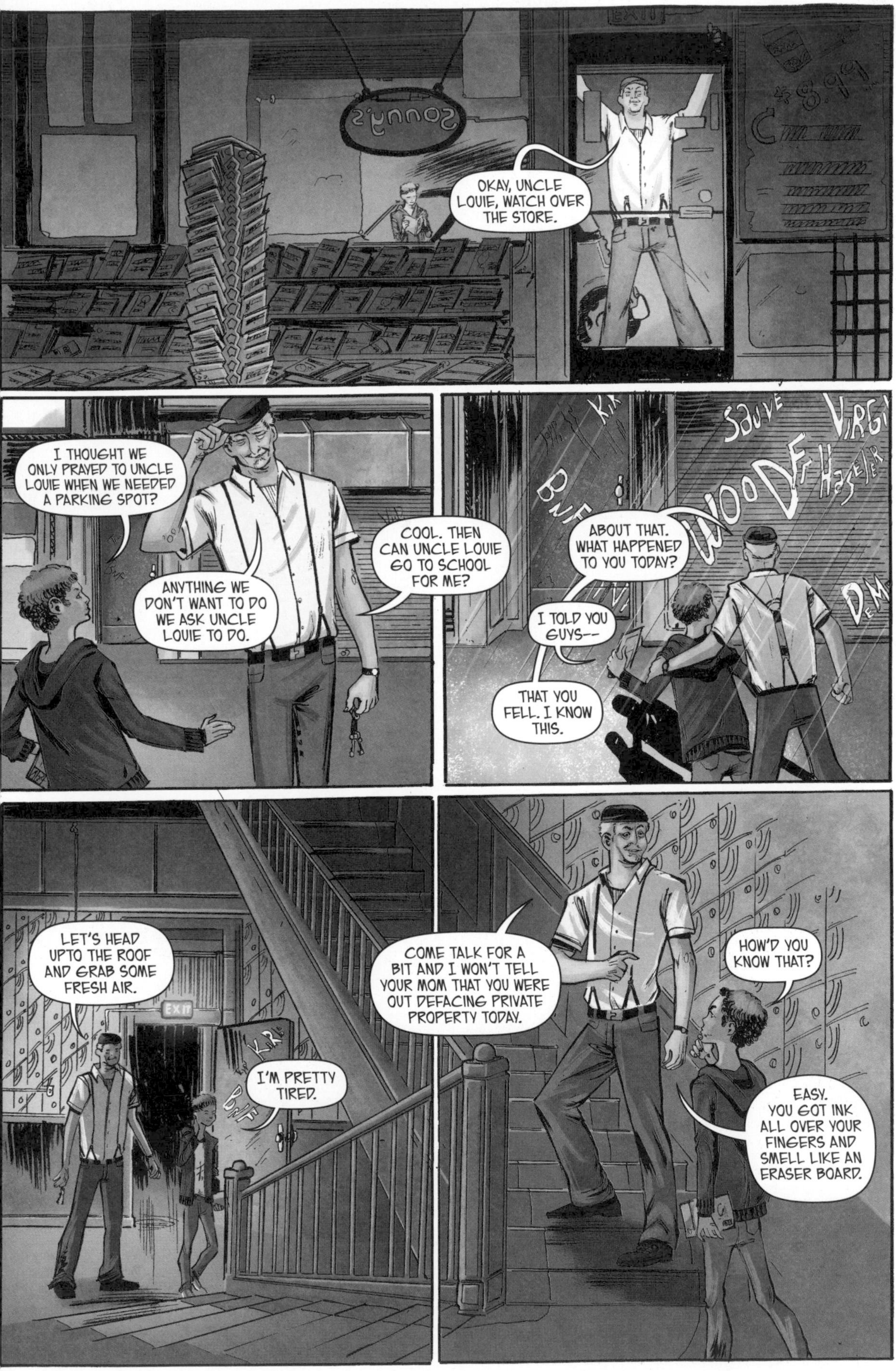
OKAY, UNCLE LOUIE, WATCH OVER THE STORE.
I THOUGHT WE ONLY PRAYED TO UNCLE LOUIE WHEN WE NEEDED A PARKING SPOT?
ANYTHING WE DON'T WANT TO DO WE ASK UNCLE LOUIE TO DO.
COOL. THEN CAN UNCLE LOUIE GO TO SCHOOL FOR ME?
ABOUT THAT. WHAT HAPPENED TO YOU TODAY?
I TOLD YOU GUYS--
THAT YOU FELL. I KNOW THIS.
LET'S HEAD UPTO THE ROOF AND GRAB SOME FRESH AIR.
I'M PRETTY TIRED.
COME TALK FOR A BIT AND I WON'T TELL YOUR MOM THAT YOU WERE OUT DEFACING PRIVATE PROPERTY TODAY.
HOW'D YOU KNOW THAT?
EASY. YOU GOT INK ALL OVER YOUR FINGERS AND SMELL LIKE AN ERASER BOARD.

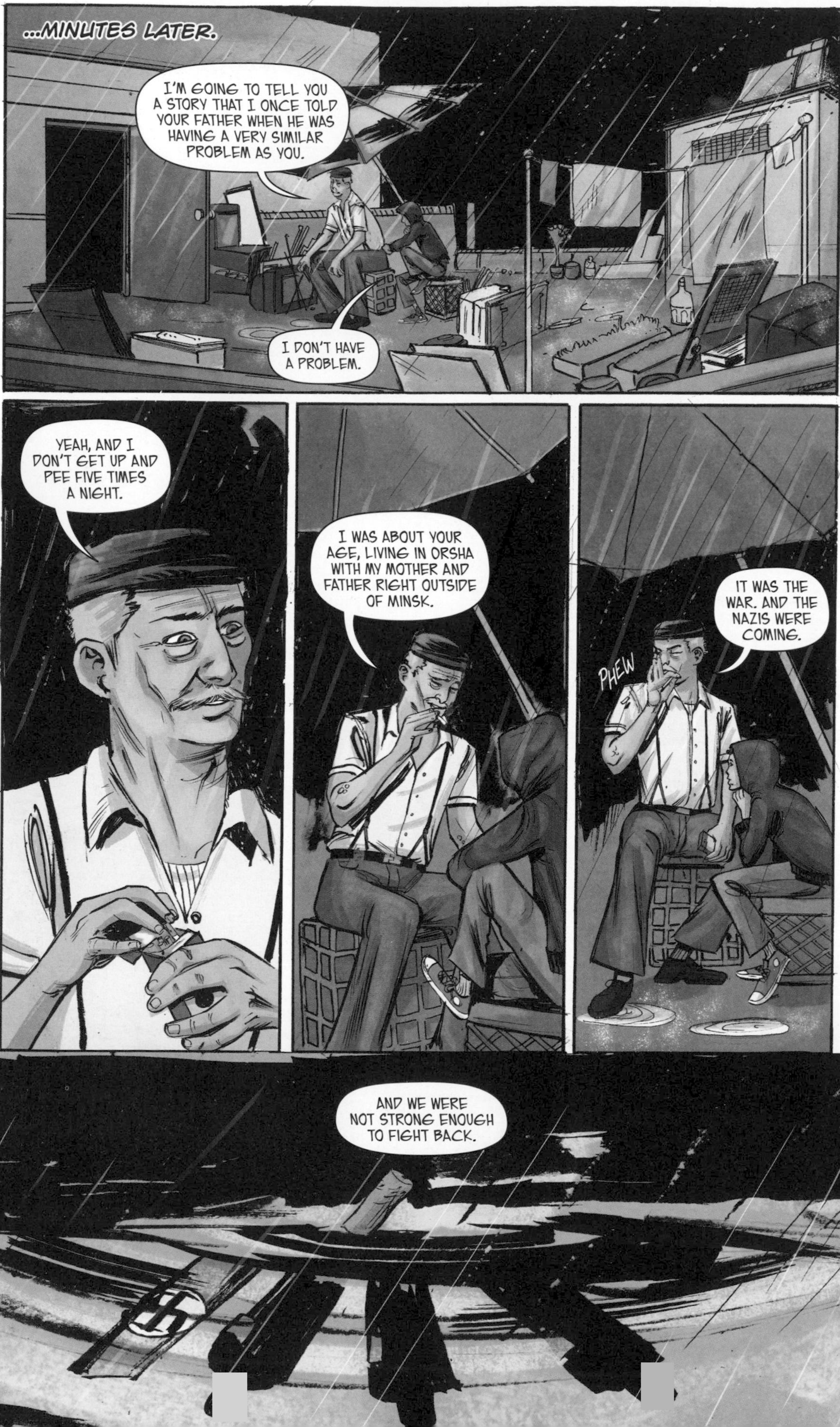
...MINUTES LATER.
I'M GOING TO TELL YOU A STORY THAT I ONCE TOLD YOUR FATHER WHEN HE WAS HAVING A VERY SIMILAR PROBLEM AS YOU.
I DON'T HAVE A PROBLEM.
YEAH, AND I DON'T GET UP AND PEE FIVE TIMES A NIGHT.
I WAS ABOUT YOUR AGE, LIVING IN ORSHA WITH MY MOTHER AND FATHER RIGHT OUTSIDE OF MINSK.
PHEW
IT WAS THE WAR. AND THE NAZIS WERE COMING.
AND WE WERE NOT STRONG ENOUGH TO FIGHT BACK.

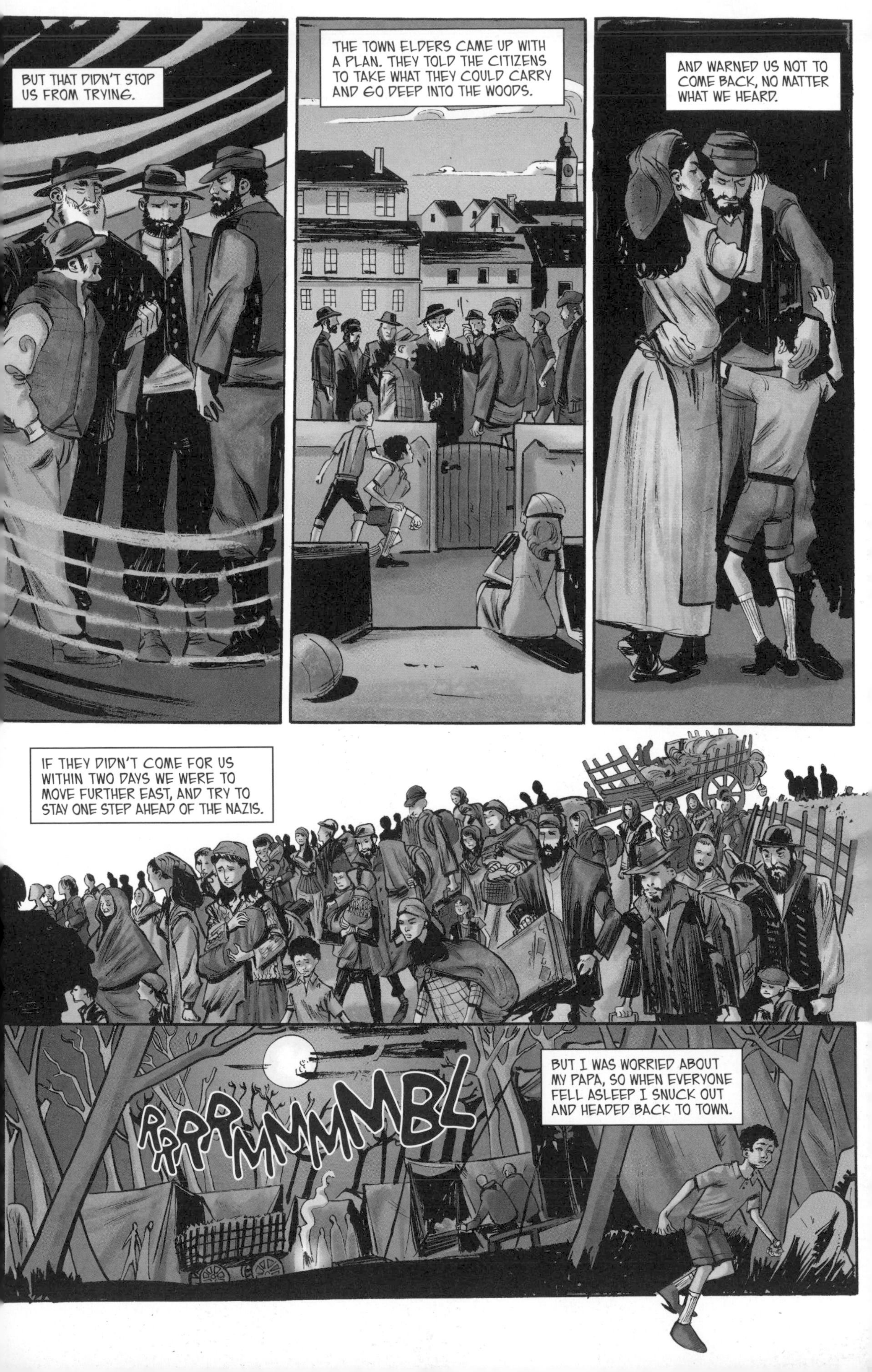
BUT THAT DIDN'T STOP US FROM TRYING.
THE TOWN ELDERS CAME UP WITH A PLAN. THEY TOLD THE CITIZENS TO TAKE WHAT THEY COULD CARRY AND GO DEEP INTO THE WOODS.
AND WARNED US NOT TO COME BACK, NO MATTER WHAT WE HEARD.
IF THEY DIDN'T COME FOR US WITHIN TWO DAYS WE WERE TO MOVE FURTHER EAST, AND TRY TO STAY ONE STEP AHEAD OF THE NAZIS.
RRRRMMMMMBL
BUT I WAS WORRIED ABOUT MY PAPA, SO WHEN EVERYONE FELL ASLEEP I SNUCK OUT AND HEADED BACK TO TOWN.

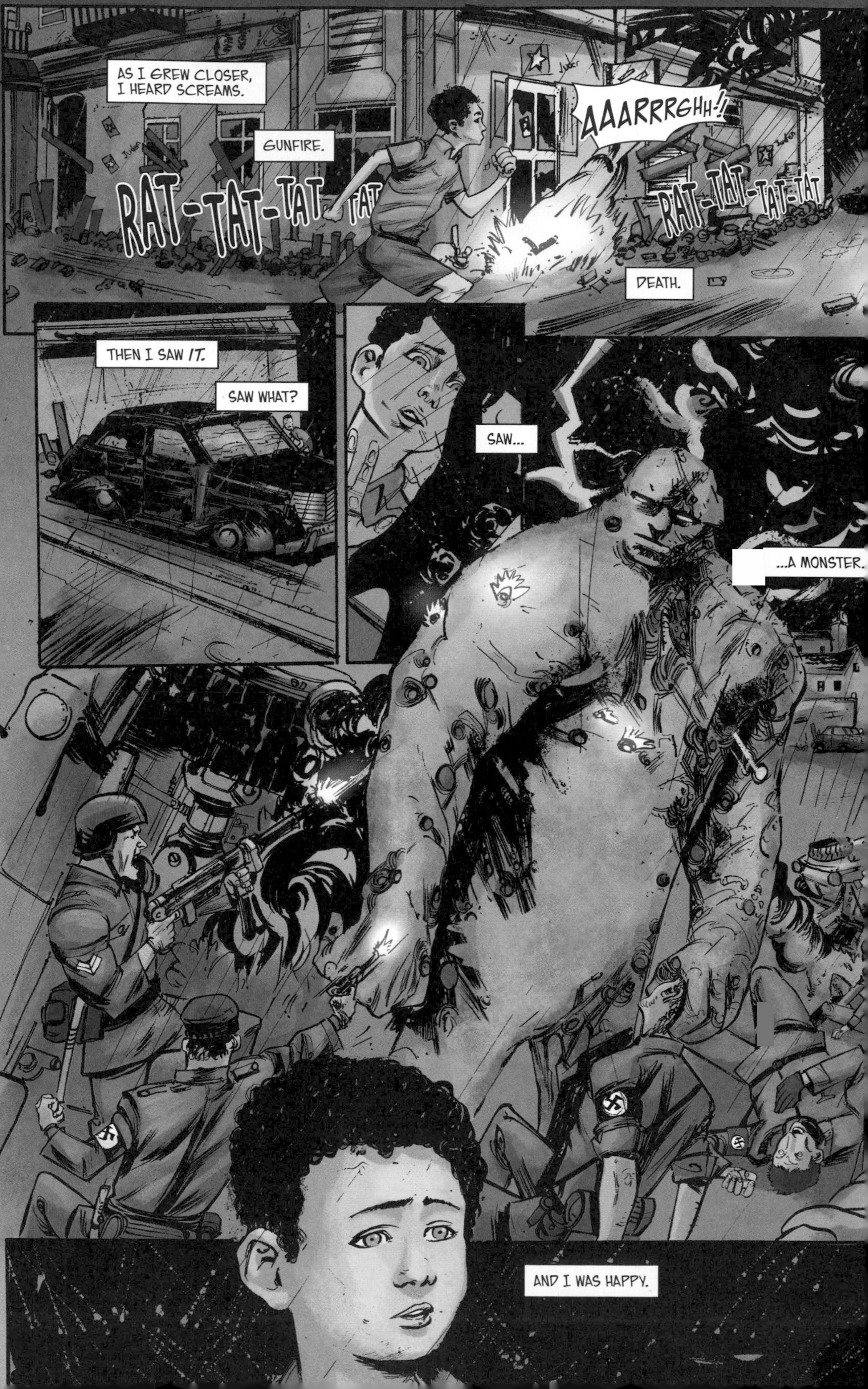
AS I GREW CLOSER, I HEARD SCREAMS.
GUNFIRE.
AAARRRGHH!!
RAT-TAT-TAT-TAT
RAT-TAT-TAT-TAT
DEATH.
THEN I SAW IT.
SAW WHAT?
SAW...
...A MONSTER.
AND I WAS HAPPY.

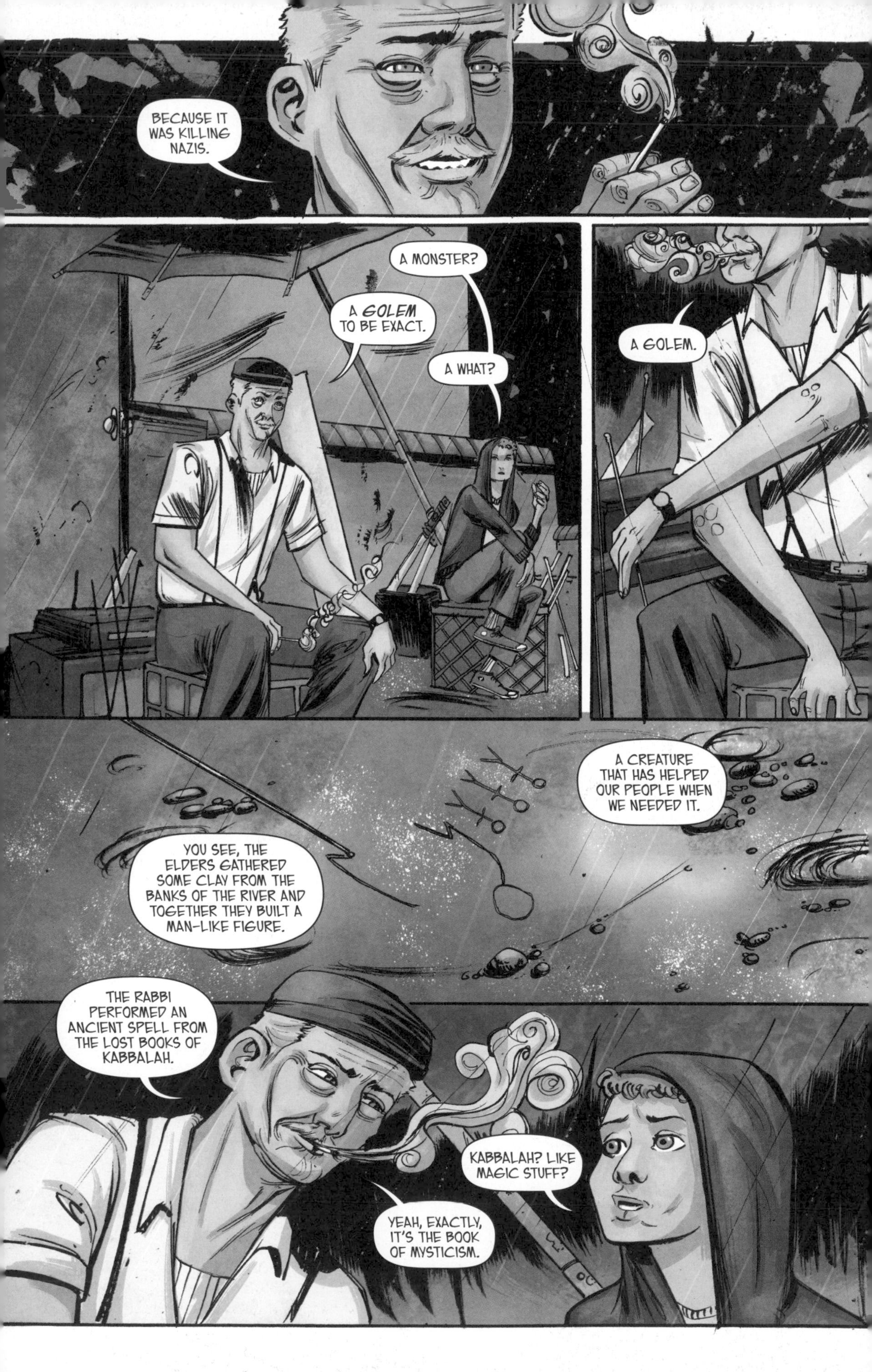
BECAUSE IT WAS KILLING NAZIS.
A MONSTER?
A GOLEM TO BE EXACT.
A WHAT?
A GOLEM.
A CREATURE THAT HAS HELPED OUR PEOPLE WHEN WE NEEDED IT.
YOU SEE, THE ELDERS GATHERED SOME CLAY FROM THE BANKS OF THE RIVER AND TOGETHER THEY BUILT A MAN-LIKE FIGURE.
THE RABBI PERFORMED AN ANCIENT SPELL FROM THE LOST BOOKS OF KABBALAH.
KABBALAH? LIKE MAGIC STUFF?
YEAH, EXACTLY, IT'S THE BOOK OF MYSTICISM.

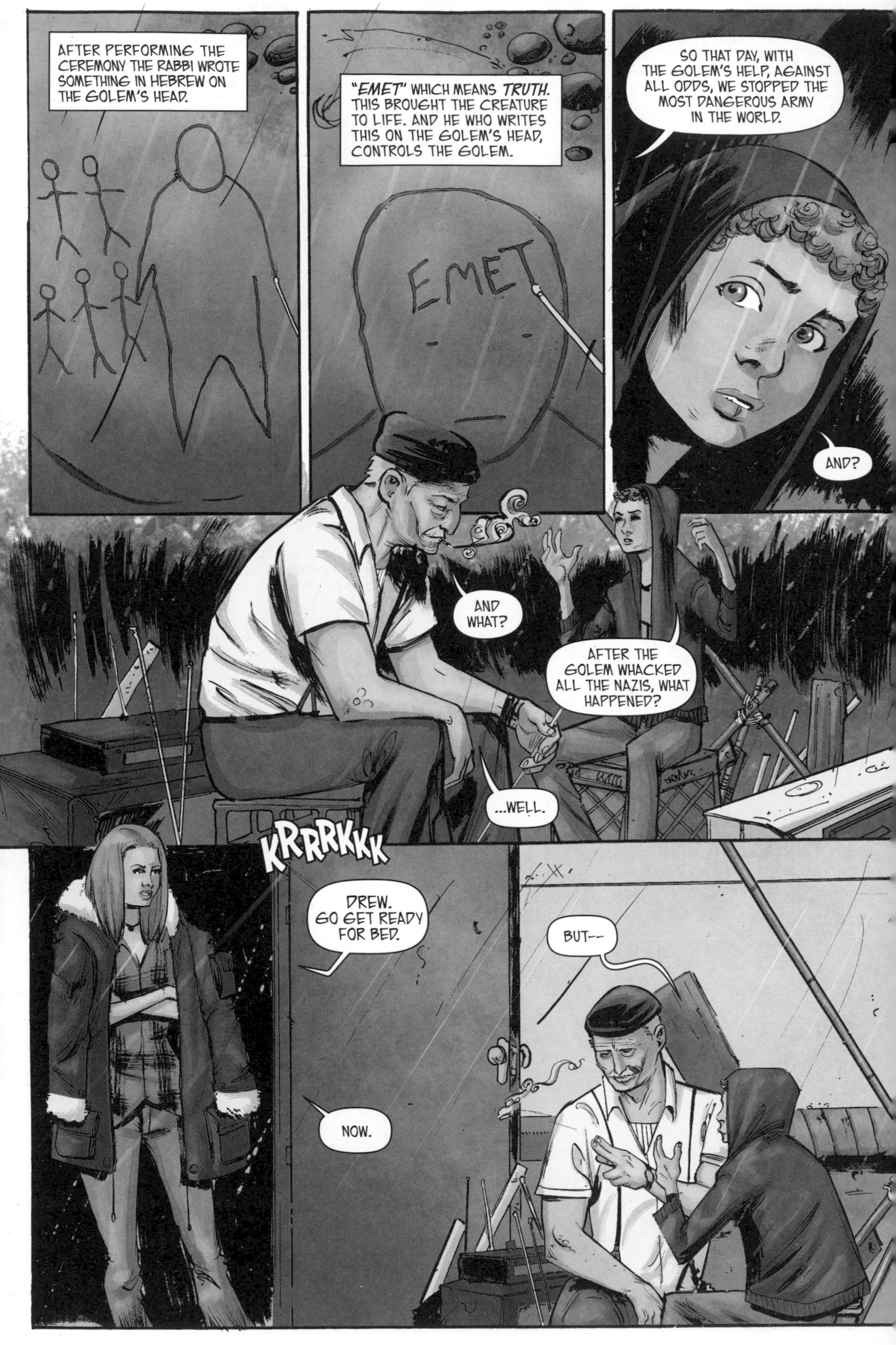
AFTER PERFORMING THE CEREMONY THE RABBI WROTE SOMETHING IN HEBREW ON THE GOLEM'S HEAD.
"EMET" WHICH MEANS TRUTH. THIS BROUGHT THE CREATURE TO LIFE. AND HE WHO WRITES THIS ON THE GOLEM'S HEAD, CONTROLS THE GOLEM.
EMET
SO THAT DAY, WITH THE GOLEM'S HELP, AGAINST ALL ODDS, WE STOPPED THE MOST DANGEROUS ARMY IN THE WORLD.
AND?
AND WHAT?
AFTER THE GOLEM WHACKED ALL THE NAZIS, WHAT HAPPENED?
...WELL.
KRRRKKK
DREW. GO GET READY FOR BED.
BUT--
NOW.

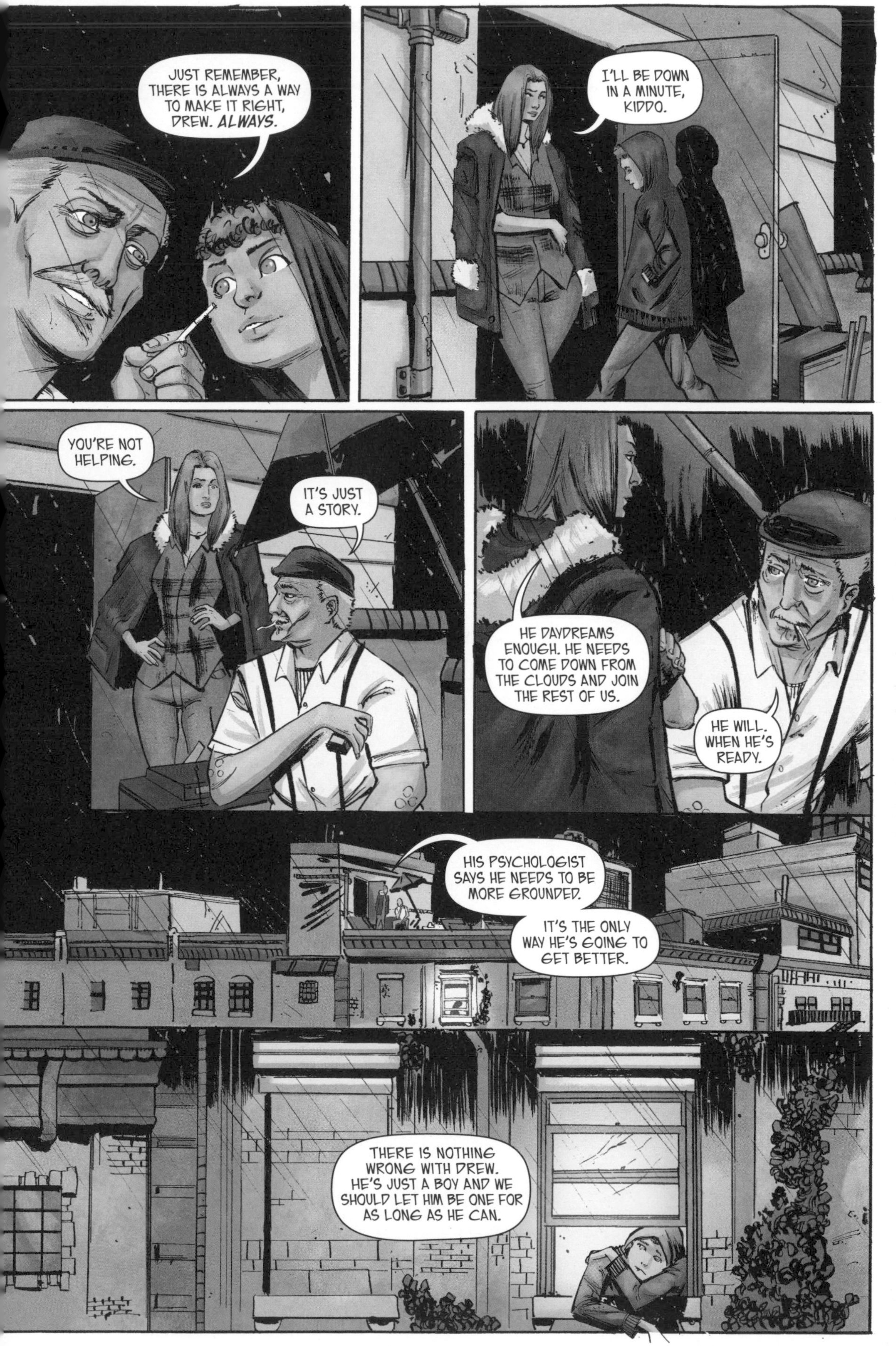
JUST REMEMBER, THERE IS ALWAYS A WAY TO MAKE IT RIGHT, DREW. *ALWAYS.*
I'LL BE DOWN IN A MINUTE, KIDDO.
YOU'RE NOT HELPING.
IT'S JUST A STORY.
HE DAYDREAMS ENOUGH. HE NEEDS TO COME DOWN FROM THE CLOUDS AND JOIN THE REST OF US.
HE WILL. WHEN HE'S READY.
HIS PSYCHOLOGIST SAYS HE NEEDS TO BE MORE GROUNDED.
IT'S THE ONLY WAY HE'S GOING TO GET BETTER.
THERE IS NOTHING WRONG WITH DREW. HE'S JUST A BOY AND WE SHOULD LET HIM BE ONE FOR AS LONG AS HE CAN.

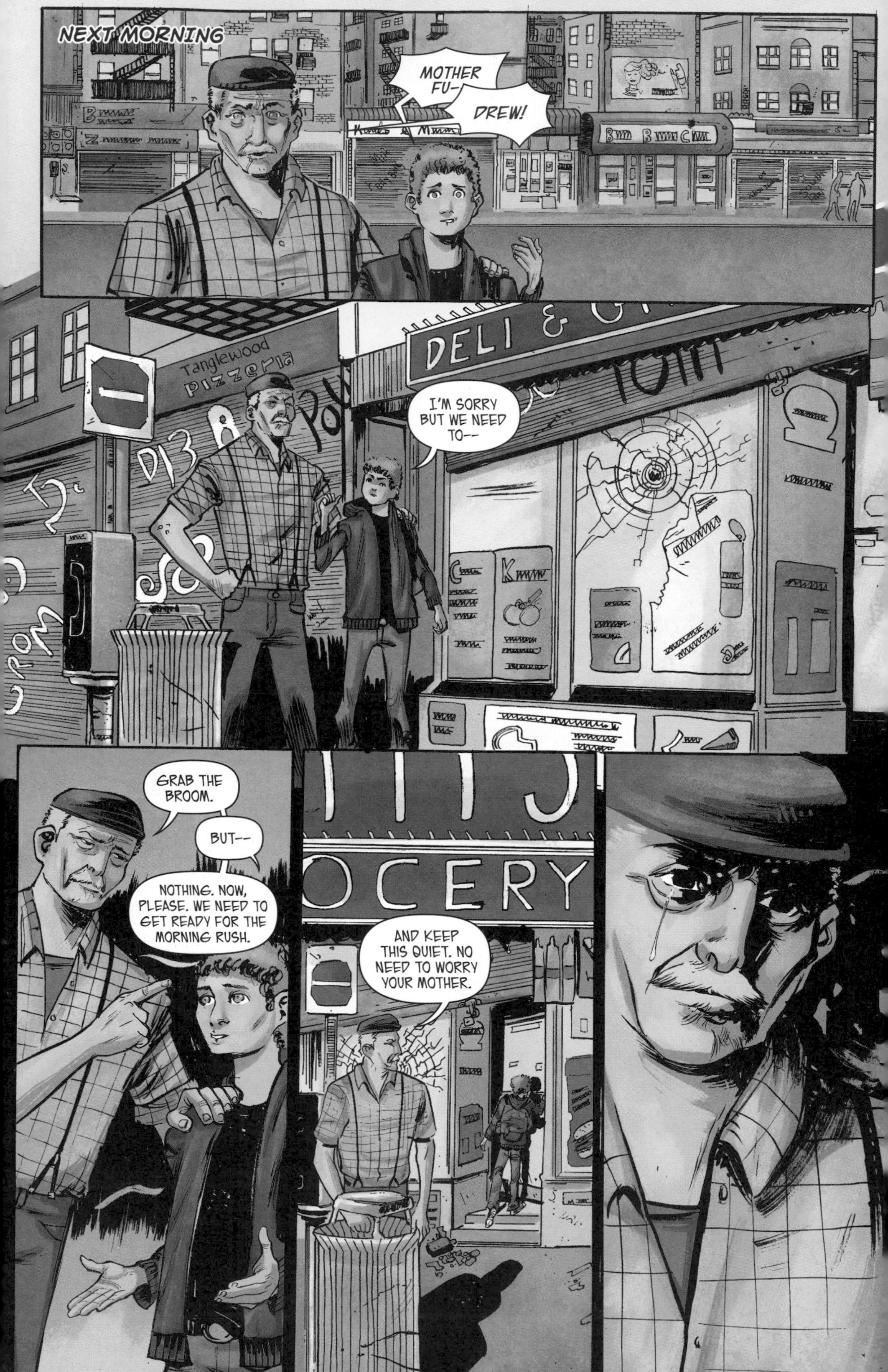
NEXT MORNING
MOTHER FU–
DREW!
Tanglewood Pizzeria
DELI &
I'M SORRY BUT WE NEED TO––
GRAB THE BROOM.
BUT––
NOTHING. NOW, PLEASE. WE NEED TO GET READY FOR THE MORNING RUSH.
OCERY
AND KEEP THIS QUIET. NO NEED TO WORRY YOUR MOTHER.

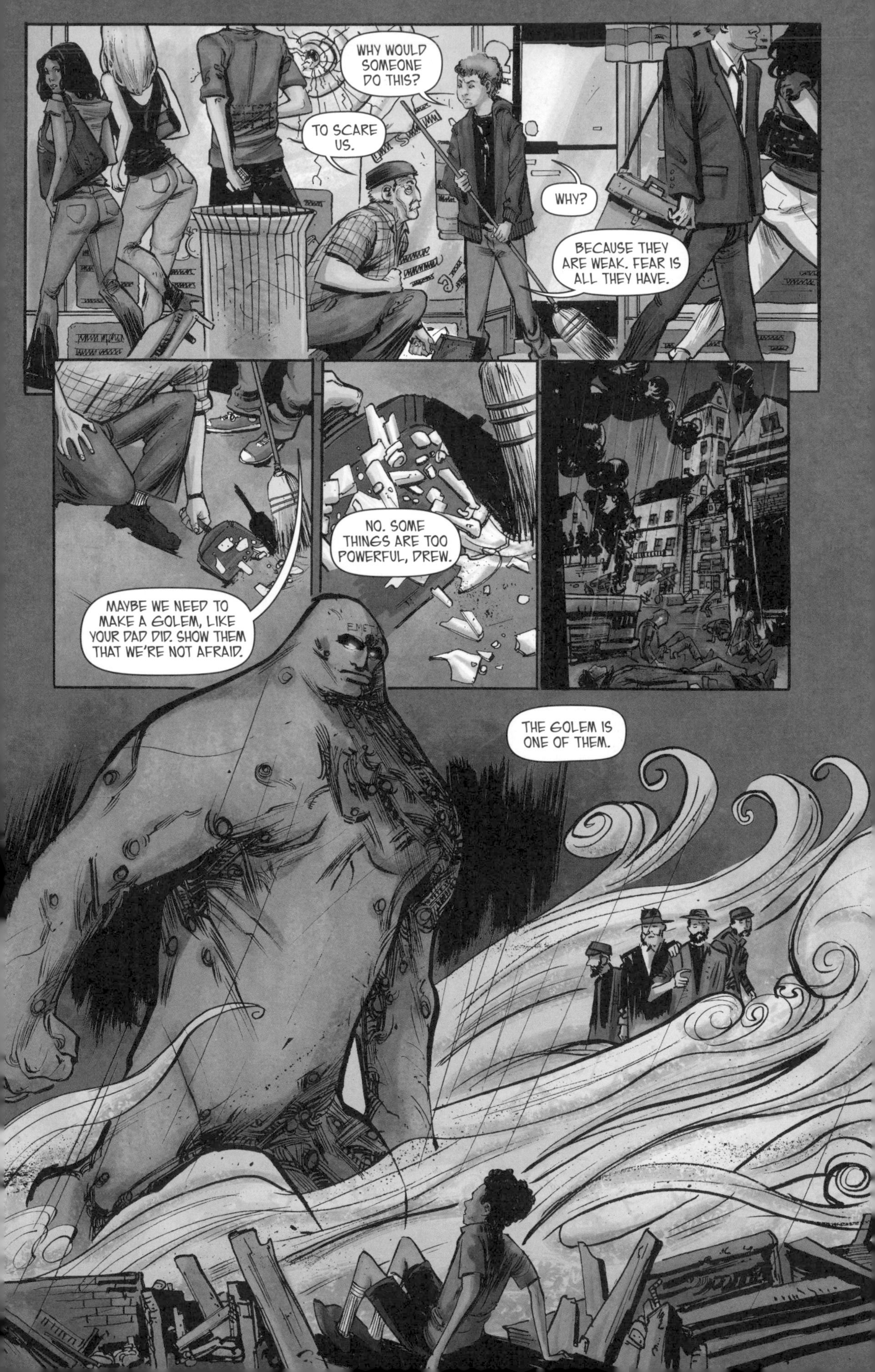
WHY WOULD SOMEONE DO THIS?
TO SCARE US.
WHY?
BECAUSE THEY ARE WEAK. FEAR IS ALL THEY HAVE.
MAYBE WE NEED TO MAKE A GOLEM, LIKE YOUR DAD DID. SHOW THEM THAT WE'RE NOT AFRAID.
NO. SOME THINGS ARE TOO POWERFUL, DREW.
THE GOLEM IS ONE OF THEM.
EMET

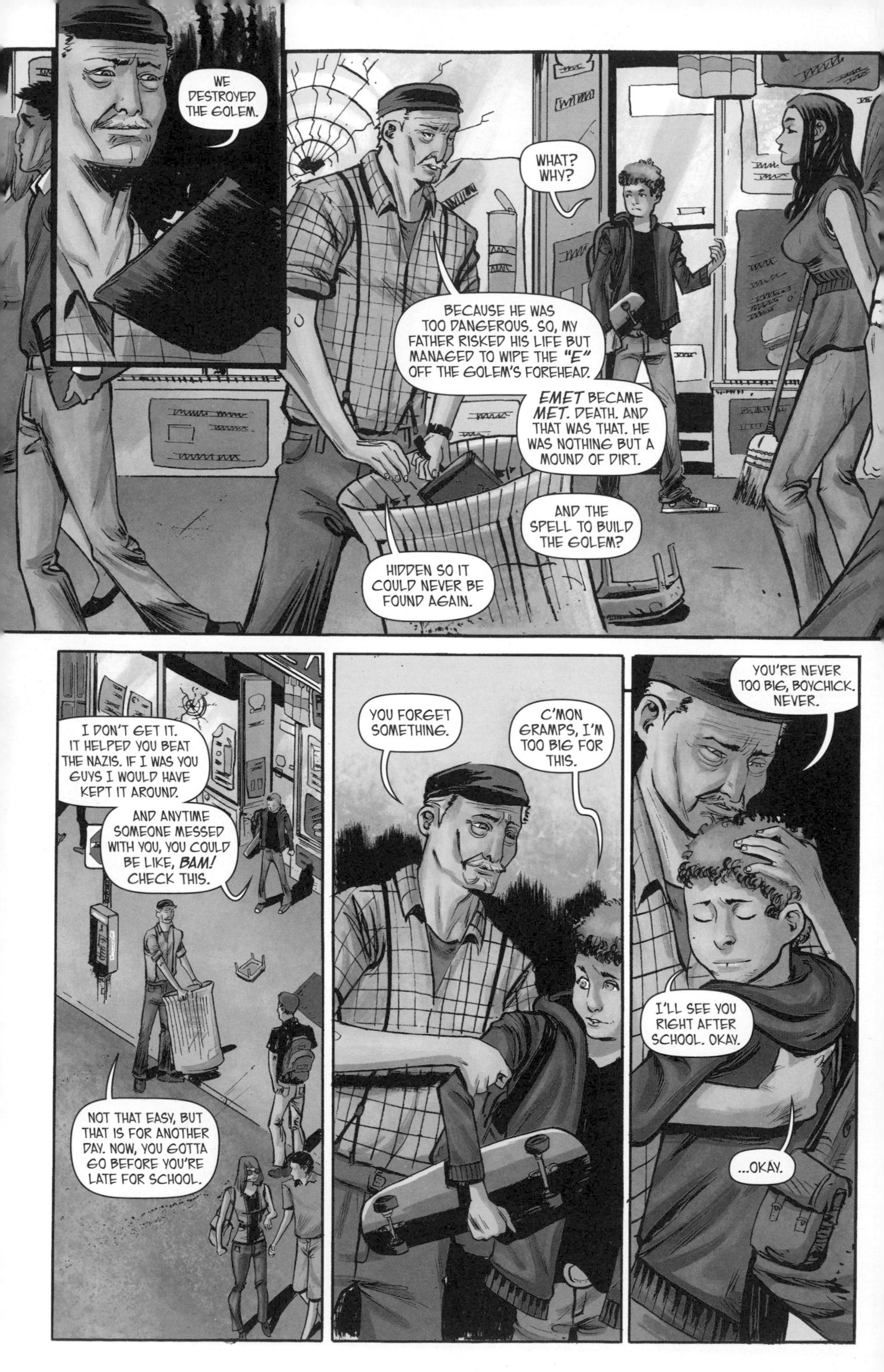
WE DESTROYED THE GOLEM.
WHAT? WHY?
BECAUSE HE WAS TOO DANGEROUS. SO, MY FATHER RISKED HIS LIFE BUT MANAGED TO WIPE THE "E" OFF THE GOLEM'S FOREHEAD.
EMET BECAME MET. DEATH. AND THAT WAS THAT. HE WAS NOTHING BUT A MOUND OF DIRT.
AND THE SPELL TO BUILD THE GOLEM?
HIDDEN SO IT COULD NEVER BE FOUND AGAIN.
I DON'T GET IT. IT HELPED YOU BEAT THE NAZIS. IF I WAS YOU GUYS I WOULD HAVE KEPT IT AROUND.
AND ANYTIME SOMEONE MESSED WITH YOU, YOU COULD BE LIKE, BAM! CHECK THIS.
NOT THAT EASY, BUT THAT IS FOR ANOTHER DAY. NOW, YOU GOTTA GO BEFORE YOU'RE LATE FOR SCHOOL.
YOU FORGET SOMETHING.
C'MON GRAMPS, I'M TOO BIG FOR THIS.
YOU'RE NEVER TOO BIG, BOYCHICK. NEVER.
I'LL SEE YOU RIGHT AFTER SCHOOL. OKAY.
...OKAY.

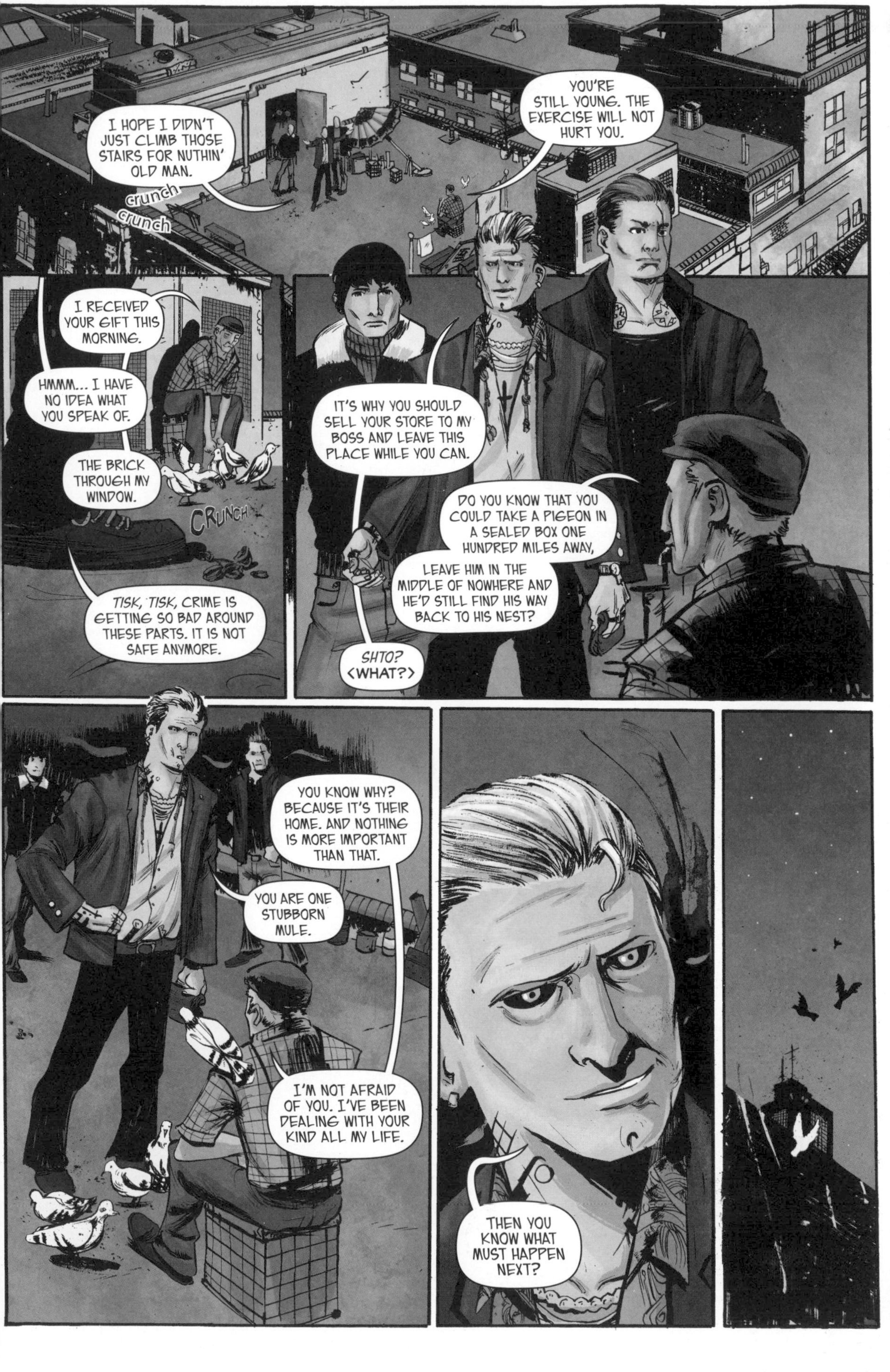
I HOPE I DIDN'T JUST CLIMB THOSE STAIRS FOR NUTHIN' OLD MAN.
crunch
crunch
YOU'RE STILL YOUNG. THE EXERCISE WILL NOT HURT YOU.
I RECEIVED YOUR GIFT THIS MORNING.
HMMM... I HAVE NO IDEA WHAT YOU SPEAK OF.
THE BRICK THROUGH MY WINDOW.
CRUNCH
TISK, TISK, CRIME IS GETTING SO BAD AROUND THESE PARTS. IT IS NOT SAFE ANYMORE.
IT'S WHY YOU SHOULD SELL YOUR STORE TO MY BOSS AND LEAVE THIS PLACE WHILE YOU CAN.
DO YOU KNOW THAT YOU COULD TAKE A PIGEON IN A SEALED BOX ONE HUNDRED MILES AWAY,
LEAVE HIM IN THE MIDDLE OF NOWHERE AND HE'D STILL FIND HIS WAY BACK TO HIS NEST?
SHTO? <WHAT?>
YOU KNOW WHY? BECAUSE IT'S THEIR HOME. AND NOTHING IS MORE IMPORTANT THAN THAT.
YOU ARE ONE STUBBORN MULE.
I'M NOT AFRAID OF YOU. I'VE BEEN DEALING WITH YOUR KIND ALL MY LIFE.
THEN YOU KNOW WHAT MUST HAPPEN NEXT?

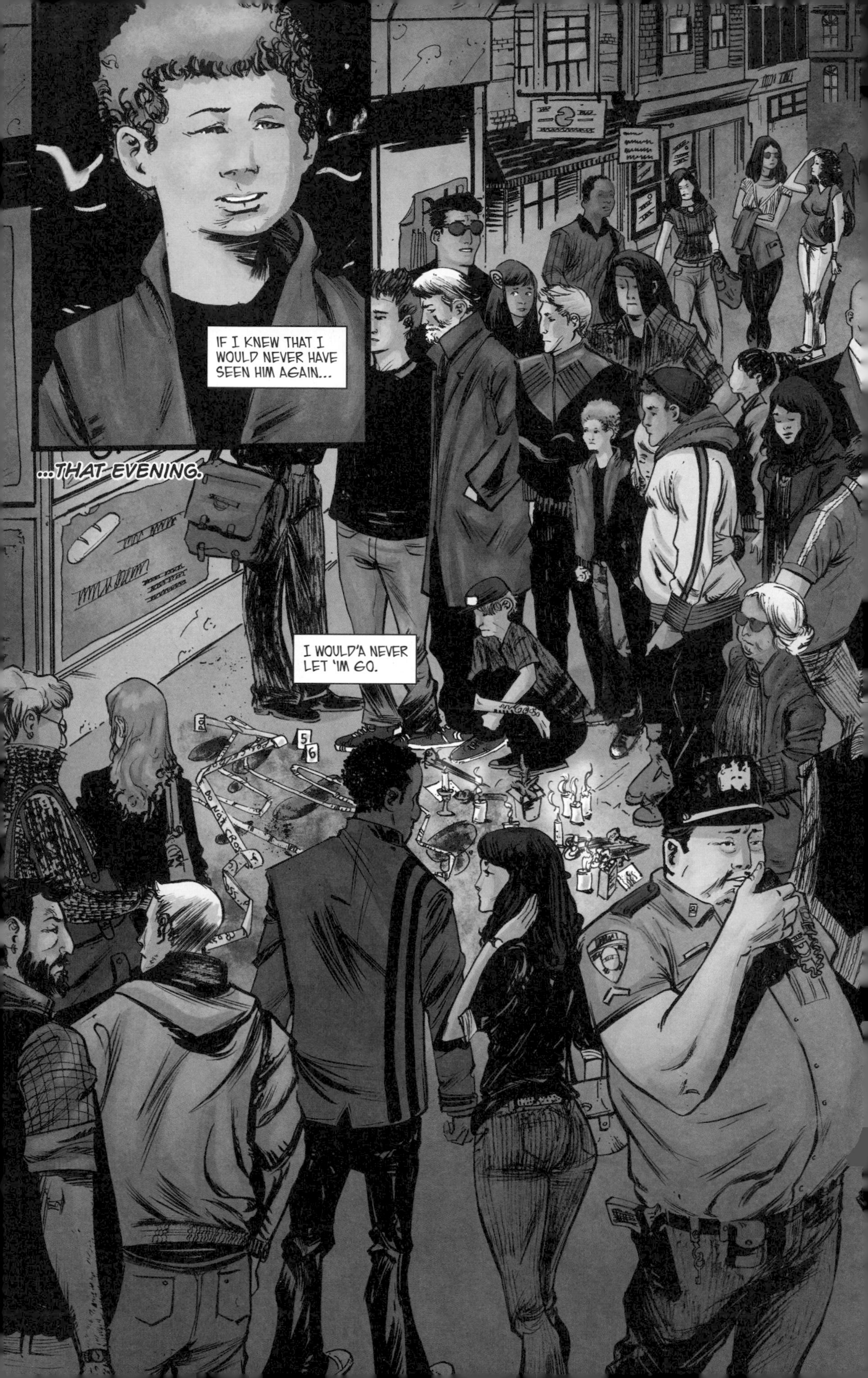
IF I KNEW THAT I WOULD NEVER HAVE SEEN HIM AGAIN...
...THAT EVENING.
I WOULD'A NEVER LET 'IM GO.

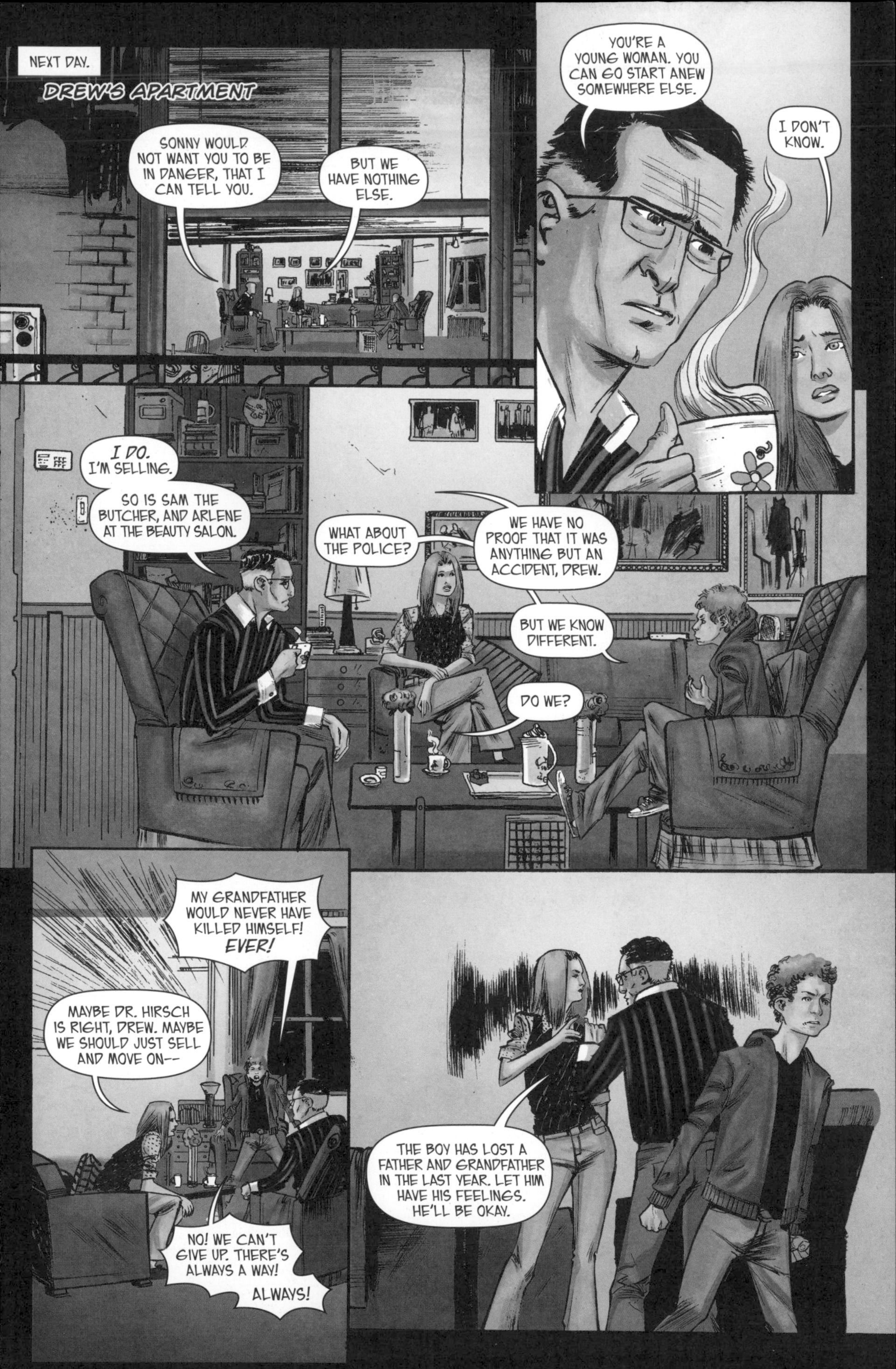
NEXT DAY.
DREW'S APARTMENT
SONNY WOULD NOT WANT YOU TO BE IN DANGER, THAT I CAN TELL YOU.
BUT WE HAVE NOTHING ELSE.
YOU'RE A YOUNG WOMAN. YOU CAN GO START ANEW SOMEWHERE ELSE.
I DON'T KNOW.
I DO. I'M SELLING.
SO IS SAM THE BUTCHER, AND ARLENE AT THE BEAUTY SALON.
WHAT ABOUT THE POLICE?
WE HAVE NO PROOF THAT IT WAS ANYTHING BUT AN ACCIDENT, DREW.
BUT WE KNOW DIFFERENT.
DO WE?
MY GRANDFATHER WOULD NEVER HAVE KILLED HIMSELF! EVER!
MAYBE DR. HIRSCH IS RIGHT, DREW. MAYBE WE SHOULD JUST SELL AND MOVE ON--
NO! WE CAN'T GIVE UP. THERE'S ALWAYS A WAY!
ALWAYS!
THE BOY HAS LOST A FATHER AND GRANDFATHER IN THE LAST YEAR. LET HIM HAVE HIS FEELINGS. HE'LL BE OKAY.

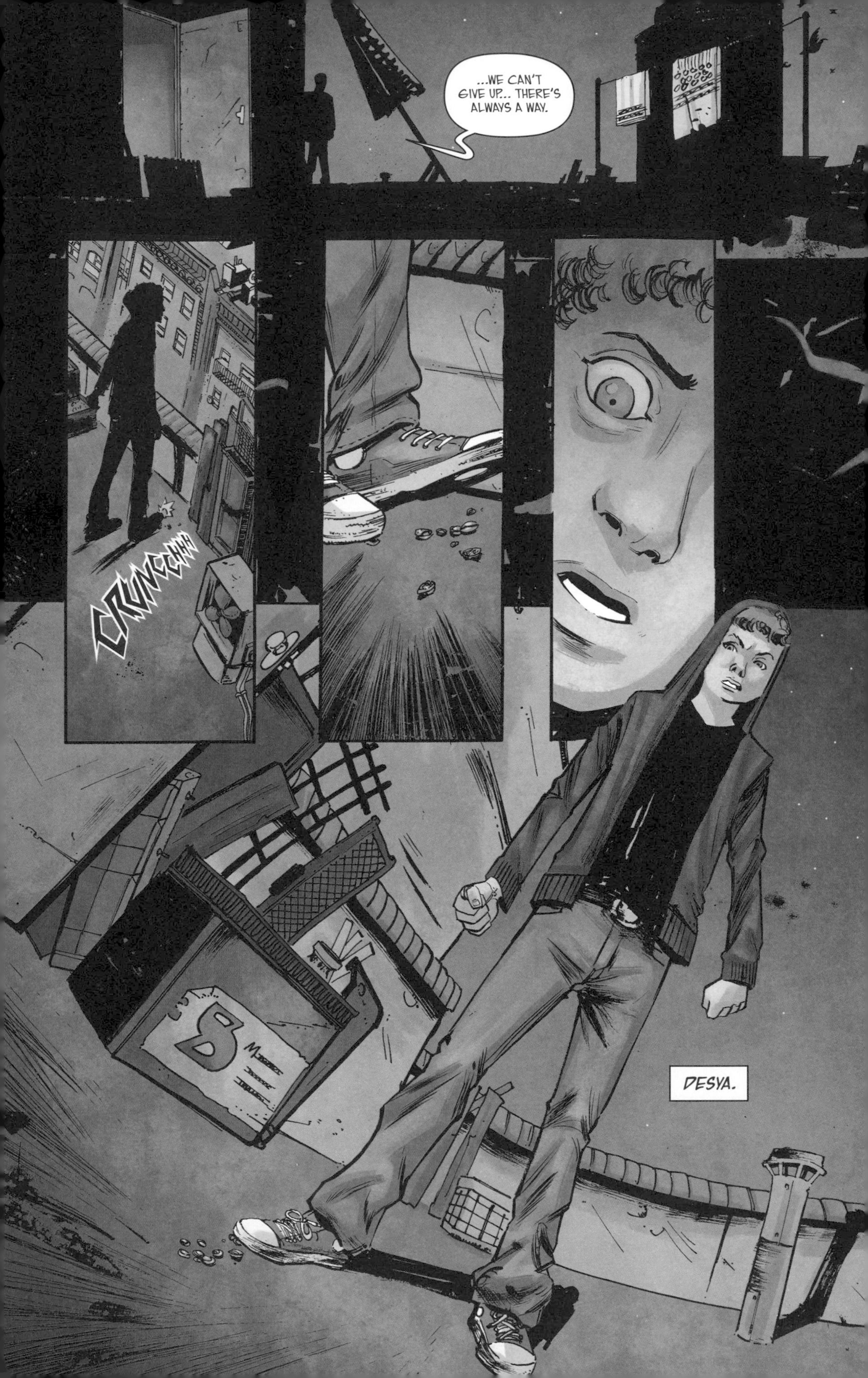
...WE CAN'T GIVE UP... THERE'S ALWAYS A WAY.
CRUNCHHH
DESYA.

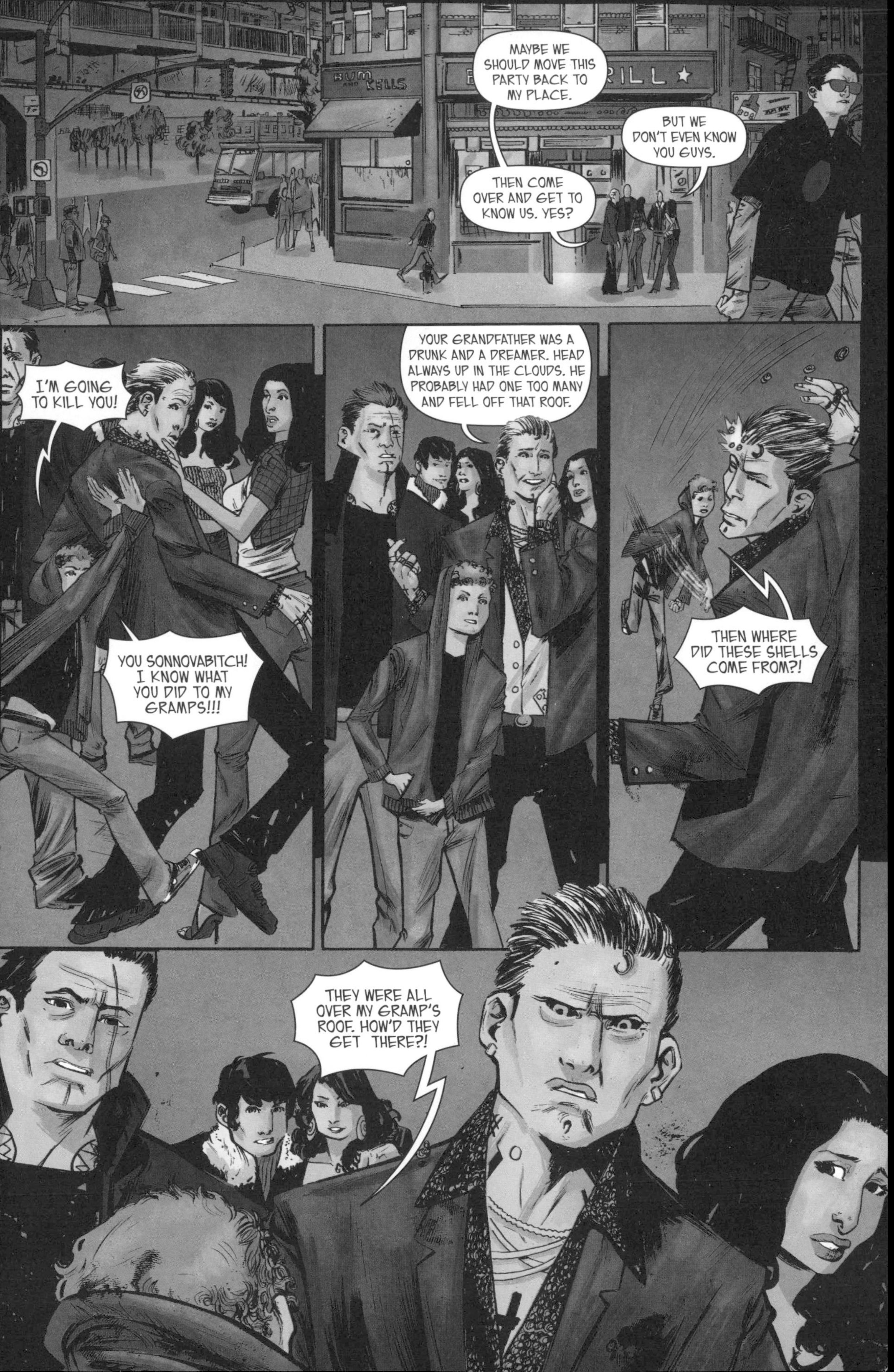
MAYBE WE SHOULD MOVE THIS PARTY BACK TO MY PLACE.
BUT WE DON'T EVEN KNOW YOU GUYS.
THEN COME OVER AND GET TO KNOW US. YES?
I'M GOING TO KILL YOU!
YOU SONNOVABITCH! I KNOW WHAT YOU DID TO MY GRAMPS!!!
YOUR GRANDFATHER WAS A DRUNK AND A DREAMER. HEAD ALWAYS UP IN THE CLOUDS. HE PROBABLY HAD ONE TOO MANY AND FELL OFF THAT ROOF.
THEN WHERE DID THESE SHELLS COME FROM?!
THEY WERE ALL OVER MY GRAMP'S ROOF. HOW'D THEY GET THERE?!

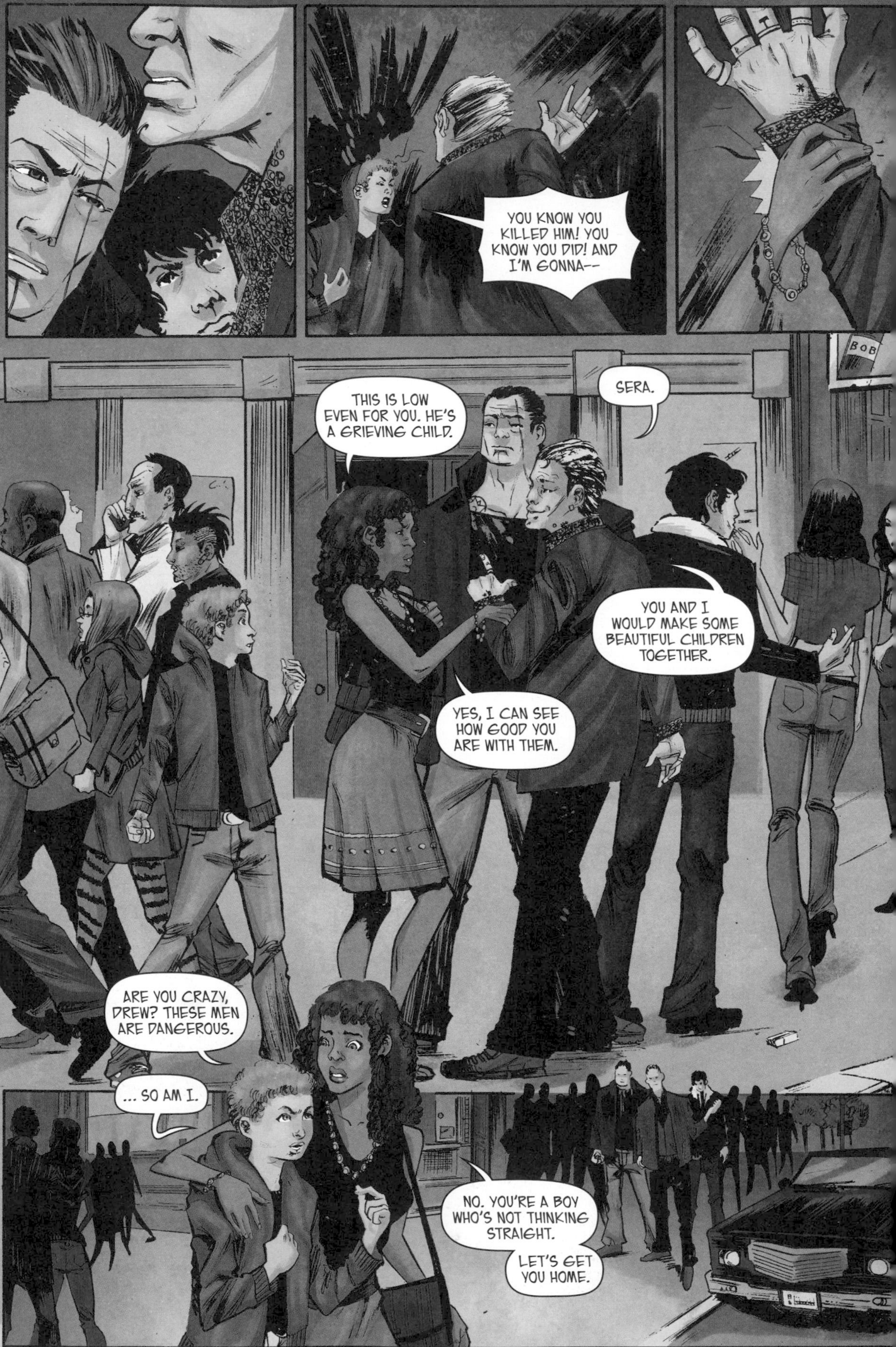
YOU KNOW YOU KILLED HIM! YOU KNOW YOU DID! AND I'M GONNA--
BOB
THIS IS LOW EVEN FOR YOU. HE'S A GRIEVING CHILD.
SERA.
YOU AND I WOULD MAKE SOME BEAUTIFUL CHILDREN TOGETHER.
YES, I CAN SEE HOW GOOD YOU ARE WITH THEM.
ARE YOU CRAZY, DREW? THESE MEN ARE DANGEROUS.
... SO AM I.
NO. YOU'RE A BOY WHO'S NOT THINKING STRAIGHT.
LET'S GET YOU HOME.

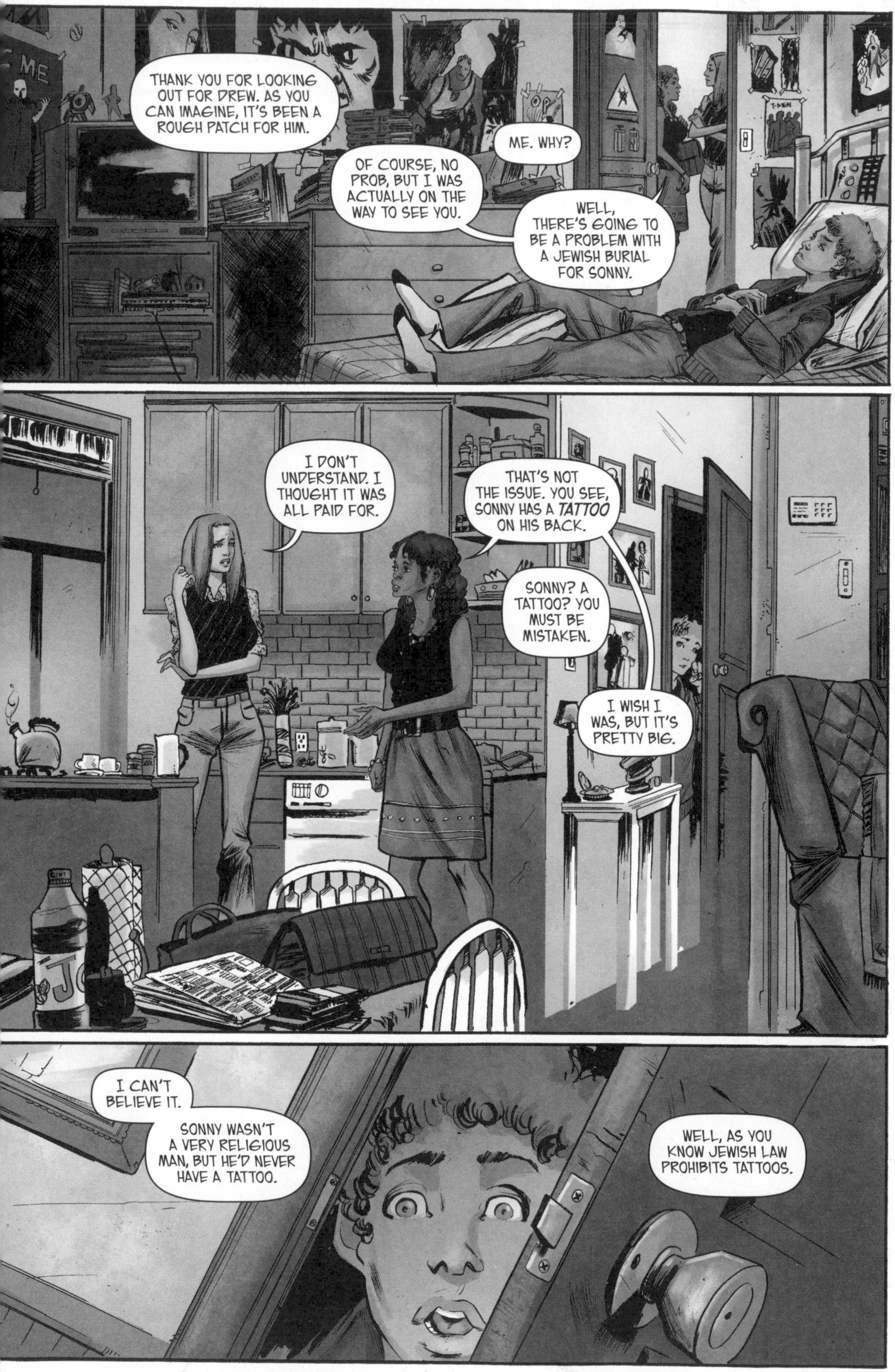
THANK YOU FOR LOOKING OUT FOR DREW. AS YOU CAN IMAGINE, IT'S BEEN A ROUGH PATCH FOR HIM.
OF COURSE, NO PROB, BUT I WAS ACTUALLY ON THE WAY TO SEE YOU.
ME. WHY?
WELL, THERE'S GOING TO BE A PROBLEM WITH A JEWISH BURIAL FOR SONNY.
I DON'T UNDERSTAND. I THOUGHT IT WAS ALL PAID FOR.
THAT'S NOT THE ISSUE. YOU SEE, SONNY HAS A *TATTOO* ON HIS BACK.
SONNY? A TATTOO? YOU MUST BE MISTAKEN.
I WISH I WAS, BUT IT'S PRETTY BIG.
I CAN'T BELIEVE IT.
SONNY WASN'T A VERY RELIGIOUS MAN, BUT HE'D NEVER HAVE A TATTOO.
WELL, AS YOU KNOW JEWISH LAW PROHIBITS TATTOOS.

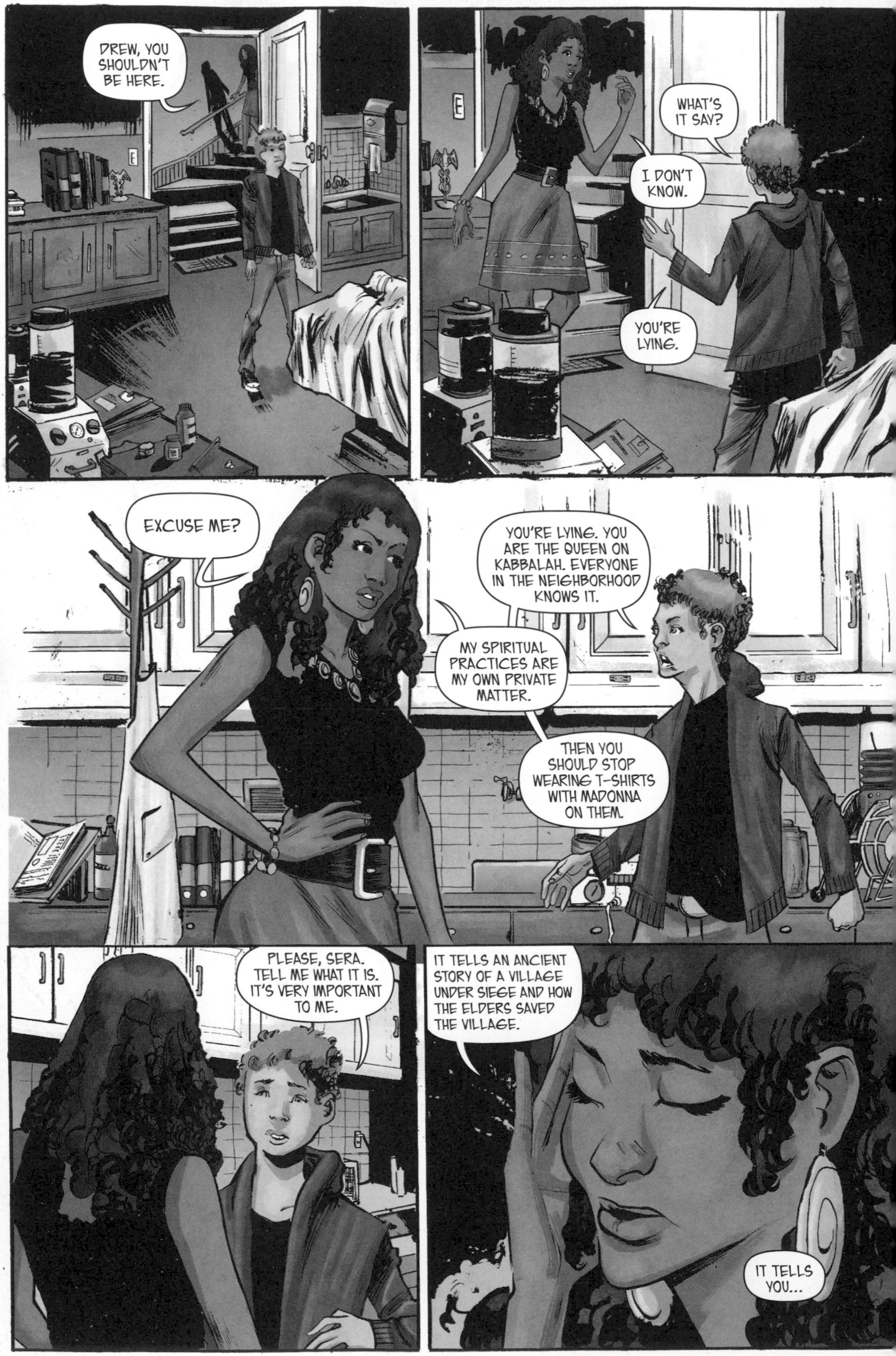
DREW, YOU SHOULDN'T BE HERE.
WHAT'S IT SAY?
I DON'T KNOW.
YOU'RE LYING.
EXCUSE ME?
YOU'RE LYING. YOU ARE THE QUEEN ON KABBALAH. EVERYONE IN THE NEIGHBORHOOD KNOWS IT.
MY SPIRITUAL PRACTICES ARE MY OWN PRIVATE MATTER.
THEN YOU SHOULD STOP WEARING T-SHIRTS WITH MADONNA ON THEM.
PLEASE, SERA. TELL ME WHAT IT IS. IT'S VERY IMPORTANT TO ME.
IT TELLS AN ANCIENT STORY OF A VILLAGE UNDER SIEGE AND HOW THE ELDERS SAVED THE VILLAGE.
IT TELLS YOU...

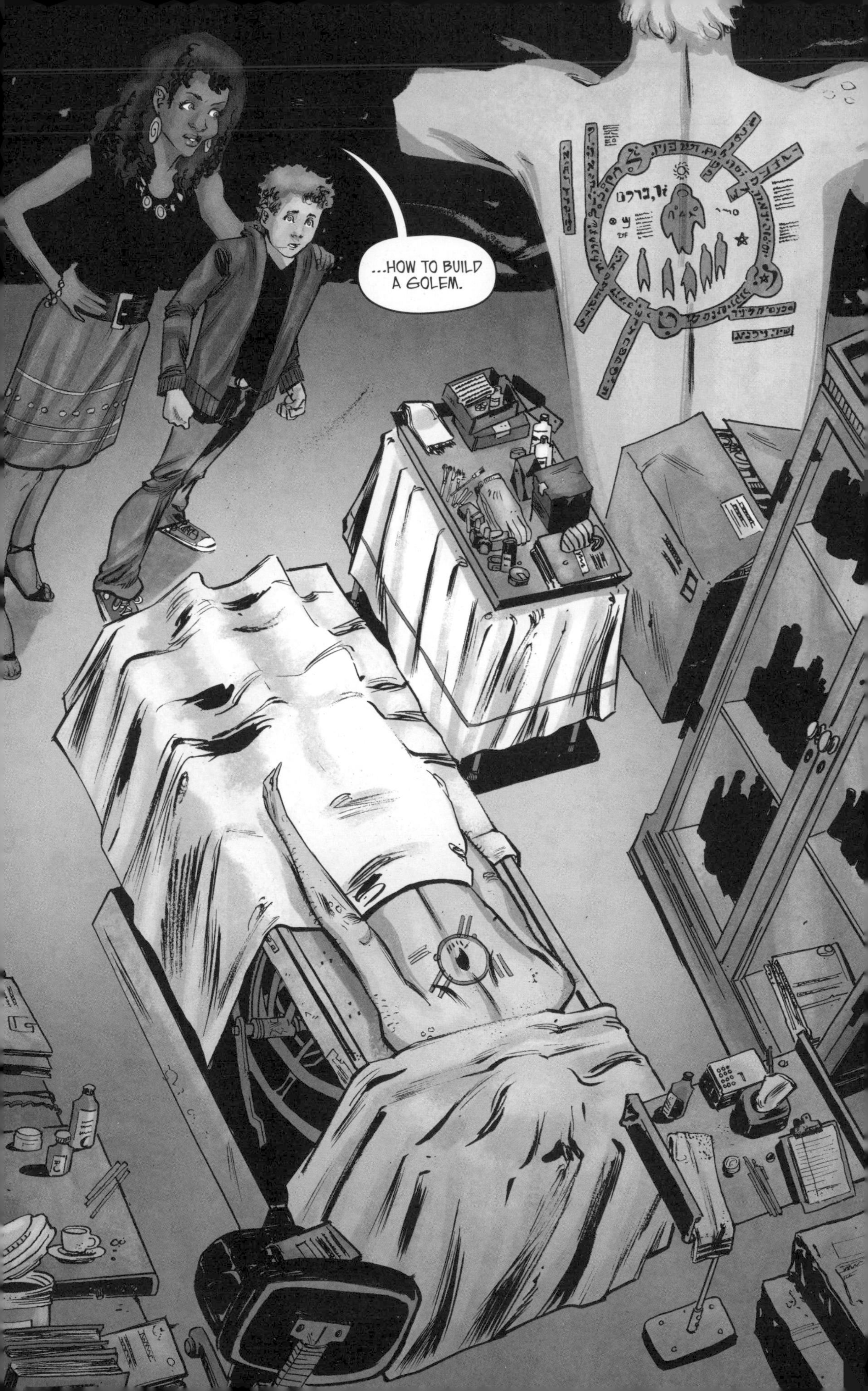
...HOW TO BUILD A GOLEM.

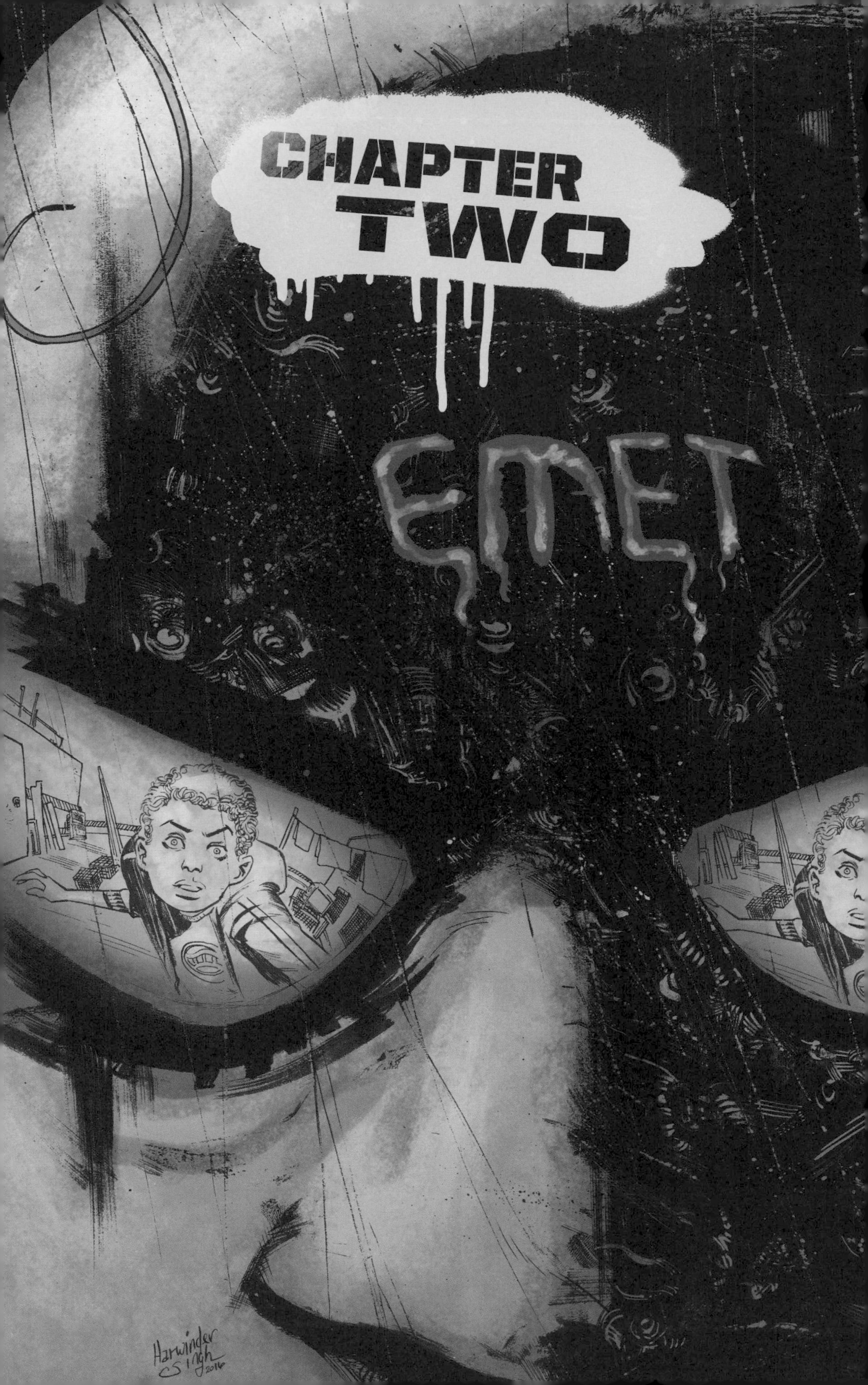
CHAPTER TWO
EMET
Harwinder Singh 2016

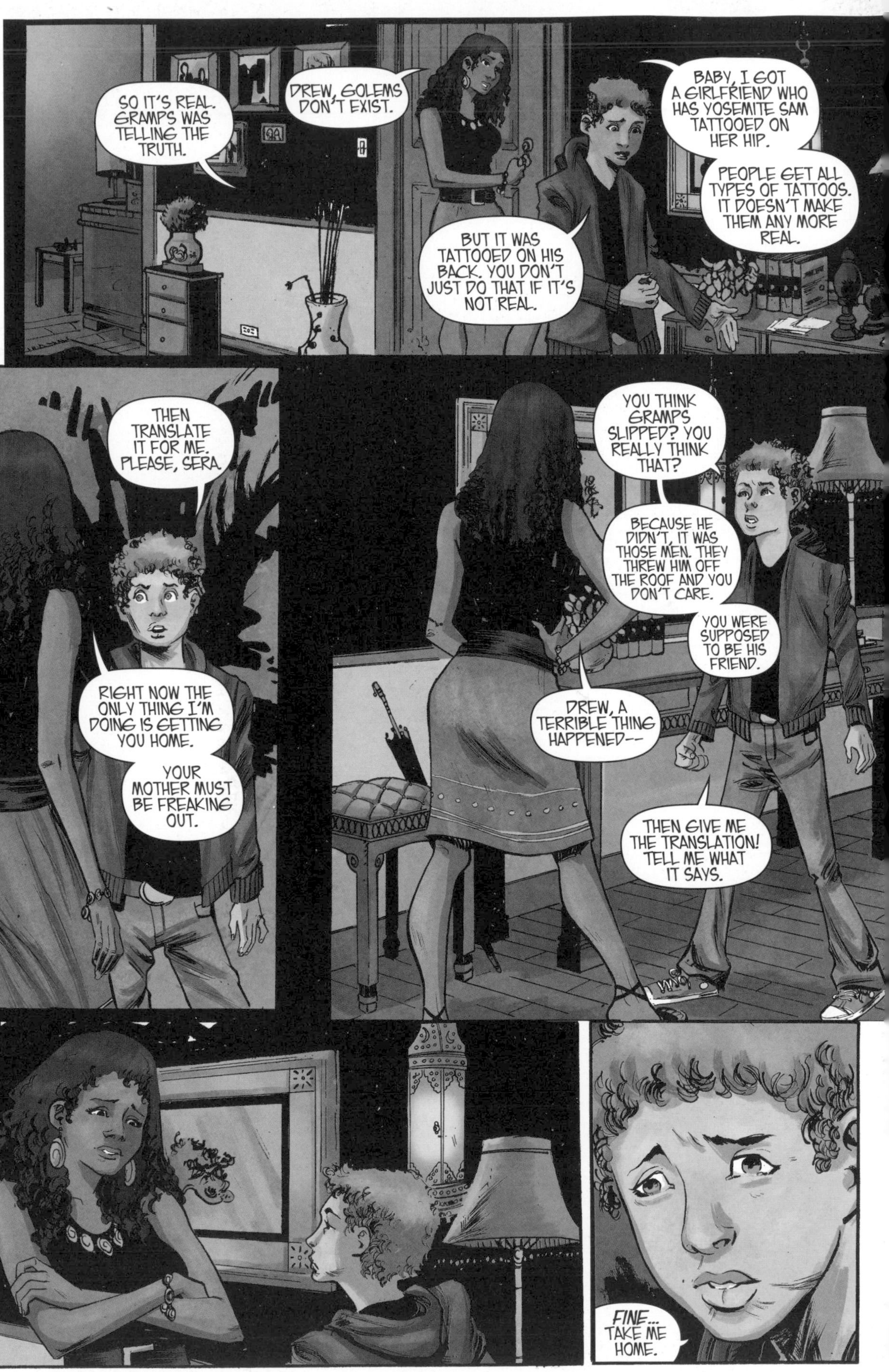
SO IT'S REAL. GRAMPS WAS TELLING THE TRUTH.
DREW, GOLEMS DON'T EXIST.
BUT IT WAS TATTOOED ON HIS BACK. YOU DON'T JUST DO THAT IF IT'S NOT REAL.
BABY, I GOT A GIRLFRIEND WHO HAS YOSEMITE SAM TATTOOED ON HER HIP.
PEOPLE GET ALL TYPES OF TATTOOS. IT DOESN'T MAKE THEM ANY MORE REAL.
THEN TRANSLATE IT FOR ME. PLEASE, SERA.
RIGHT NOW THE ONLY THING I'M DOING IS GETTING YOU HOME.
YOUR MOTHER MUST BE FREAKING OUT.
YOU THINK GRAMPS SLIPPED? YOU REALLY THINK THAT?
BECAUSE HE DIDN'T, IT WAS THOSE MEN. THEY THREW HIM OFF THE ROOF AND YOU DON'T CARE.
YOU WERE SUPPOSED TO BE HIS FRIEND.
DREW, A TERRIBLE THING HAPPENED--
THEN GIVE ME THE TRANSLATION! TELL ME WHAT IT SAYS.
FINE... TAKE ME HOME.

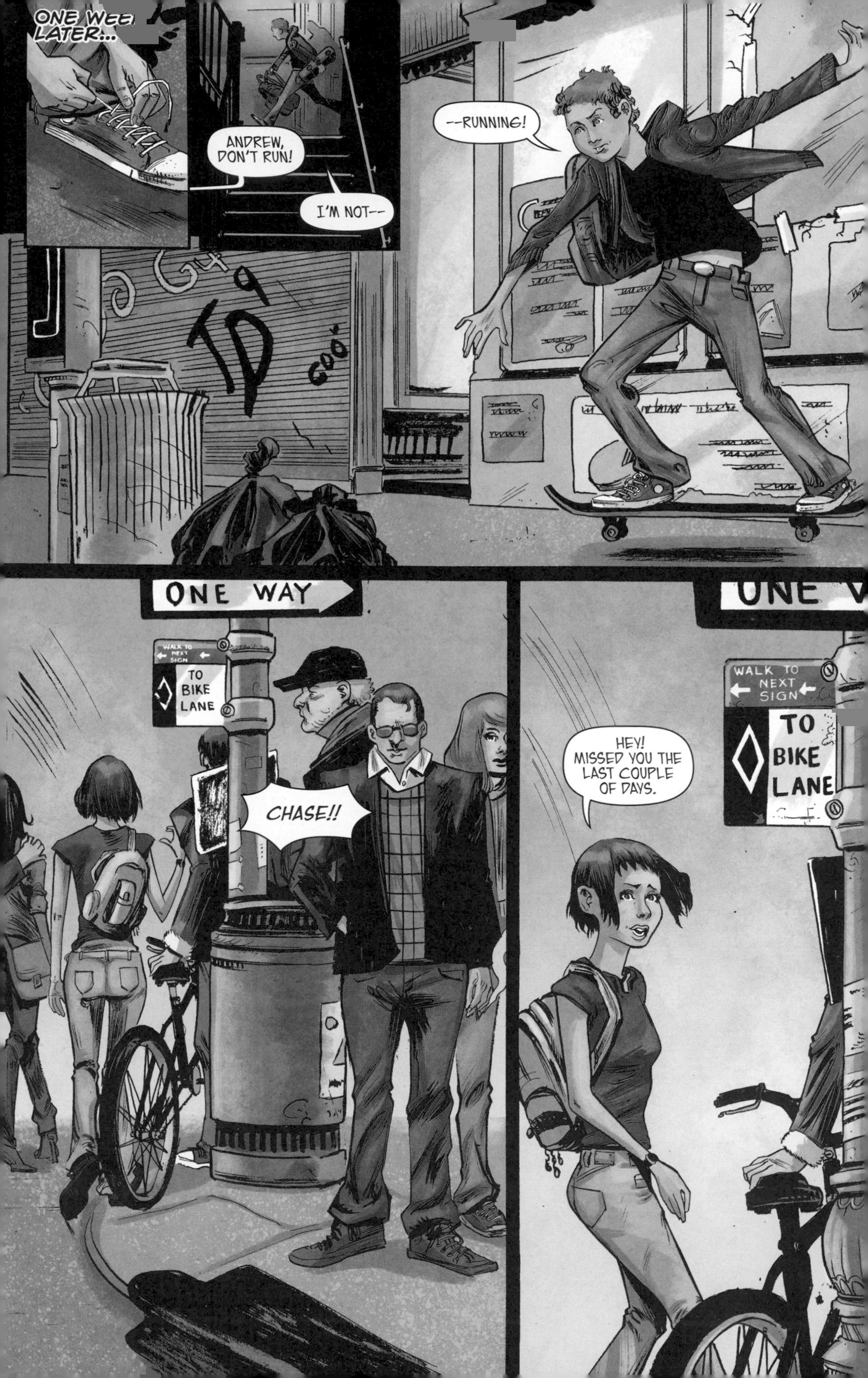
ONE WEE
LATER...
ANDREW, DON'T RUN!
I'M NOT--
--RUNNING!
ONE WAY
WALK TO NEXT SIGN
TO BIKE LANE
CHASE!!
ONE
WALK TO NEXT SIGN
TO BIKE LANE
HEY! MISSED YOU THE LAST COUPLE OF DAYS.

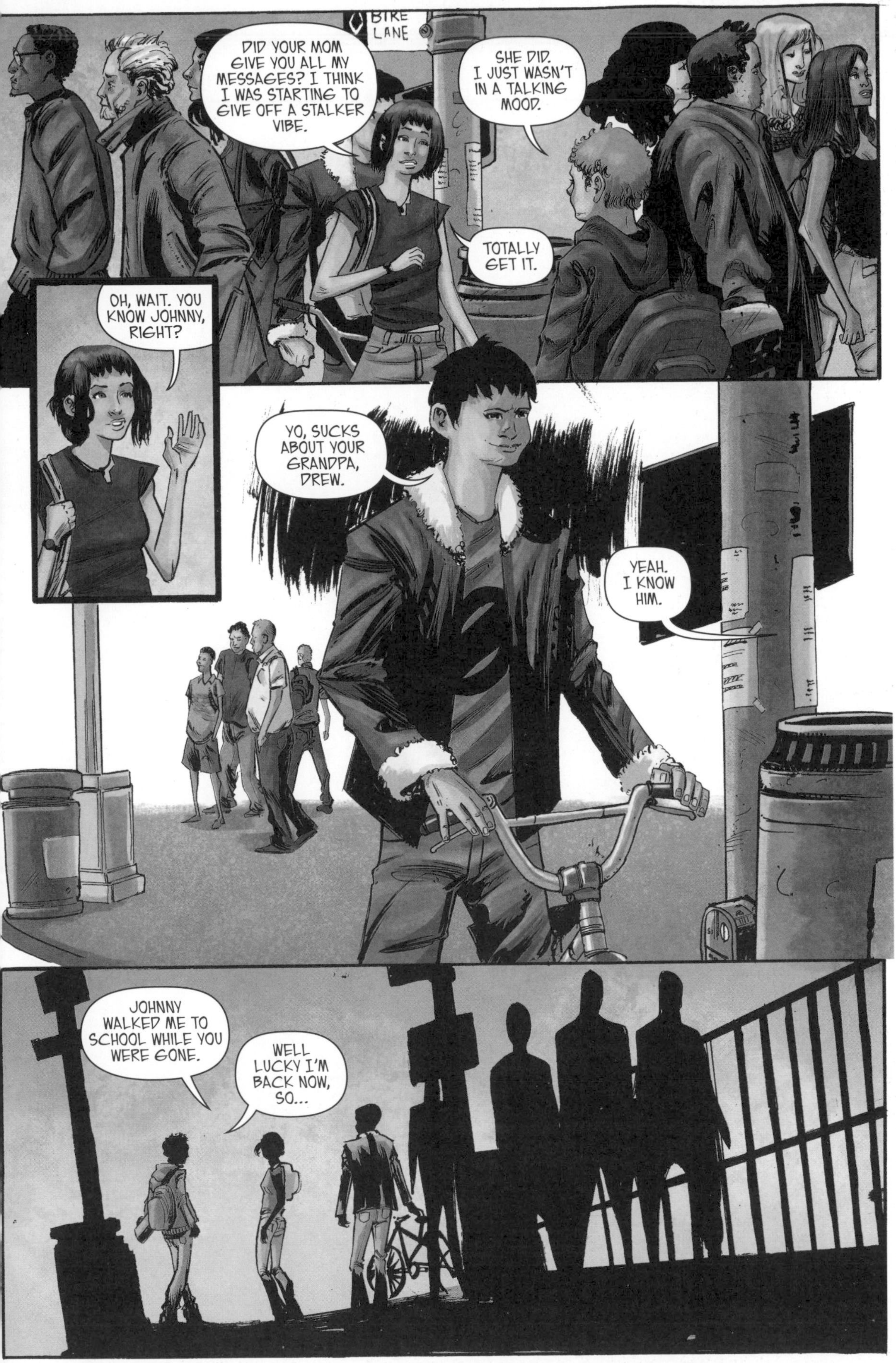
BIKE LANE
DID YOUR MOM GIVE YOU ALL MY MESSAGES? I THINK I WAS STARTING TO GIVE OFF A STALKER VIBE.
SHE DID. I JUST WASN'T IN A TALKING MOOD.
TOTALLY GET IT.
OH, WAIT. YOU KNOW JOHNNY, RIGHT?
YO, SUCKS ABOUT YOUR GRANDPA, DREW.
YEAH. I KNOW HIM.
JOHNNY WALKED ME TO SCHOOL WHILE YOU WERE GONE.
WELL LUCKY I'M BACK NOW, SO...

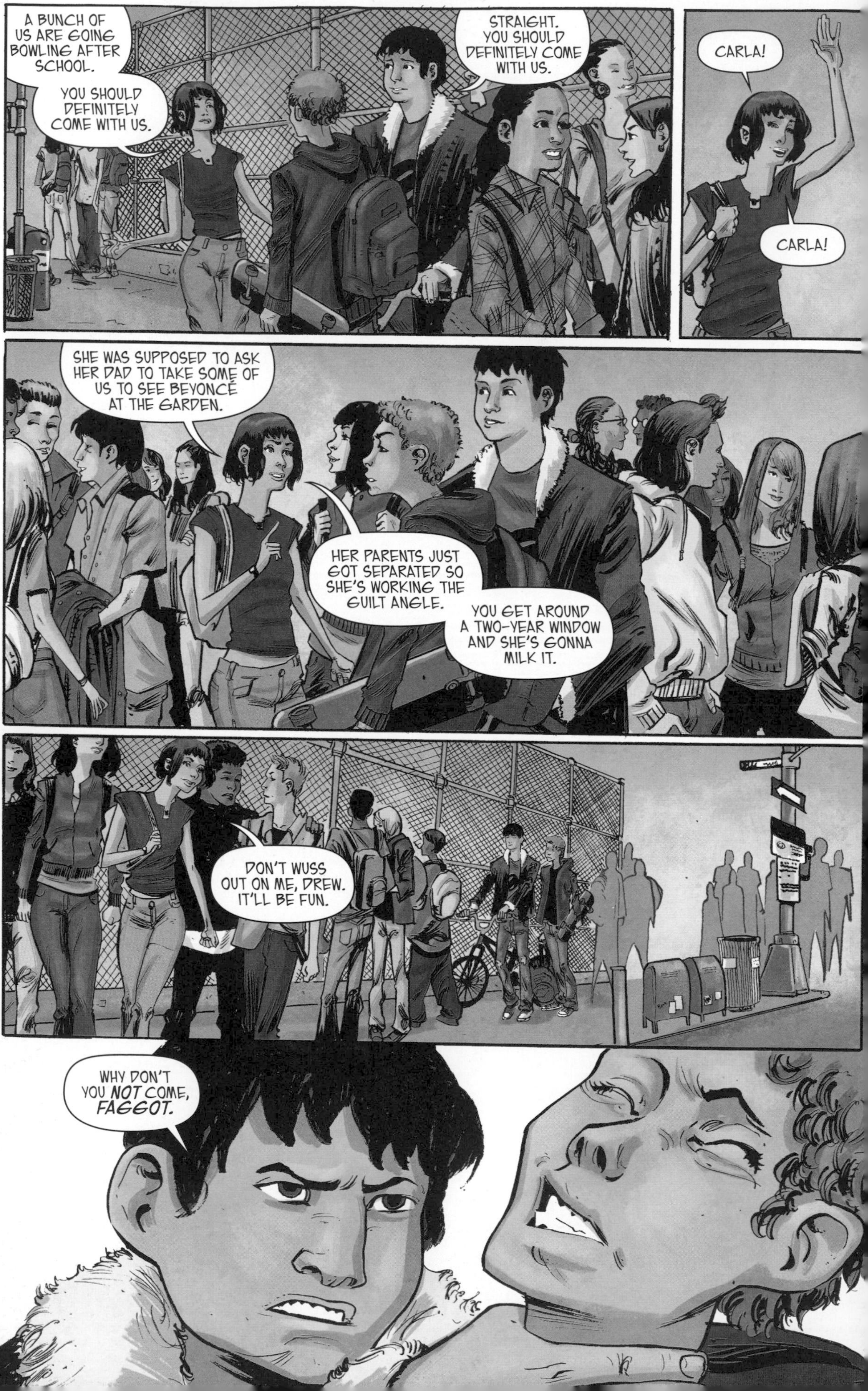

A BUNCH OF US ARE GOING BOWLING AFTER SCHOOL.
YOU SHOULD DEFINITELY COME WITH US.
STRAIGHT. YOU SHOULD DEFINITELY COME WITH US.
CARLA!
CARLA!
SHE WAS SUPPOSED TO ASK HER DAD TO TAKE SOME OF US TO SEE BEYONCÉ AT THE GARDEN.
HER PARENTS JUST GOT SEPARATED SO SHE'S WORKING THE GUILT ANGLE.
YOU GET AROUND A TWO-YEAR WINDOW AND SHE'S GONNA MILK IT.
DON'T WUSS OUT ON ME, DREW. IT'LL BE FUN.
WHY DON'T YOU ***NOT*** COME, ***FAGGOT.***

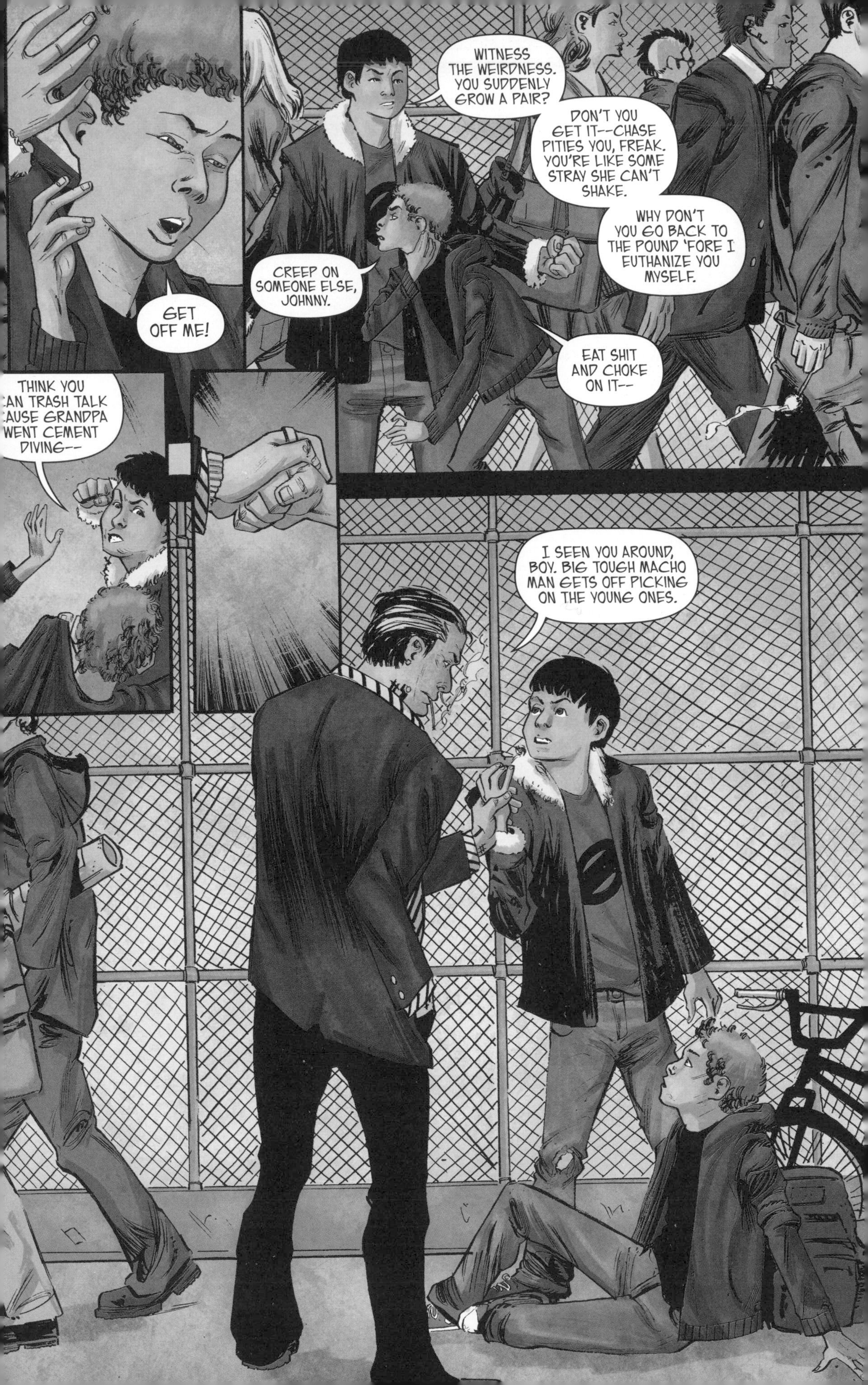
GET OFF ME!
WITNESS THE WEIRDNESS. YOU SUDDENLY GROW A PAIR?
CREEP ON SOMEONE ELSE, JOHNNY.
DON'T YOU GET IT--CHASE PITIES YOU, FREAK. YOU'RE LIKE SOME STRAY SHE CAN'T SHAKE.
WHY DON'T YOU GO BACK TO THE POUND 'FORE I EUTHANIZE YOU MYSELF.
EAT SHIT AND CHOKE ON IT--
THINK YOU CAN TRASH TALK CAUSE GRANDPA WENT CEMENT DIVING--
I SEEN YOU AROUND, BOY. BIG TOUGH MACHO MAN GETS OFF PICKING ON THE YOUNG ONES.

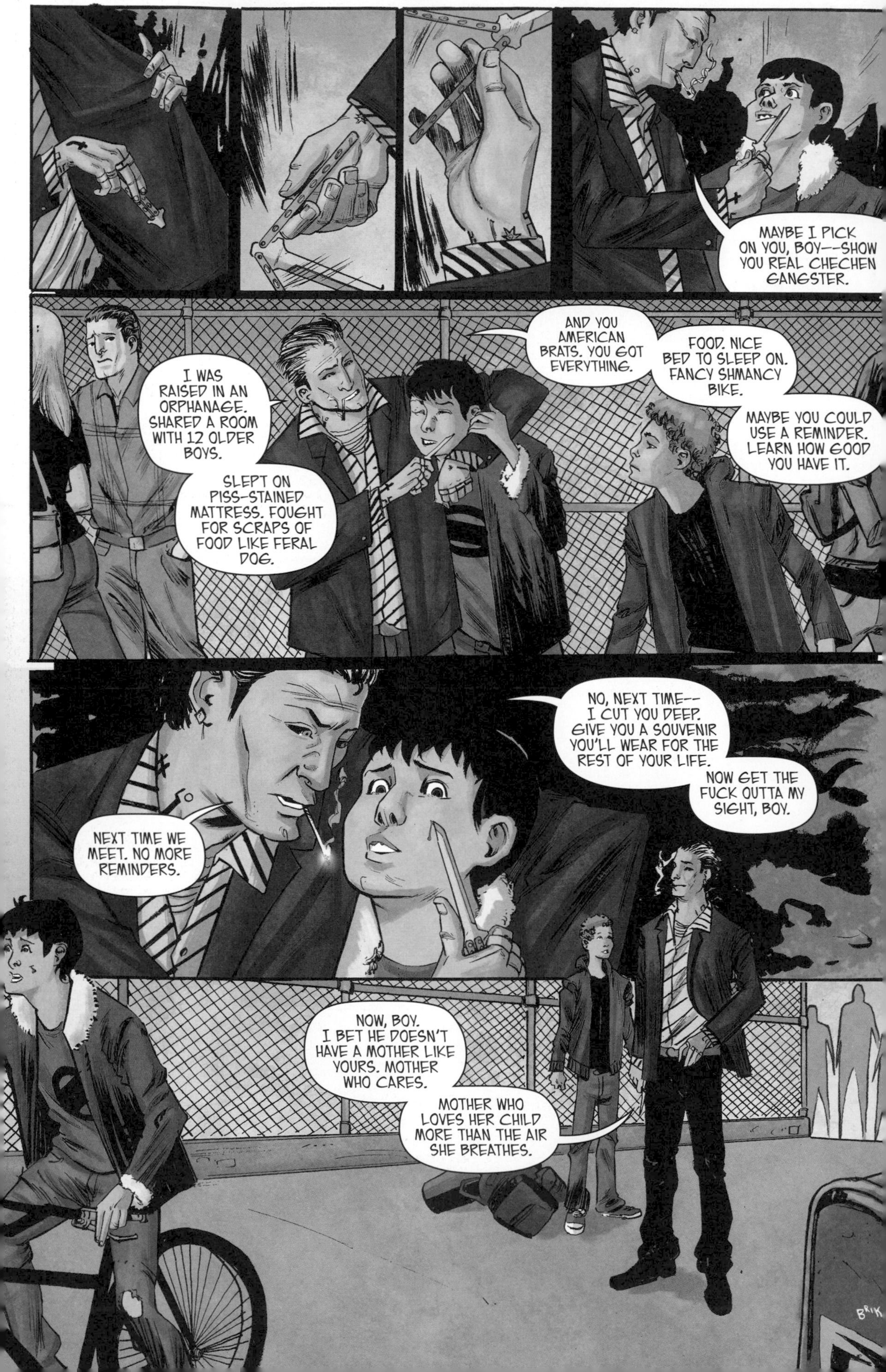
MAYBE I PICK ON YOU, BOY--SHOW YOU REAL CHECHEN GANGSTER.
I WAS RAISED IN AN ORPHANAGE. SHARED A ROOM WITH 12 OLDER BOYS.
SLEPT ON PISS-STAINED MATTRESS. FOUGHT FOR SCRAPS OF FOOD LIKE FERAL DOG.
AND YOU AMERICAN BRATS. YOU GOT EVERYTHING.
FOOD. NICE BED TO SLEEP ON. FANCY SHMANCY BIKE.
MAYBE YOU COULD USE A REMINDER. LEARN HOW GOOD YOU HAVE IT.
NEXT TIME WE MEET. NO MORE REMINDERS.
NO, NEXT TIME-- I CUT YOU DEEP. GIVE YOU A SOUVENIR YOU'LL WEAR FOR THE REST OF YOUR LIFE.
NOW GET THE FUCK OUTTA MY SIGHT, BOY.
NOW, BOY. I BET HE DOESN'T HAVE A MOTHER LIKE YOURS. MOTHER WHO CARES.
MOTHER WHO LOVES HER CHILD MORE THAN THE AIR SHE BREATHES.
BRIK

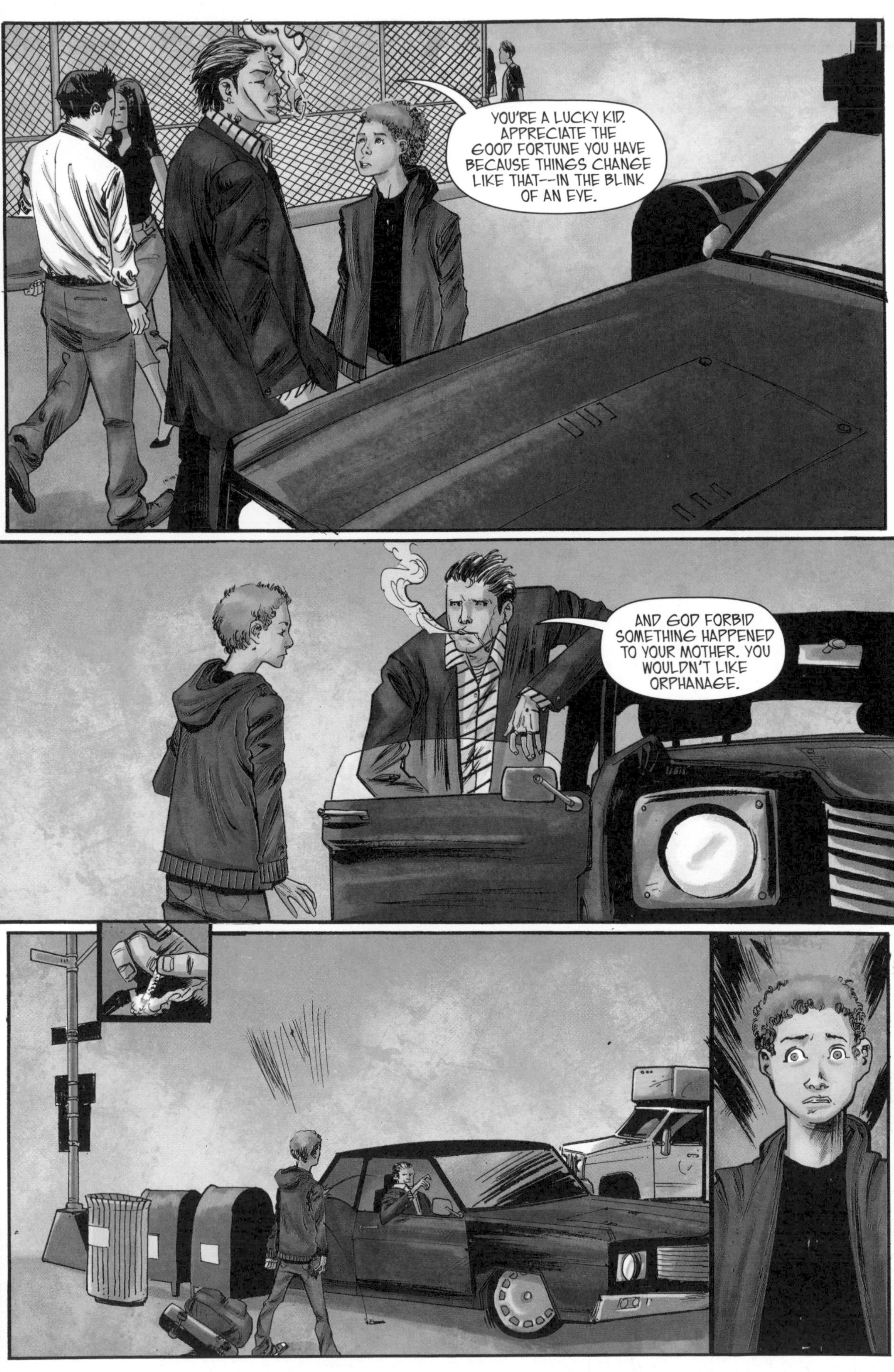
YOU'RE A LUCKY KID. APPRECIATE THE GOOD FORTUNE YOU HAVE BECAUSE THINGS CHANGE LIKE THAT--IN THE BLINK OF AN EYE.
AND GOD FORBID SOMETHING HAPPENED TO YOUR MOTHER. YOU WOULDN'T LIKE ORPHANAGE.

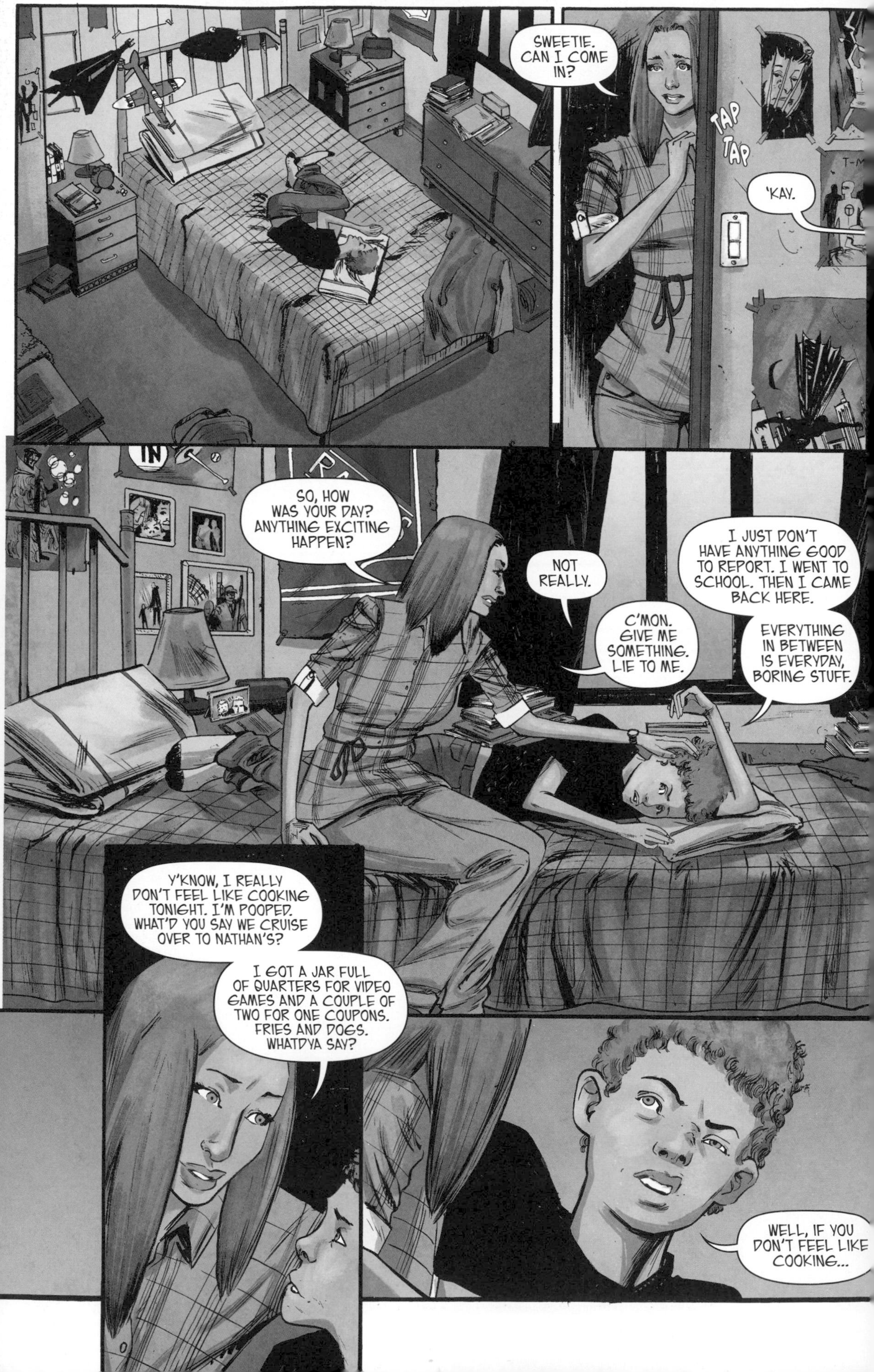
SWEETIE. CAN I COME IN?
TAP TAP
'KAY.
SO, HOW WAS YOUR DAY? ANYTHING EXCITING HAPPEN?
NOT REALLY.
C'MON. GIVE ME SOMETHING. LIE TO ME.
I JUST DON'T HAVE ANYTHING GOOD TO REPORT. I WENT TO SCHOOL. THEN I CAME BACK HERE.
EVERYTHING IN BETWEEN IS EVERYDAY, BORING STUFF.
Y'KNOW, I REALLY DON'T FEEL LIKE COOKING TONIGHT. I'M POOPED. WHAT'D YOU SAY WE CRUISE OVER TO NATHAN'S?
I GOT A JAR FULL OF QUARTERS FOR VIDEO GAMES AND A COUPLE OF TWO FOR ONE COUPONS. FRIES AND DOGS. WHATDYA SAY?
WELL, IF YOU DON'T FEEL LIKE COOKING...

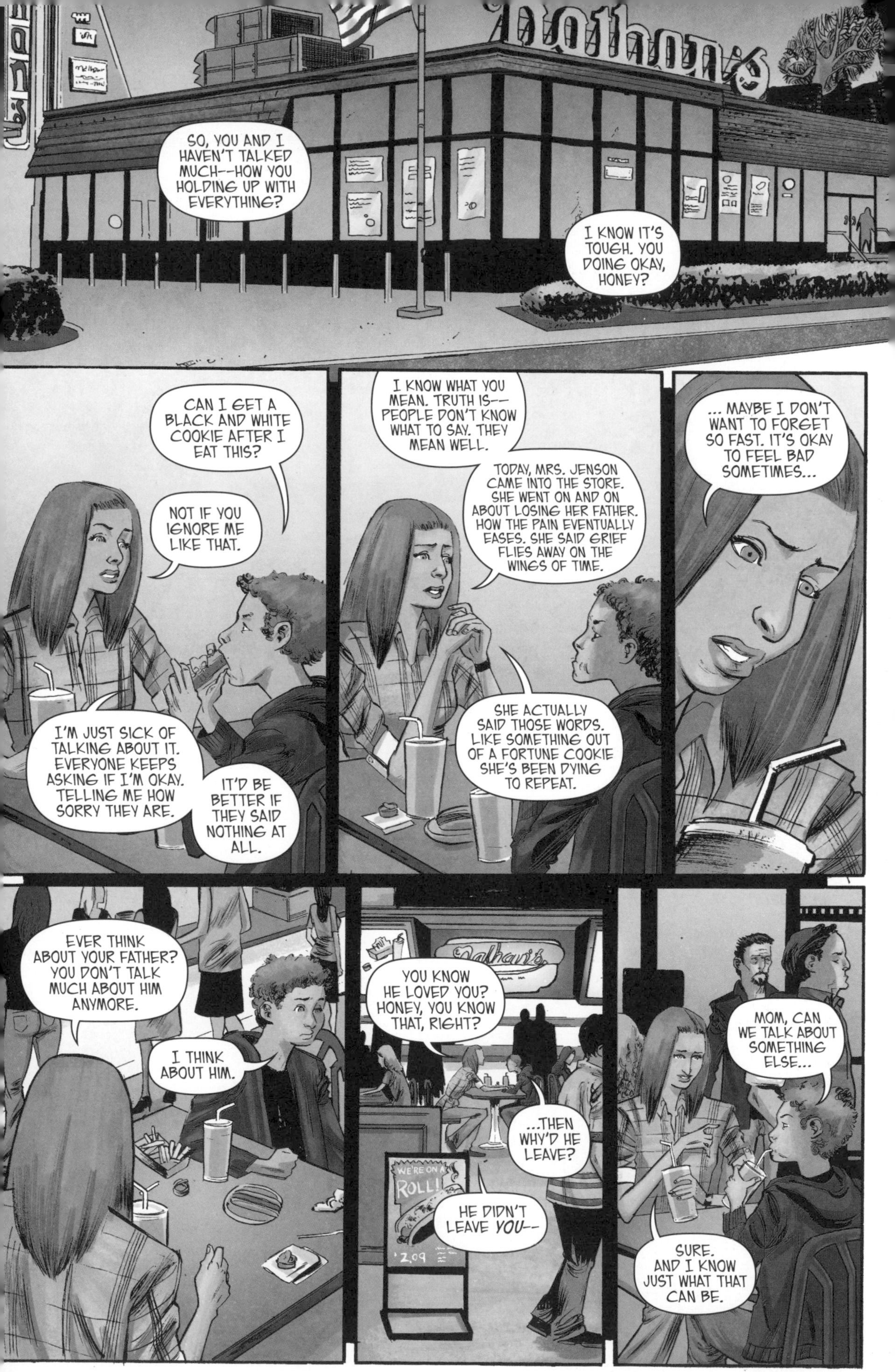

SO, YOU AND I HAVEN'T TALKED MUCH--HOW YOU HOLDING UP WITH EVERYTHING?
I KNOW IT'S TOUGH. YOU DOING OKAY, HONEY?
CAN I GET A BLACK AND WHITE COOKIE AFTER I EAT THIS?
NOT IF YOU IGNORE ME LIKE THAT.
I'M JUST SICK OF TALKING ABOUT IT. EVERYONE KEEPS ASKING IF I'M OKAY. TELLING ME HOW SORRY THEY ARE.
IT'D BE BETTER IF THEY SAID NOTHING AT ALL.
I KNOW WHAT YOU MEAN. TRUTH IS-- PEOPLE DON'T KNOW WHAT TO SAY. THEY MEAN WELL.
TODAY, MRS. JENSON CAME INTO THE STORE. SHE WENT ON AND ON ABOUT LOSING HER FATHER. HOW THE PAIN EVENTUALLY EASES. SHE SAID GRIEF FLIES AWAY ON THE WINGS OF TIME.
SHE ACTUALLY SAID THOSE WORDS. LIKE SOMETHING OUT OF A FORTUNE COOKIE SHE'S BEEN DYING TO REPEAT.
... MAYBE I DON'T WANT TO FORGET SO FAST. IT'S OKAY TO FEEL BAD SOMETIMES...
EVER THINK ABOUT YOUR FATHER? YOU DON'T TALK MUCH ABOUT HIM ANYMORE.
I THINK ABOUT HIM.
YOU KNOW HE LOVED YOU? HONEY, YOU KNOW THAT, RIGHT?
...THEN WHY'D HE LEAVE?
HE DIDN'T LEAVE *YOU*--
WE'RE ON A ROLL!
MOM, CAN WE TALK ABOUT SOMETHING ELSE...
SURE. AND I KNOW JUST WHAT THAT CAN BE.

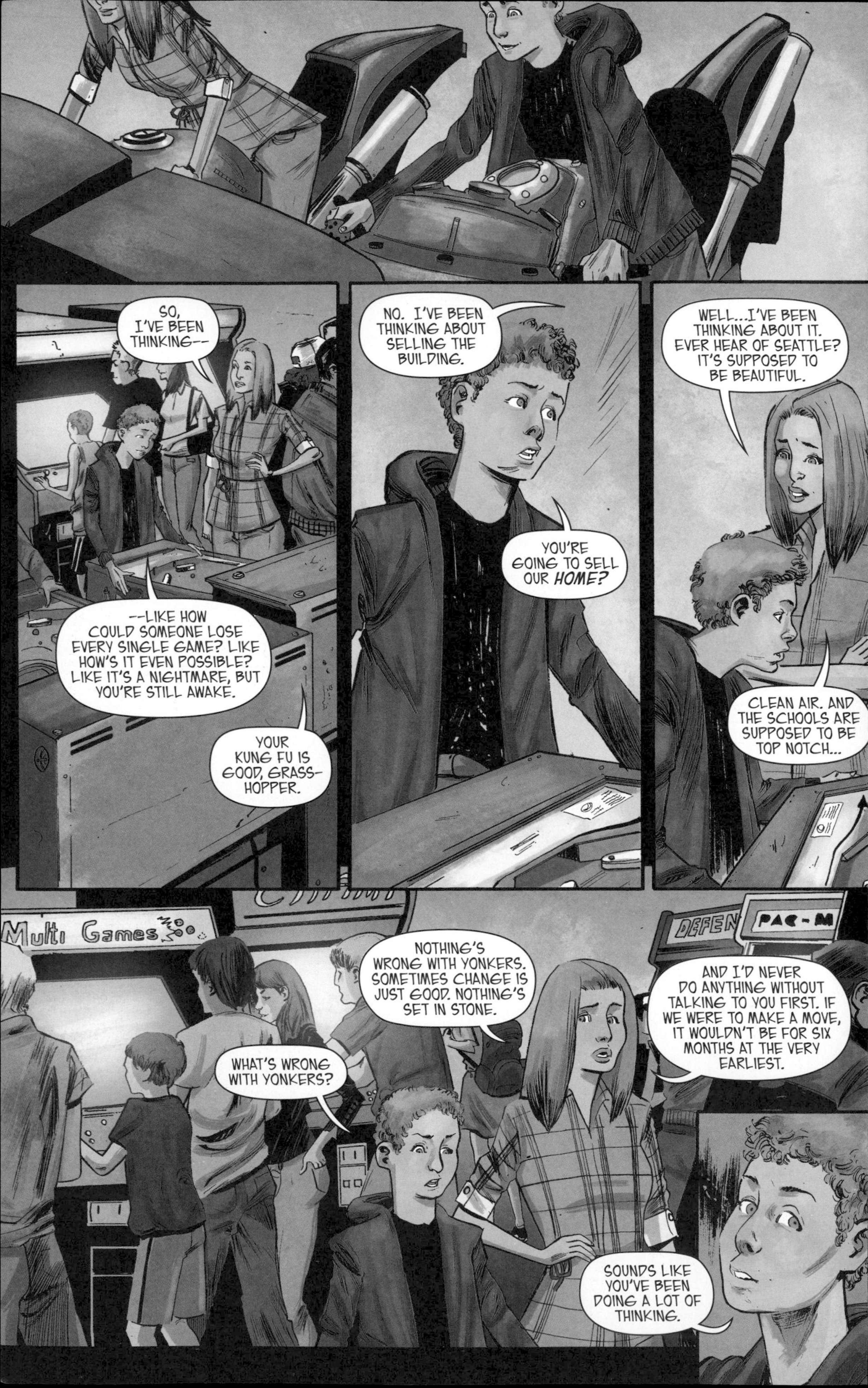
SO, I'VE BEEN THINKING--
--LIKE HOW COULD SOMEONE LOSE EVERY SINGLE GAME? LIKE HOW'S IT EVEN POSSIBLE? LIKE IT'S A NIGHTMARE, BUT YOU'RE STILL AWAKE.
YOUR KUNG FU IS GOOD, GRASS-HOPPER.
NO. I'VE BEEN THINKING ABOUT SELLING THE BUILDING.
YOU'RE GOING TO SELL OUR *HOME?*
WELL...I'VE BEEN THINKING ABOUT IT. EVER HEAR OF SEATTLE? IT'S SUPPOSED TO BE BEAUTIFUL.
CLEAN AIR. AND THE SCHOOLS ARE SUPPOSED TO BE TOP NOTCH...
Multi Games
DEFEN
PAC-M
WHAT'S WRONG WITH YONKERS?
NOTHING'S WRONG WITH YONKERS. SOMETIMES CHANGE IS JUST GOOD. NOTHING'S SET IN STONE.
AND I'D NEVER DO ANYTHING WITHOUT TALKING TO YOU FIRST. IF WE WERE TO MAKE A MOVE, IT WOULDN'T BE FOR SIX MONTHS AT THE VERY EARLIEST.
SOUNDS LIKE YOU'VE BEEN DOING A LOT OF THINKING.

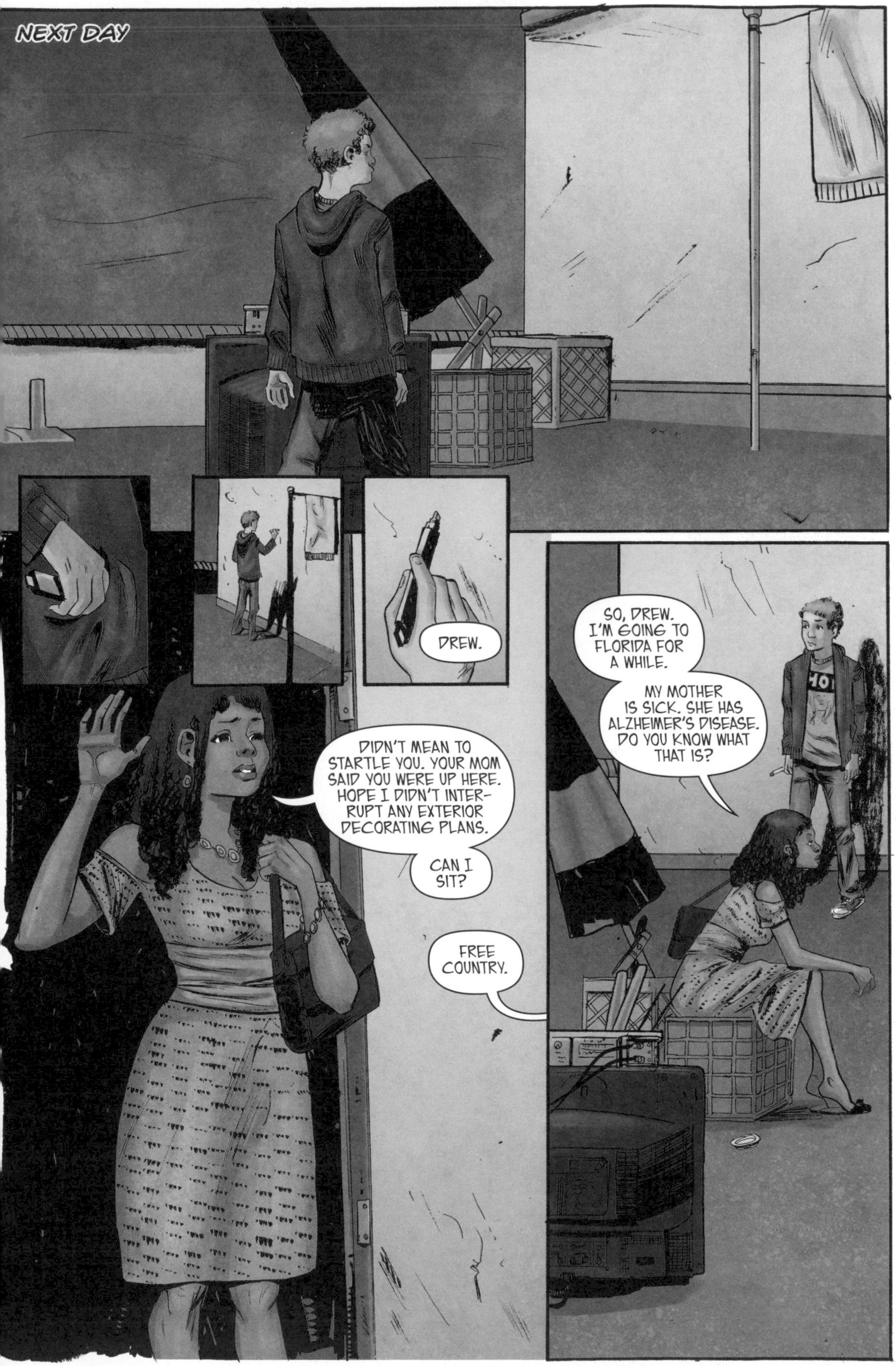
NEXT DAY
DREW.
DIDN'T MEAN TO STARTLE YOU. YOUR MOM SAID YOU WERE UP HERE. HOPE I DIDN'T INTER-RUPT ANY EXTERIOR DECORATING PLANS.
CAN I SIT?
FREE COUNTRY.
SO, DREW. I'M GOING TO FLORIDA FOR A WHILE.
MY MOTHER IS SICK. SHE HAS ALZHEIMER'S DISEASE. DO YOU KNOW WHAT THAT IS?

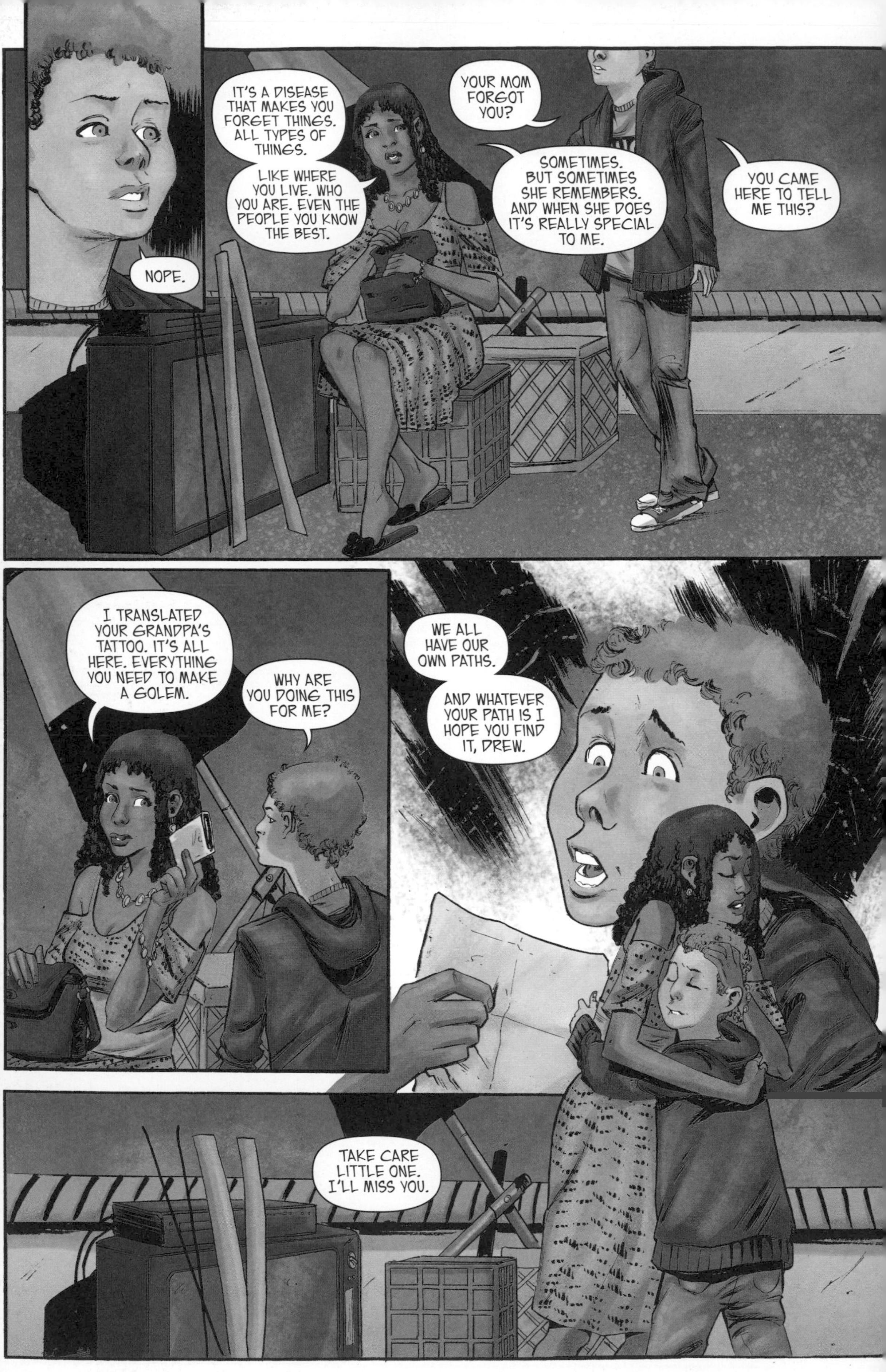
IT'S A DISEASE THAT MAKES YOU FORGET THINGS. ALL TYPES OF THINGS.
LIKE WHERE YOU LIVE. WHO YOU ARE. EVEN THE PEOPLE YOU KNOW THE BEST.
NOPE.
YOUR MOM FORGOT YOU?
SOMETIMES. BUT SOMETIMES SHE REMEMBERS. AND WHEN SHE DOES IT'S REALLY SPECIAL TO ME.
YOU CAME HERE TO TELL ME THIS?
I TRANSLATED YOUR GRANDPA'S TATTOO. IT'S ALL HERE. EVERYTHING YOU NEED TO MAKE A GOLEM.
WHY ARE YOU DOING THIS FOR ME?
WE ALL HAVE OUR OWN PATHS.
AND WHATEVER YOUR PATH IS I HOPE YOU FIND IT, DREW.
TAKE CARE LITTLE ONE. I'LL MISS YOU.

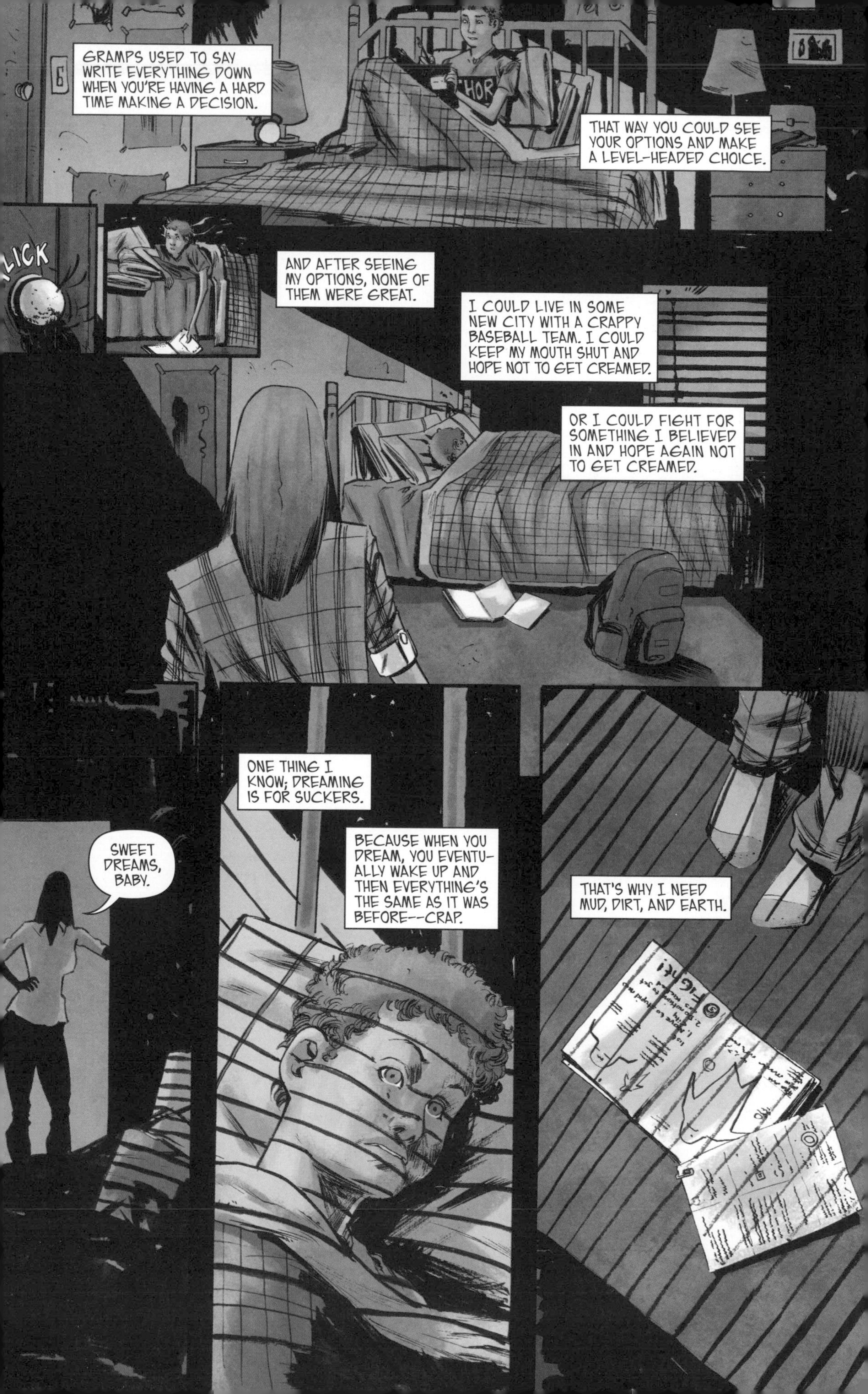
GRAMPS USED TO SAY WRITE EVERYTHING DOWN WHEN YOU'RE HAVING A HARD TIME MAKING A DECISION.
THAT WAY YOU COULD SEE YOUR OPTIONS AND MAKE A LEVEL-HEADED CHOICE.
LICK
AND AFTER SEEING MY OPTIONS, NONE OF THEM WERE GREAT.
I COULD LIVE IN SOME NEW CITY WITH A CRAPPY BASEBALL TEAM. I COULD KEEP MY MOUTH SHUT AND HOPE NOT TO GET CREAMED.
OR I COULD FIGHT FOR SOMETHING I BELIEVED IN AND HOPE AGAIN NOT TO GET CREAMED.
SWEET DREAMS, BABY.
ONE THING I KNOW; DREAMING IS FOR SUCKERS.
BECAUSE WHEN YOU DREAM, YOU EVENTU-ALLY WAKE UP AND THEN EVERYTHING'S THE SAME AS IT WAS BEFORE--CRAP.
THAT'S WHY I NEED MUD, DIRT, AND EARTH.

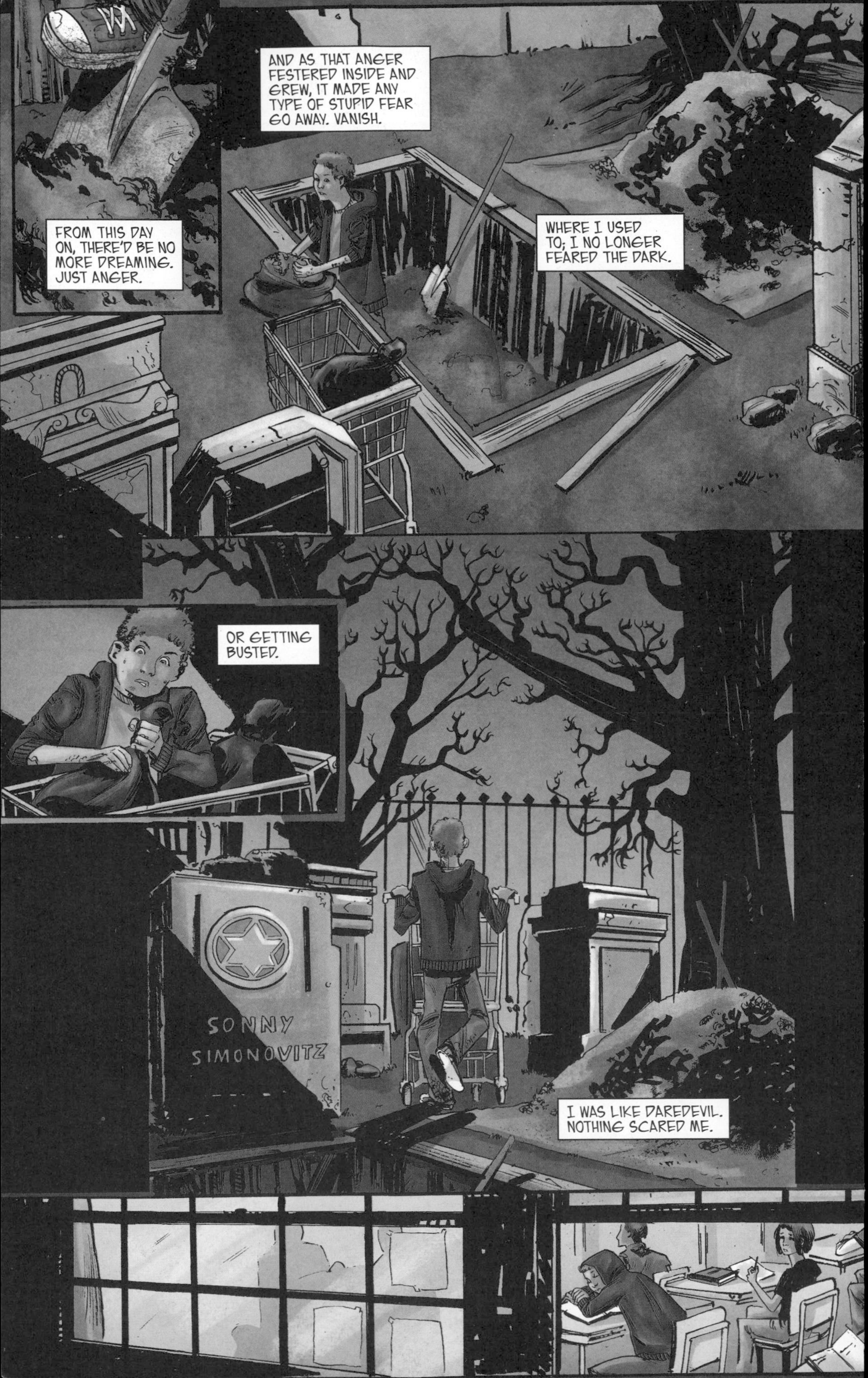
AND AS THAT ANGER FESTERED INSIDE AND GREW, IT MADE ANY TYPE OF STUPID FEAR GO AWAY. VANISH.
FROM THIS DAY ON, THERE'D BE NO MORE DREAMING. JUST ANGER.
WHERE I USED TO; I NO LONGER FEARED THE DARK.
OR GETTING BUSTED.
SONNY SIMONOVITZ
I WAS LIKE DAREDEVIL. NOTHING SCARED ME.

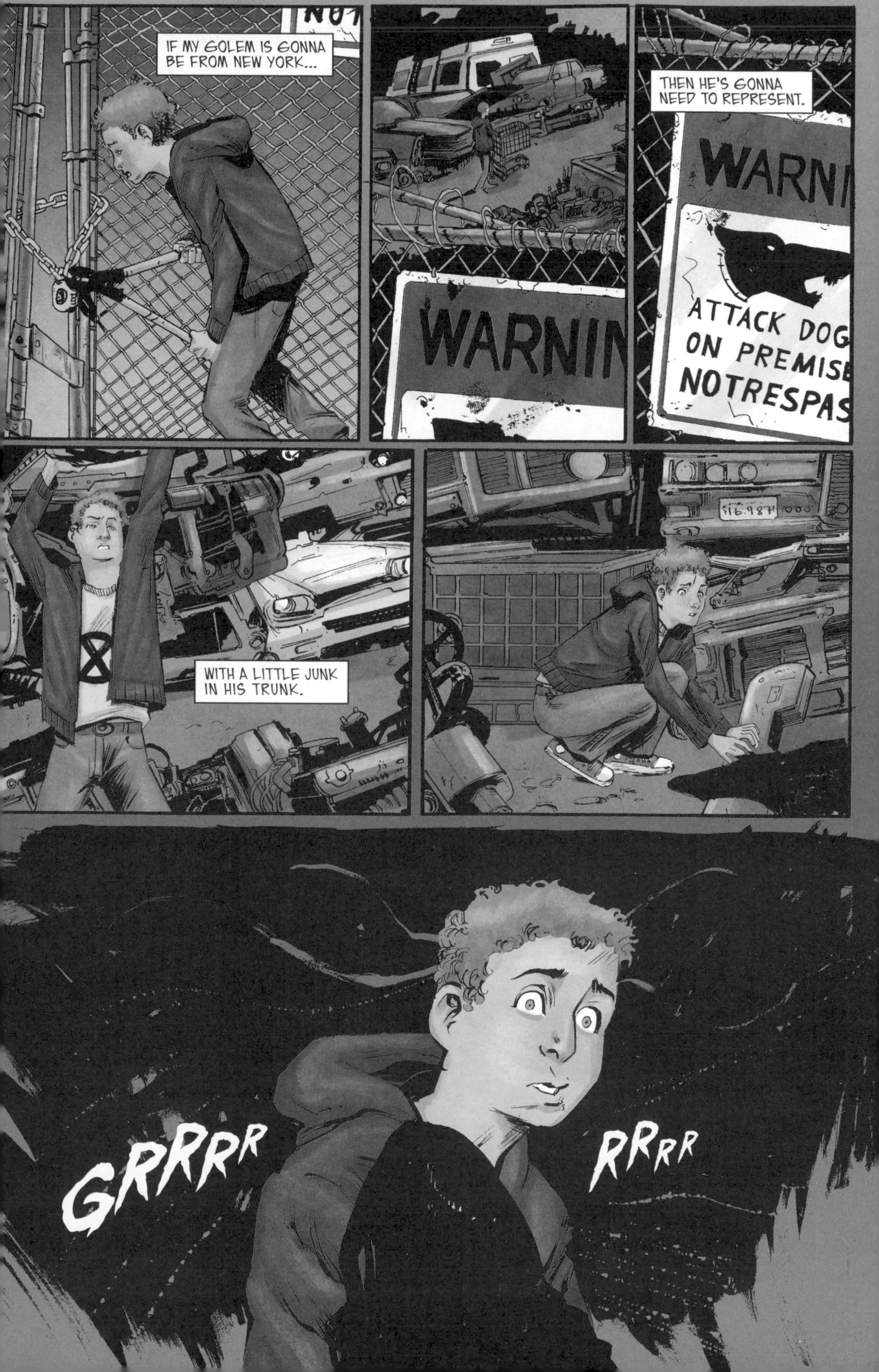
IF MY GOLEM IS GONNA BE FROM NEW YORK...
WARNIN
THEN HE'S GONNA NEED TO REPRESENT.
WARNI
ATTACK DOG
ON PREMISE
NOTRESPAS
WITH A LITTLE JUNK IN HIS TRUNK.
GRRRR
RRRR

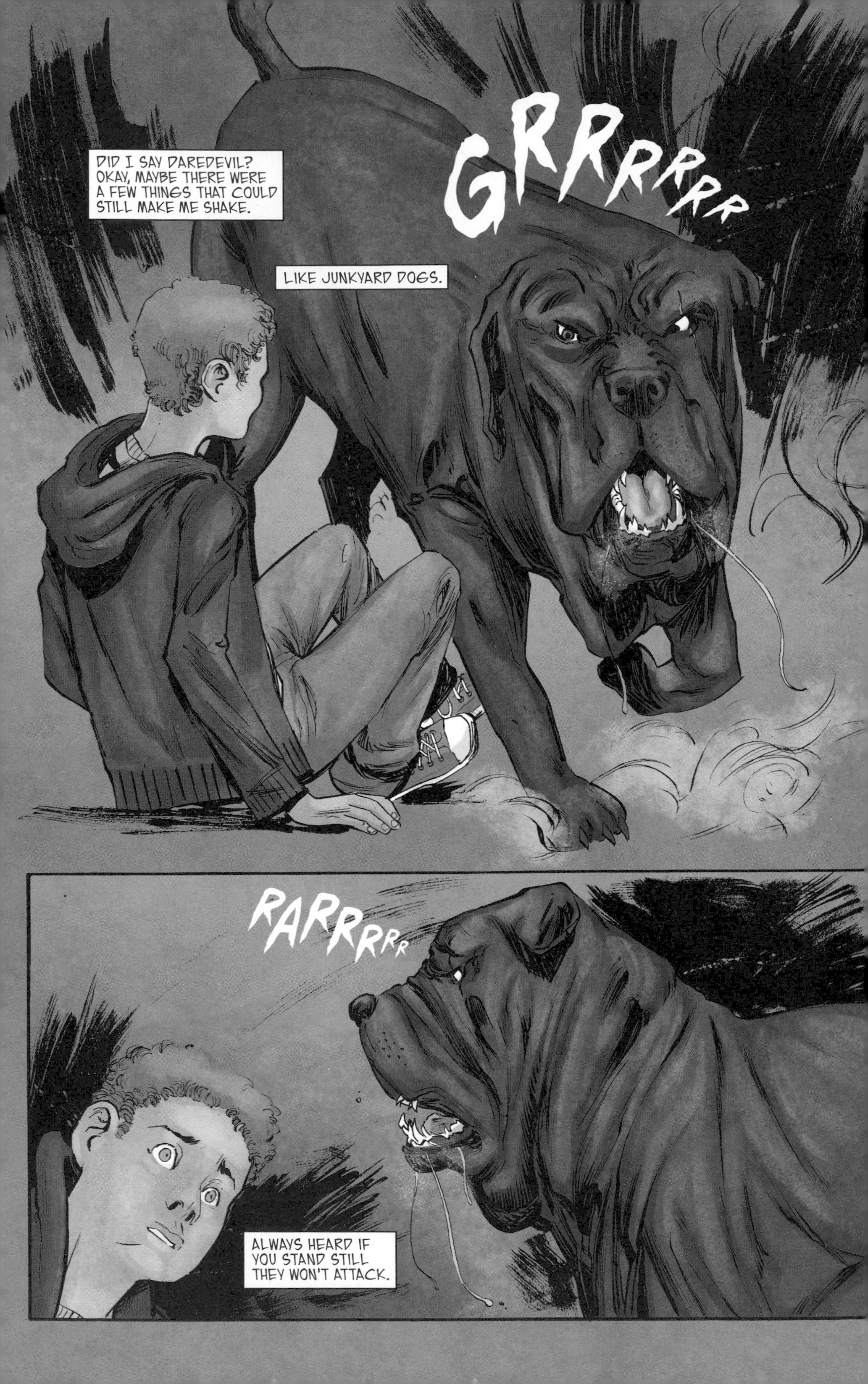
DID I SAY DAREDEVIL? OKAY, MAYBE THERE WERE A FEW THINGS THAT COULD STILL MAKE ME SHAKE.
GRRRRRR
LIKE JUNKYARD DOGS.
RARRRRR
ALWAYS HEARD IF YOU STAND STILL THEY WON'T ATTACK.

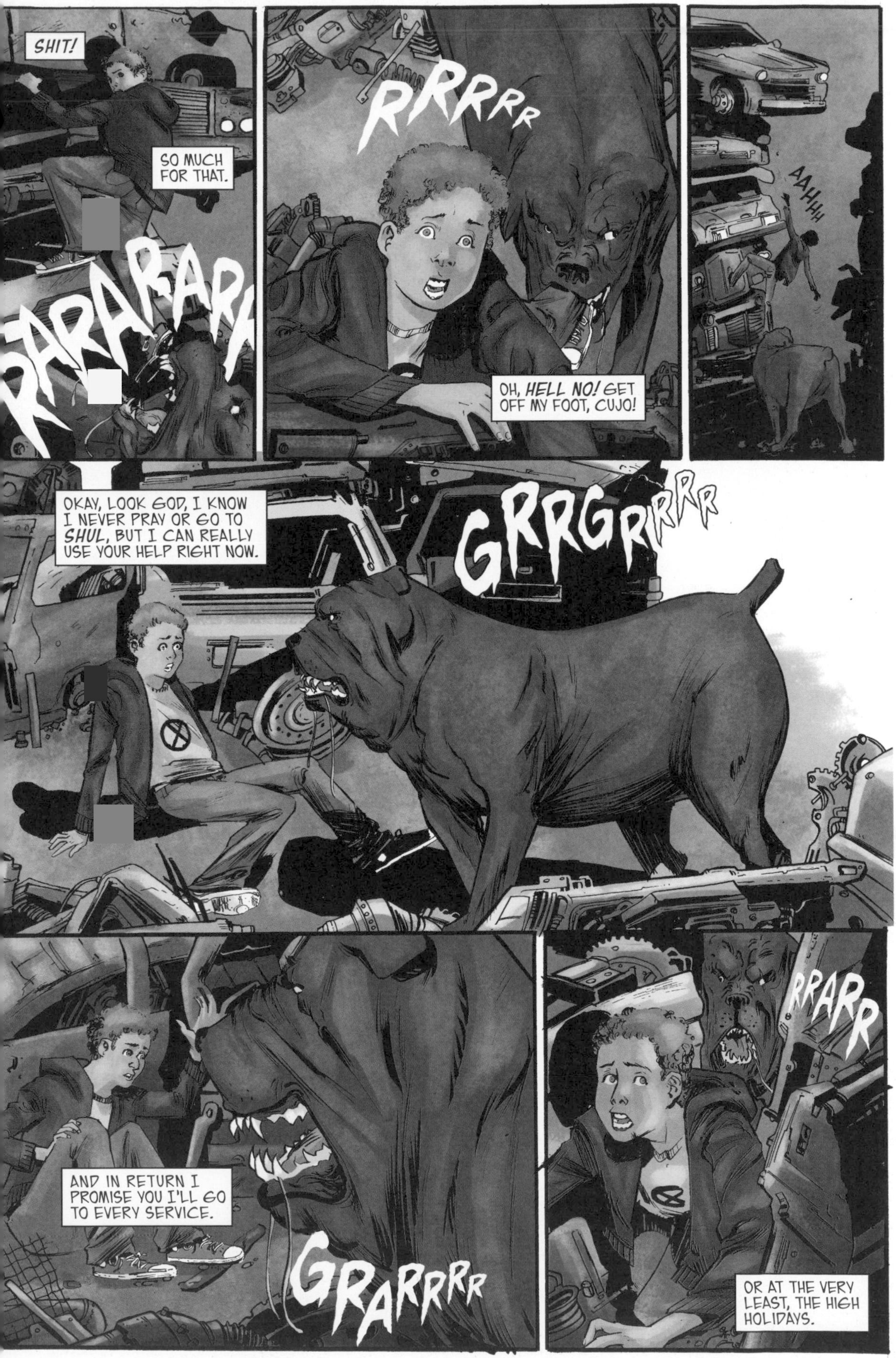
SHIT!
SO MUCH FOR THAT.
RARARARARK
RRRRRR
OH, HELL NO! GET OFF MY FOOT, CUJO!
AAHHH
OKAY, LOOK GOD, I KNOW I NEVER PRAY OR GO TO SHUL, BUT I CAN REALLY USE YOUR HELP RIGHT NOW.
GRRGRRRR
AND IN RETURN I PROMISE YOU I'LL GO TO EVERY SERVICE.
GRARRRR
RRARR
OR AT THE VERY LEAST, THE HIGH HOLIDAYS.

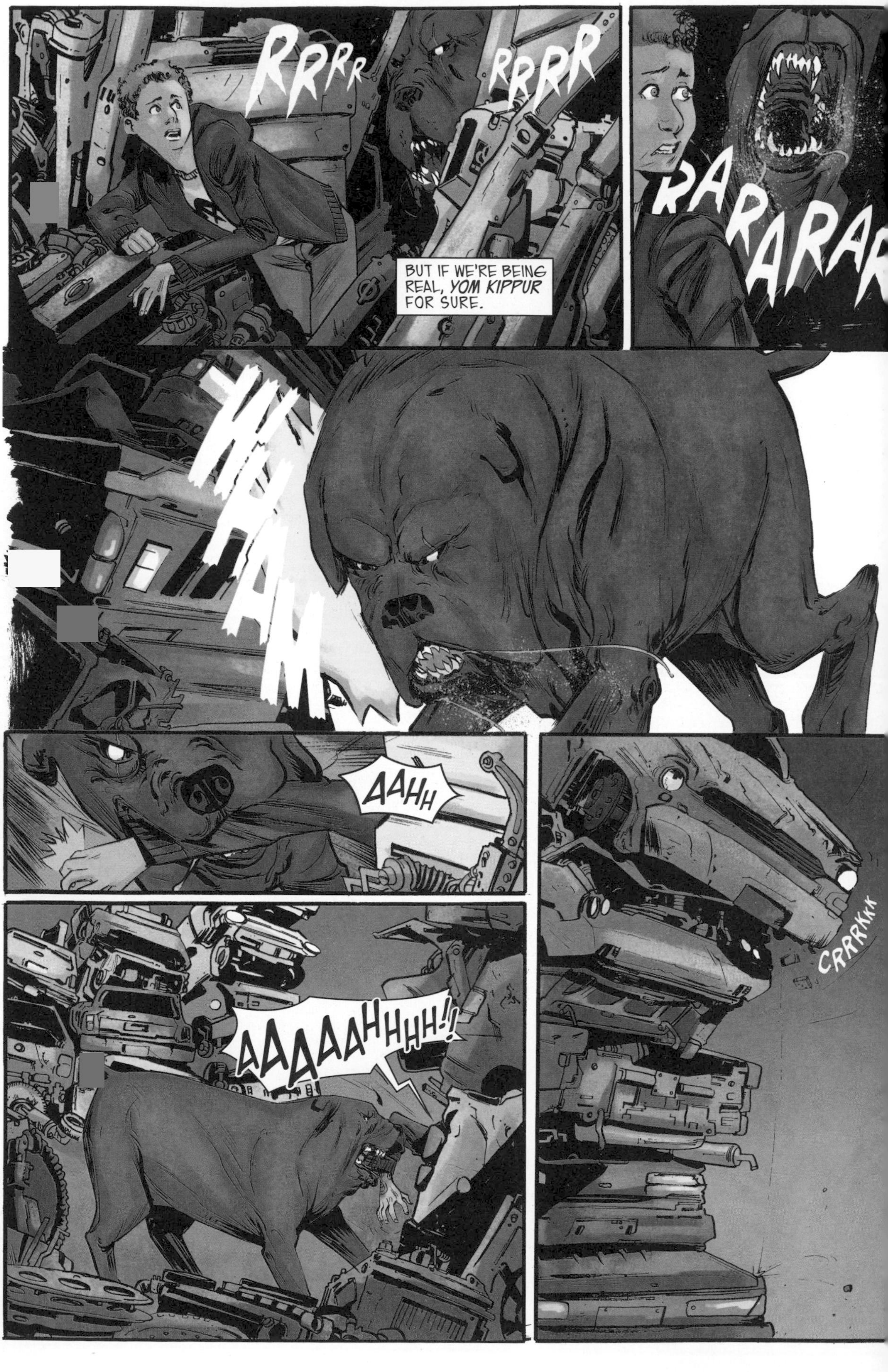
RRRR
RRRR
BUT IF WE'RE BEING REAL, *YOM KIPPUR* FOR SURE.
RARARAR
WHAM
AAHH
AAAAAHHHH!!
CRRRKKK

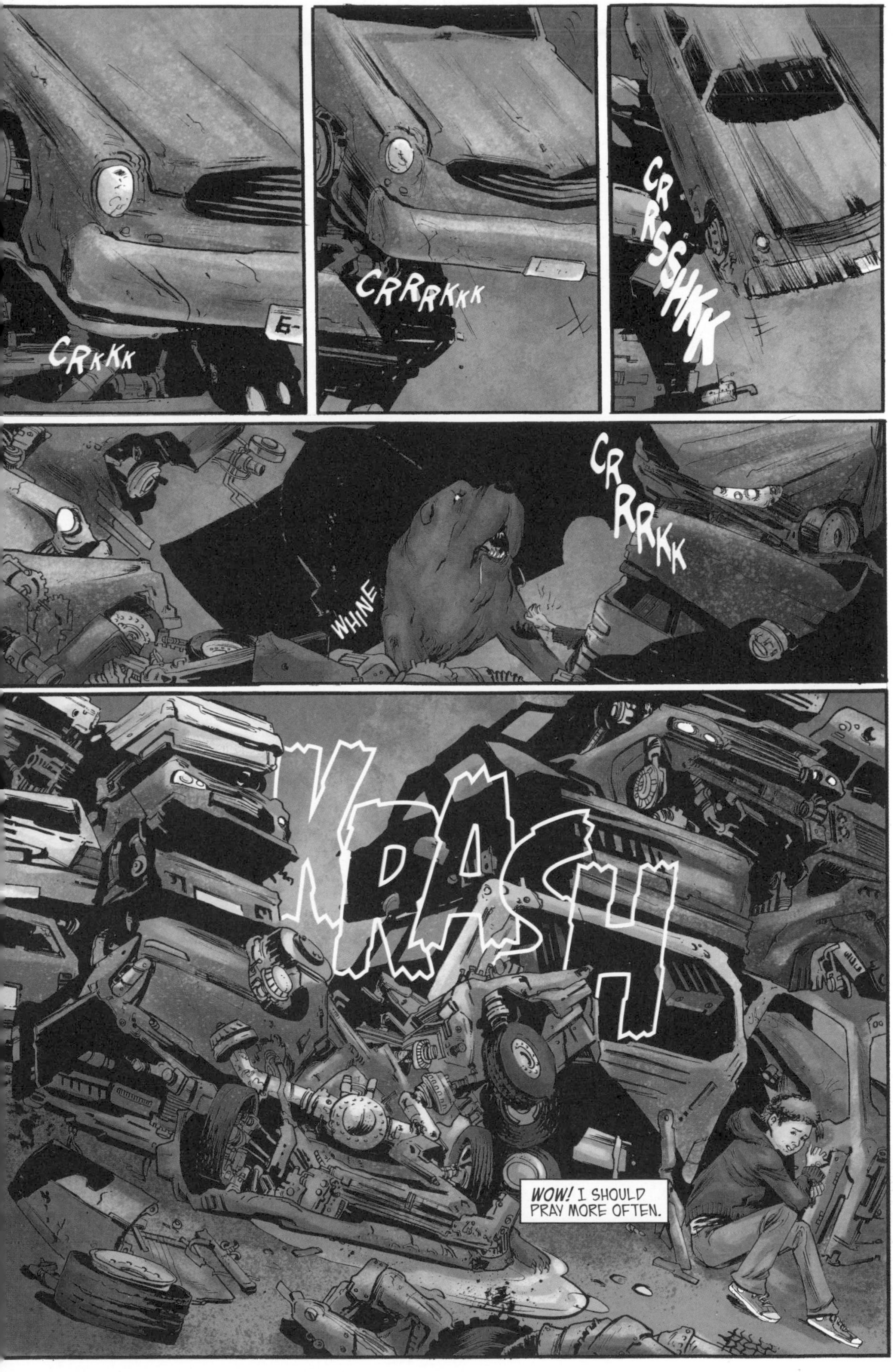
CRKKK
CRRRKKK
CRRSSHKKK
CRRRKK
WHINE
KRASH
WOW! I SHOULD PRAY MORE OFTEN.

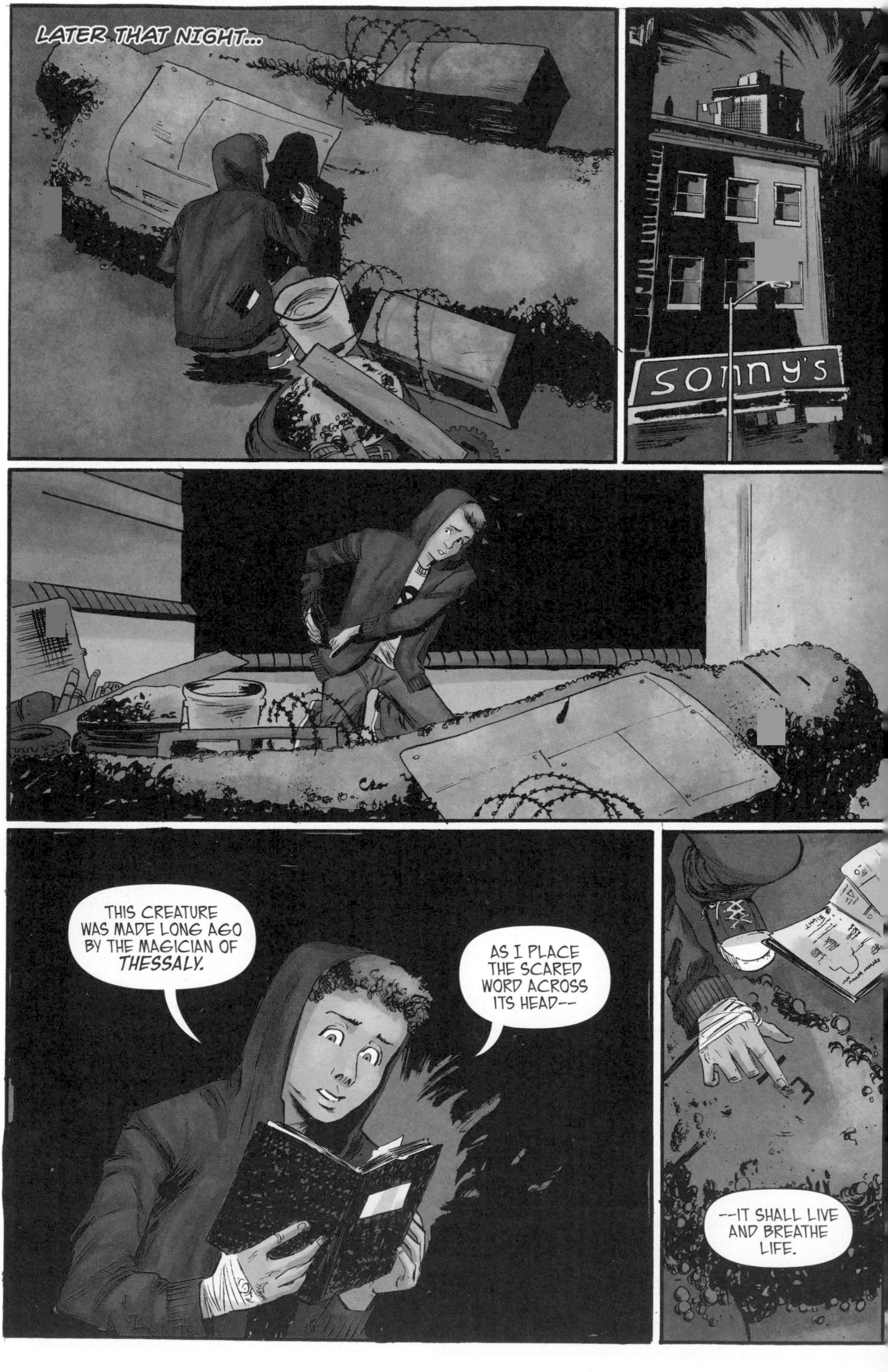

LATER THAT NIGHT...
SONNY'S
THIS CREATURE WAS MADE LONG AGO BY THE MAGICIAN OF THESSALY.
AS I PLACE THE SCARED WORD ACROSS ITS HEAD--
--IT SHALL LIVE AND BREATHE LIFE.

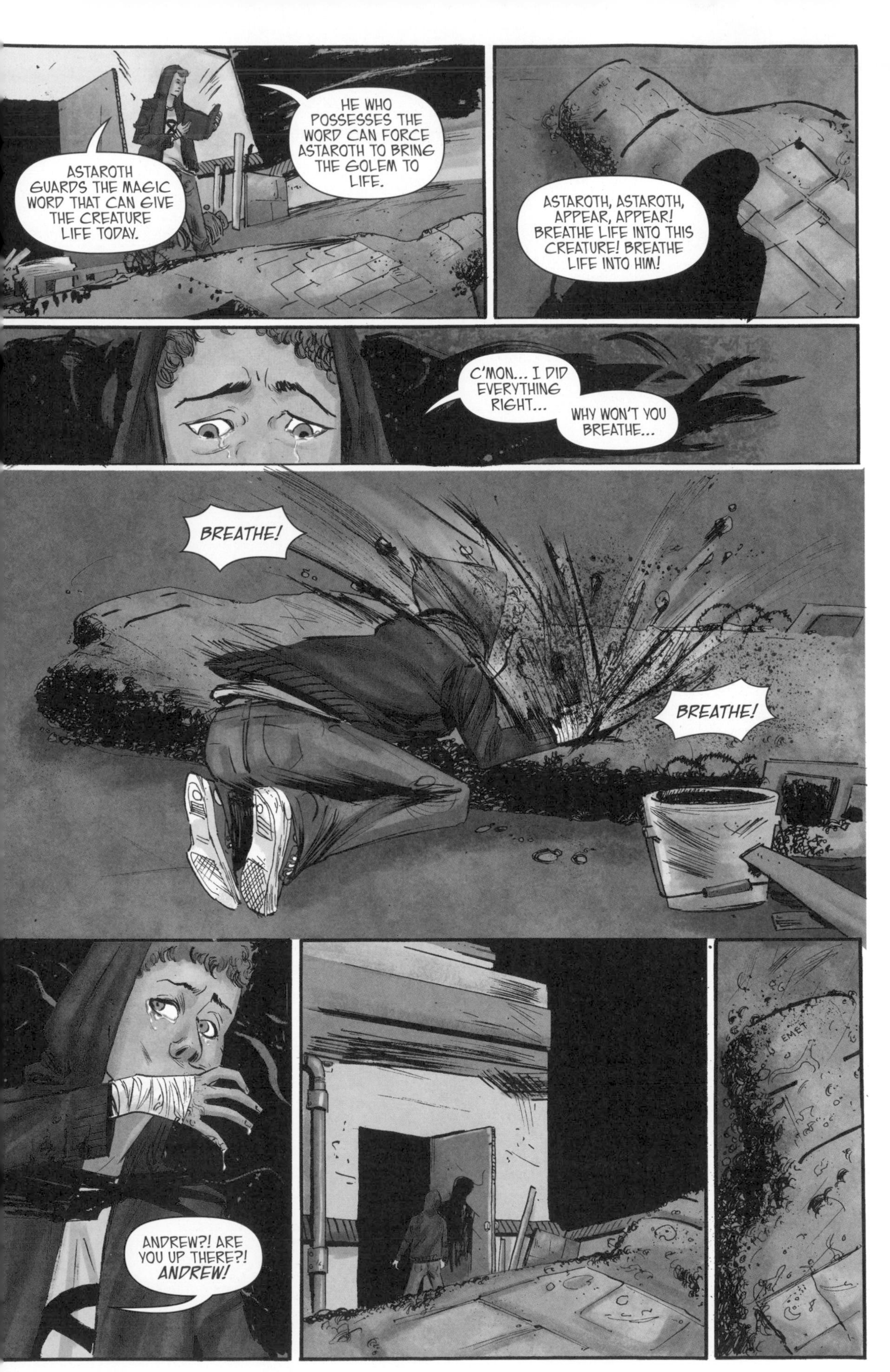
ASTAROTH GUARDS THE MAGIC WORD THAT CAN GIVE THE CREATURE LIFE TODAY.
HE WHO POSSESSES THE WORD CAN FORCE ASTAROTH TO BRING THE GOLEM TO LIFE.
EMET
ASTAROTH, ASTAROTH, APPEAR, APPEAR! BREATHE LIFE INTO THIS CREATURE! BREATHE LIFE INTO HIM!
C'MON... I DID EVERYTHING RIGHT...
WHY WON'T YOU BREATHE...
BREATHE!
BREATHE!
ANDREW?! ARE YOU UP THERE?! ANDREW!
EMET

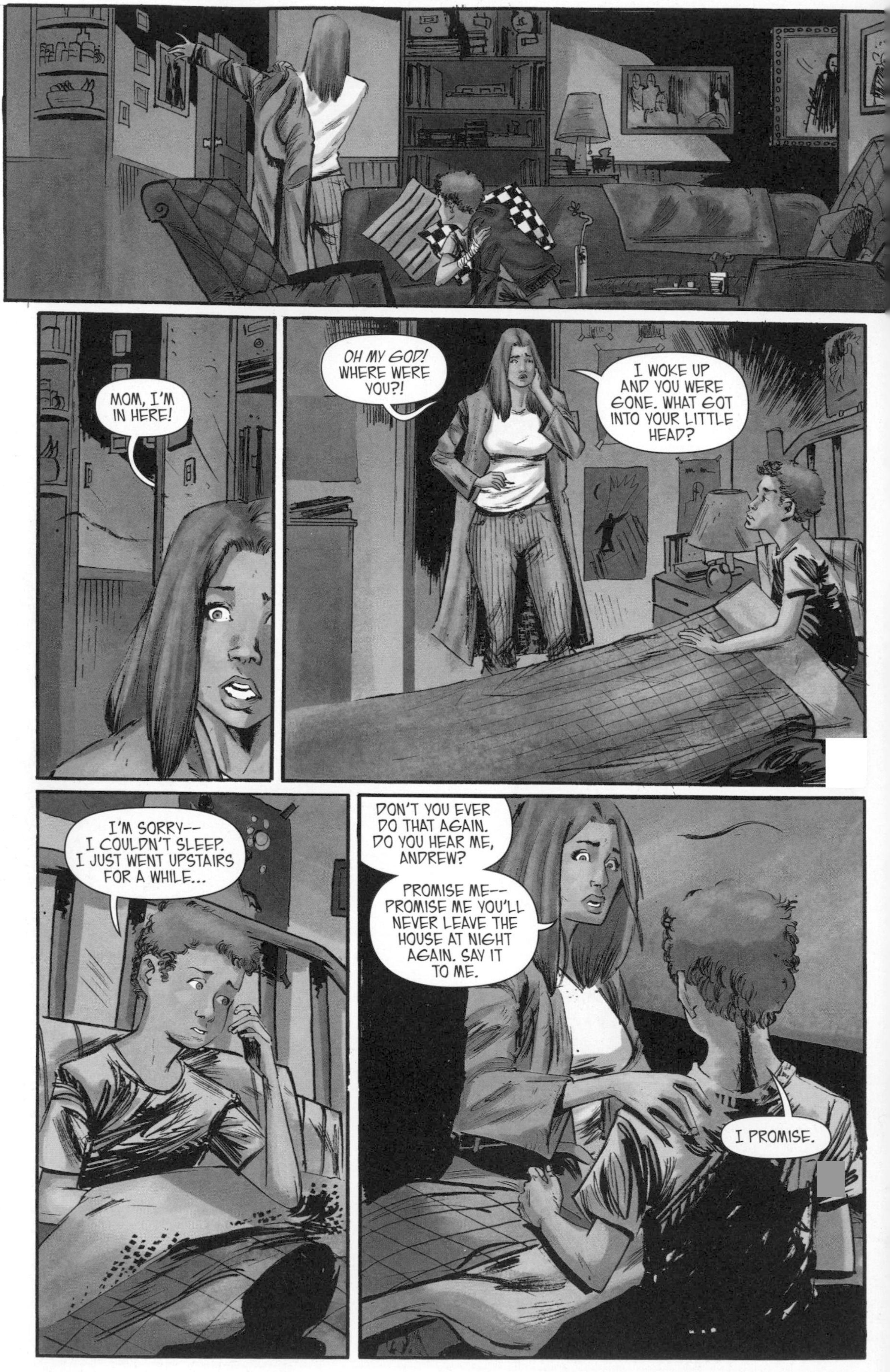
MOM, I'M IN HERE!
OH MY GOD! WHERE WERE YOU?!
I WOKE UP AND YOU WERE GONE. WHAT GOT INTO YOUR LITTLE HEAD?
I'M SORRY-- I COULDN'T SLEEP. I JUST WENT UPSTAIRS FOR A WHILE...
DON'T YOU EVER DO THAT AGAIN. DO YOU HEAR ME, ANDREW?
PROMISE ME-- PROMISE ME YOU'LL NEVER LEAVE THE HOUSE AT NIGHT AGAIN. SAY IT TO ME.
I PROMISE.

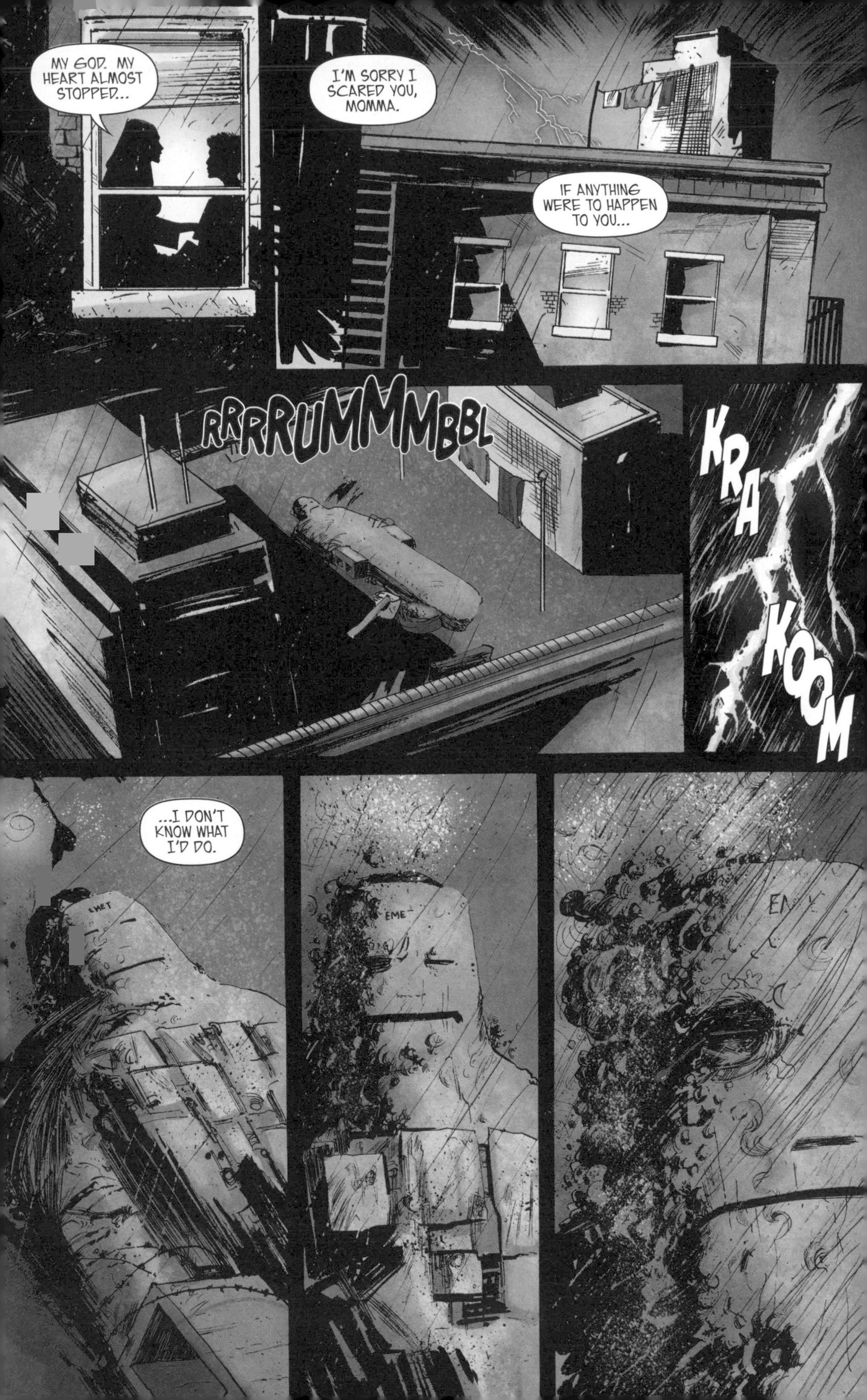
MY GOD. MY HEART ALMOST STOPPED...
I'M SORRY I SCARED YOU, MOMMA.
IF ANYTHING WERE TO HAPPEN TO YOU...
RRRRUMMMBBL
KRAKOOM
...I DON'T KNOW WHAT I'D DO.
EMET
EME

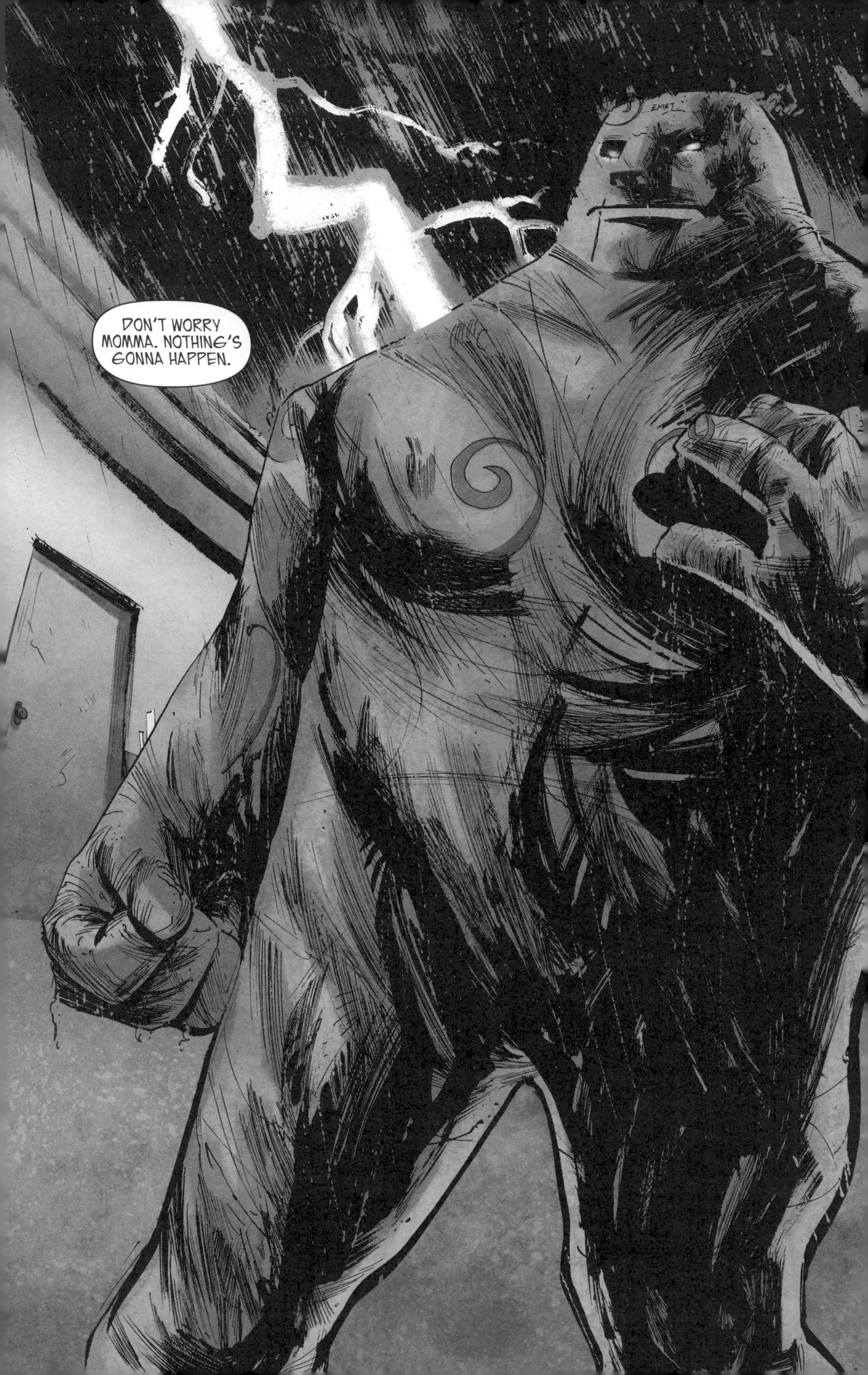
EMET
DON'T WORRY MOMMA. NOTHING'S GONNA HAPPEN.

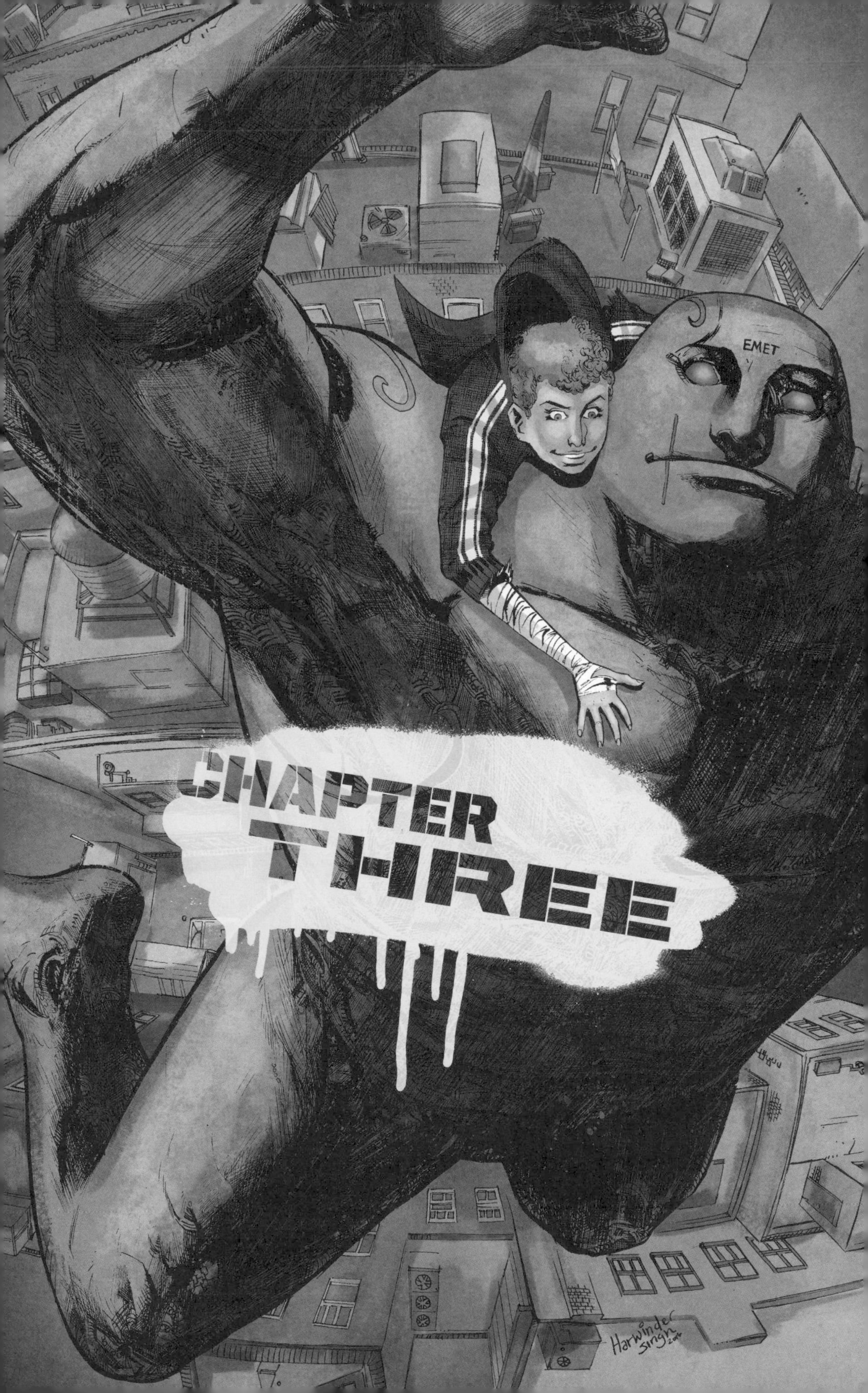
EMET
CHAPTER THREE
Harwinder Singh

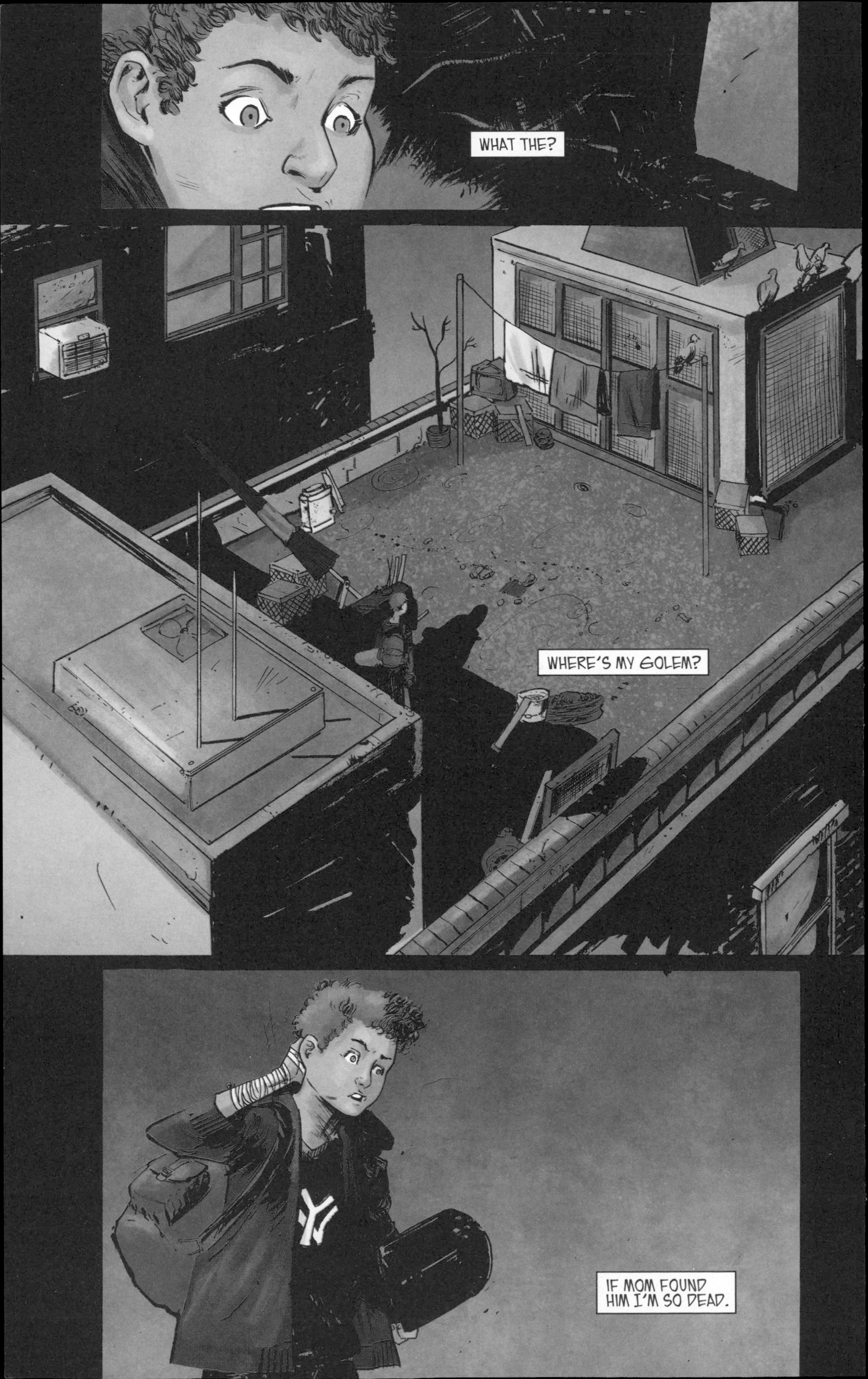
WHAT THE?
WHERE'S MY GOLEM?
IF MOM FOUND HIM I'M SO DEAD.

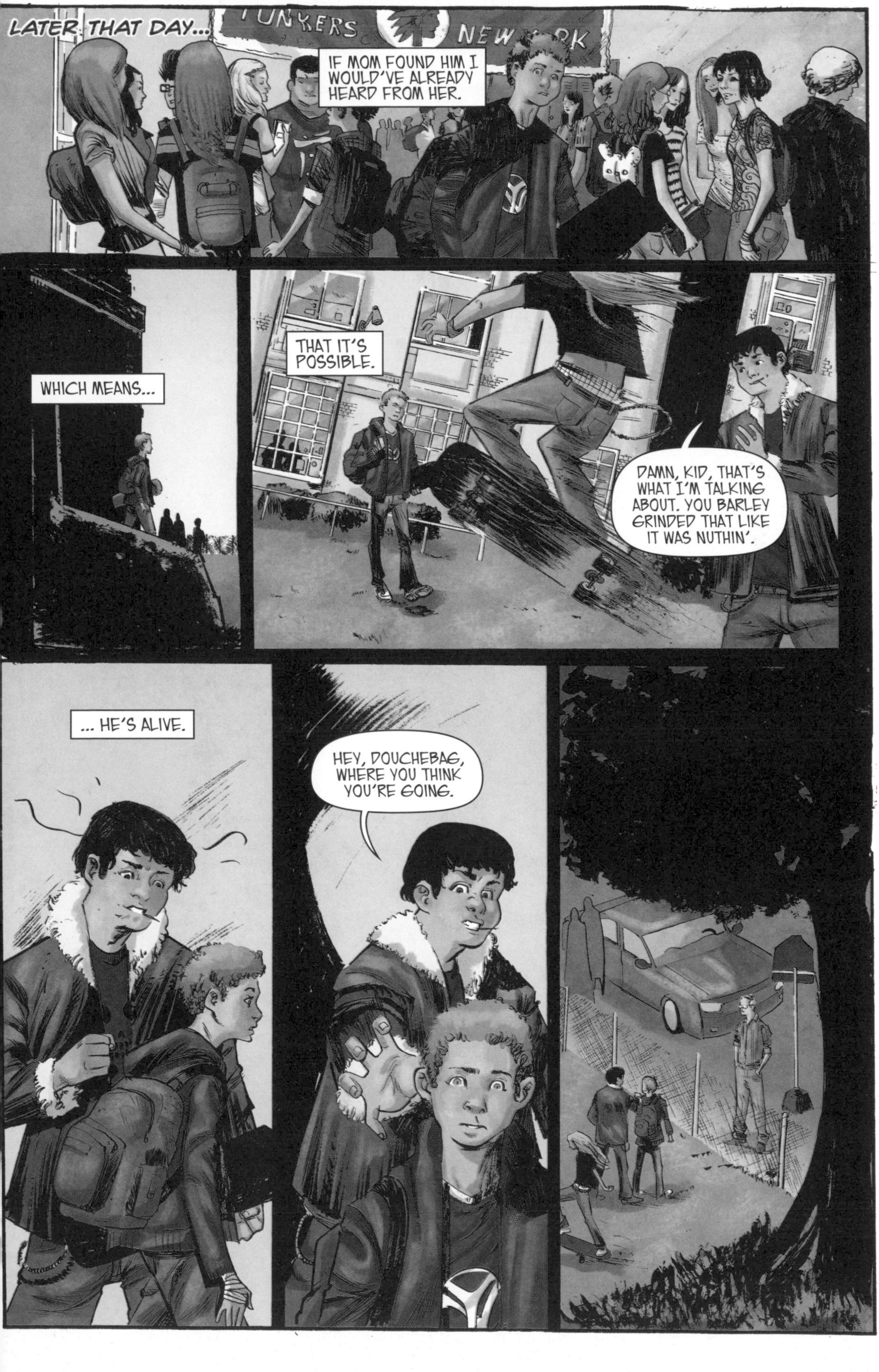
LATER THAT DAY...
YONKERS NEW YORK
IF MOM FOUND HIM I WOULD'VE ALREADY HEARD FROM HER.
WHICH MEANS...
THAT IT'S POSSIBLE.
DAMN, KID, THAT'S WHAT I'M TALKING ABOUT. YOU BARLEY GRINDED THAT LIKE IT WAS NUTHIN'.
... HE'S ALIVE.
HEY, DOUCHEBAG, WHERE YOU THINK YOU'RE GOING.

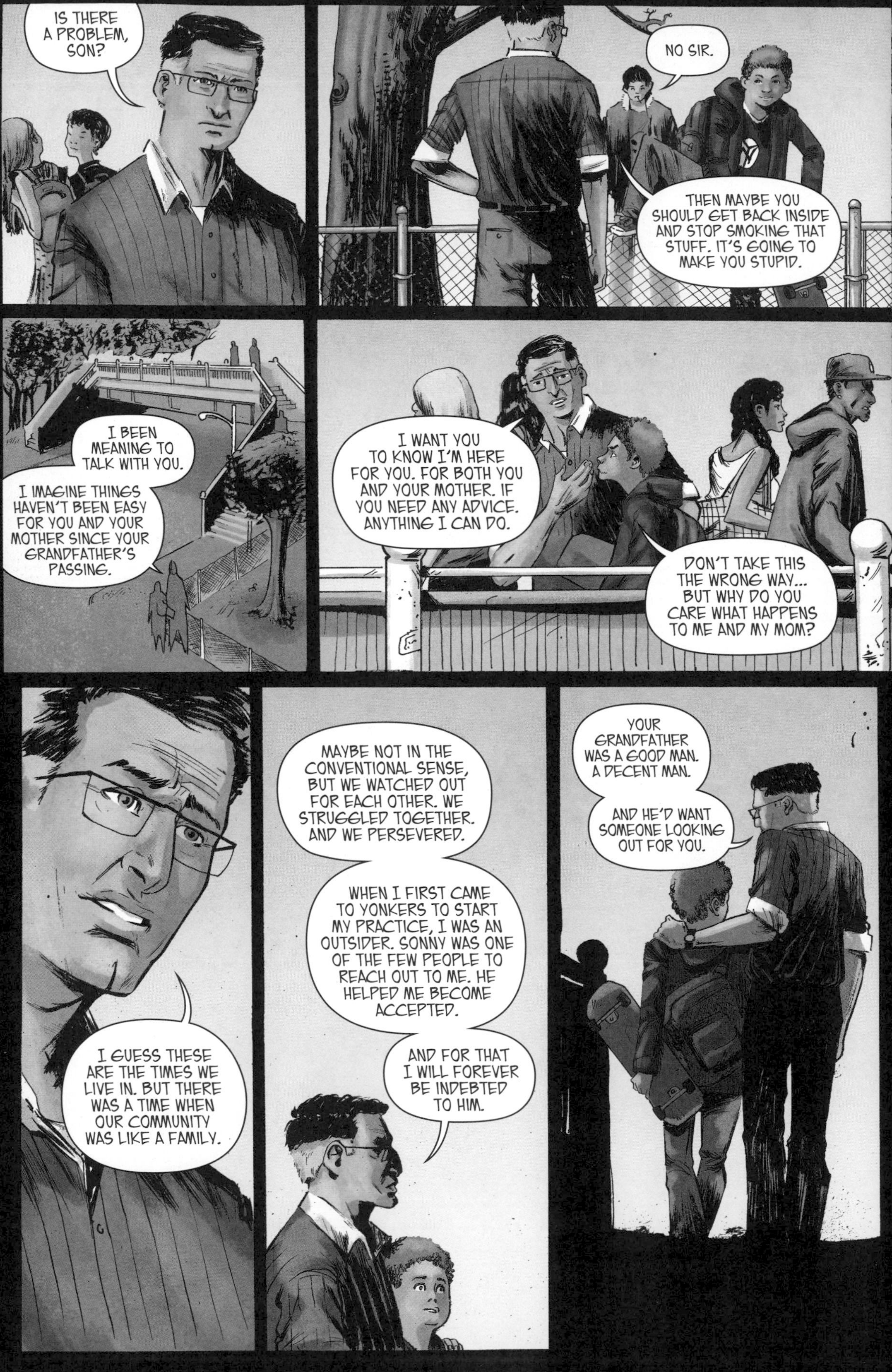
IS THERE A PROBLEM, SON?
NO SIR.
THEN MAYBE YOU SHOULD GET BACK INSIDE AND STOP SMOKING THAT STUFF. IT'S GOING TO MAKE YOU STUPID.
I BEEN MEANING TO TALK WITH YOU.
I IMAGINE THINGS HAVEN'T BEEN EASY FOR YOU AND YOUR MOTHER SINCE YOUR GRANDFATHER'S PASSING.
I WANT YOU TO KNOW I'M HERE FOR YOU. FOR BOTH YOU AND YOUR MOTHER. IF YOU NEED ANY ADVICE. ANYTHING I CAN DO.
DON'T TAKE THIS THE WRONG WAY... BUT WHY DO YOU CARE WHAT HAPPENS TO ME AND MY MOM?
I GUESS THESE ARE THE TIMES WE LIVE IN. BUT THERE WAS A TIME WHEN OUR COMMUNITY WAS LIKE A FAMILY.
MAYBE NOT IN THE CONVENTIONAL SENSE, BUT WE WATCHED OUT FOR EACH OTHER. WE STRUGGLED TOGETHER. AND WE PERSEVERED.
WHEN I FIRST CAME TO YONKERS TO START MY PRACTICE, I WAS AN OUTSIDER. SONNY WAS ONE OF THE FEW PEOPLE TO REACH OUT TO ME. HE HELPED ME BECOME ACCEPTED.
AND FOR THAT I WILL FOREVER BE INDEBTED TO HIM.
YOUR GRANDFATHER WAS A GOOD MAN. A DECENT MAN.
AND HE'D WANT SOMEONE LOOKING OUT FOR YOU.

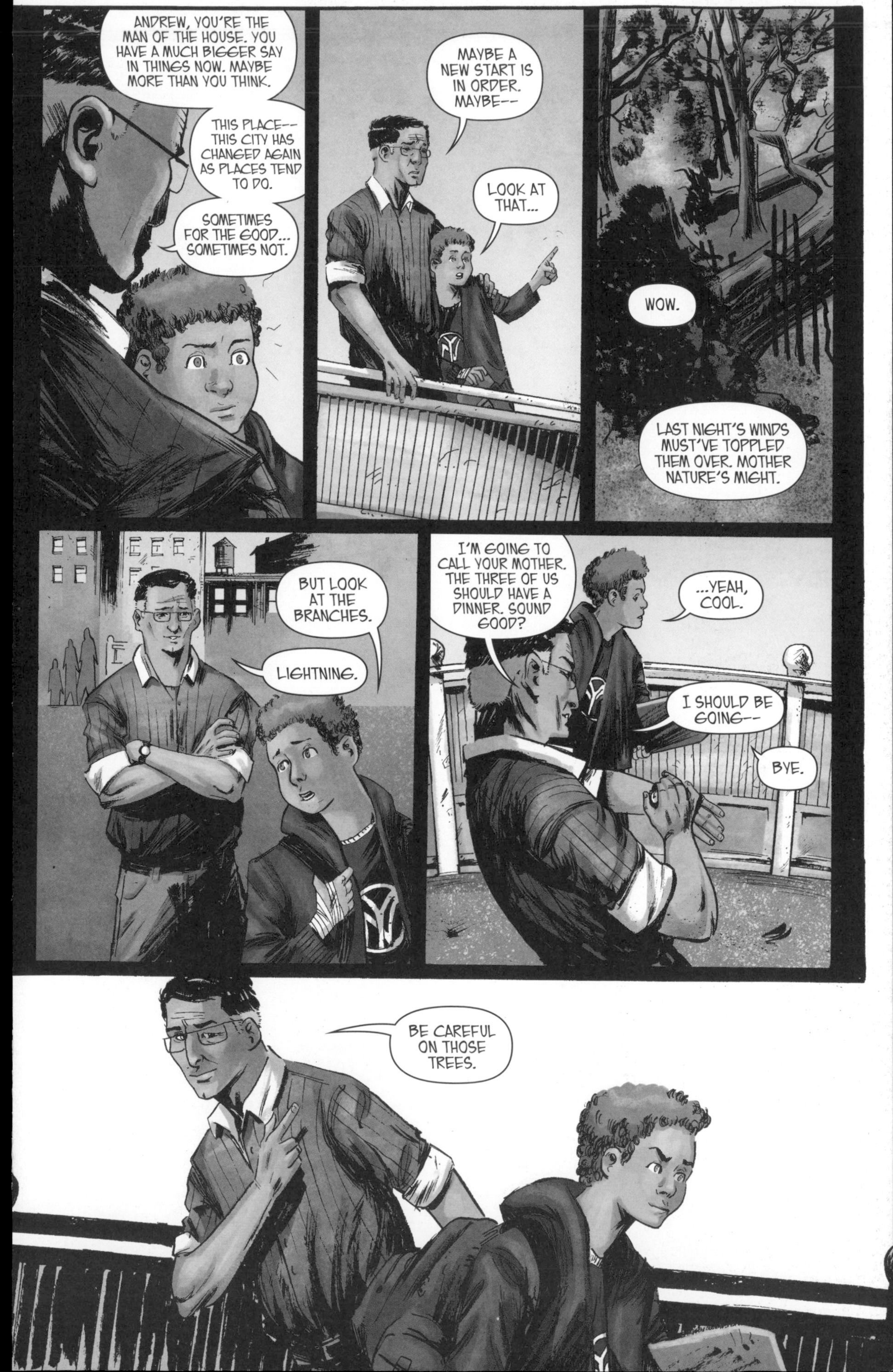
ANDREW, YOU'RE THE MAN OF THE HOUSE. YOU HAVE A MUCH BIGGER SAY IN THINGS NOW. MAYBE MORE THAN YOU THINK.
THIS PLACE-- THIS CITY HAS CHANGED AGAIN AS PLACES TEND TO DO.
SOMETIMES FOR THE GOOD... SOMETIMES NOT.
MAYBE A NEW START IS IN ORDER. MAYBE--
LOOK AT THAT...
WOW.
LAST NIGHT'S WINDS MUST'VE TOPPLED THEM OVER. MOTHER NATURE'S MIGHT.
BUT LOOK AT THE BRANCHES.
LIGHTNING.
I'M GOING TO CALL YOUR MOTHER. THE THREE OF US SHOULD HAVE A DINNER. SOUND GOOD?
...YEAH, COOL.
I SHOULD BE GOING--
BYE.
BE CAREFUL ON THOSE TREES.

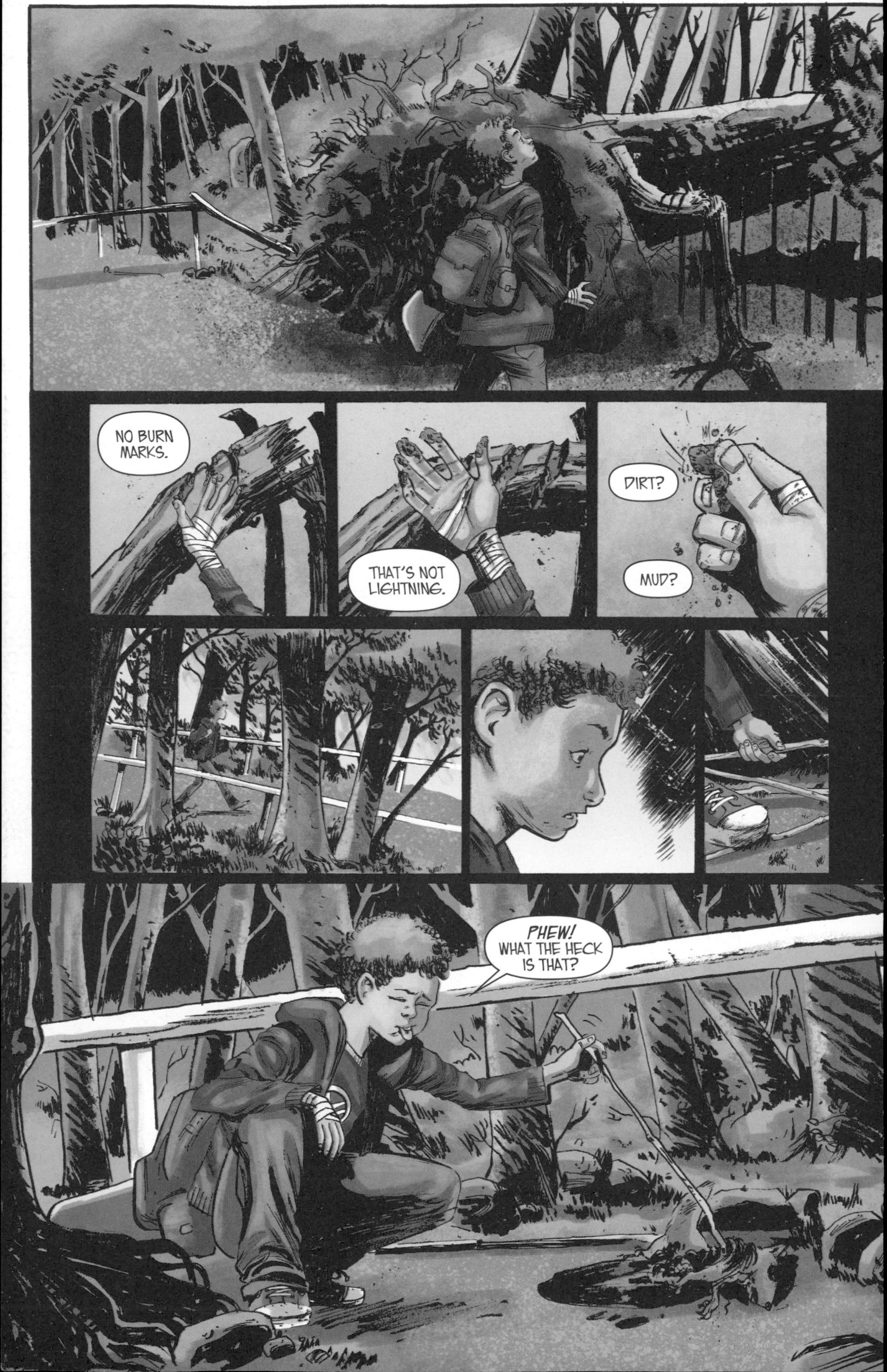
NO BURN MARKS.
THAT'S NOT LIGHTNING.
DIRT?
MUD?
PHEW! WHAT THE HECK IS THAT?

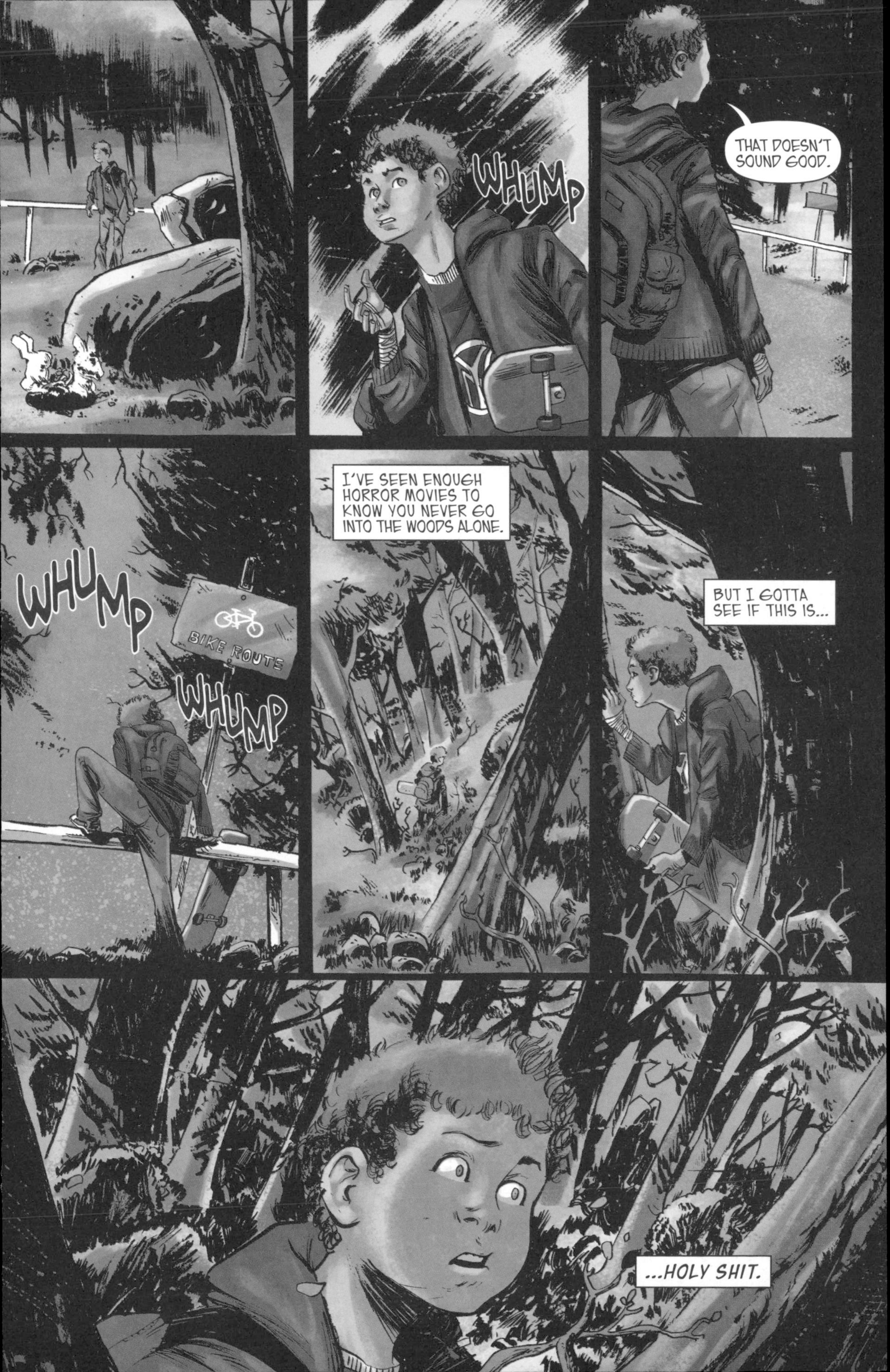
WHUMP
THAT DOESN'T SOUND GOOD.
WHUMP
BIKE ROUTE
WHUMP
I'VE SEEN ENOUGH HORROR MOVIES TO KNOW YOU NEVER GO INTO THE WOODS ALONE.
BUT I GOTTA SEE IF THIS IS...
...HOLY SHIT.

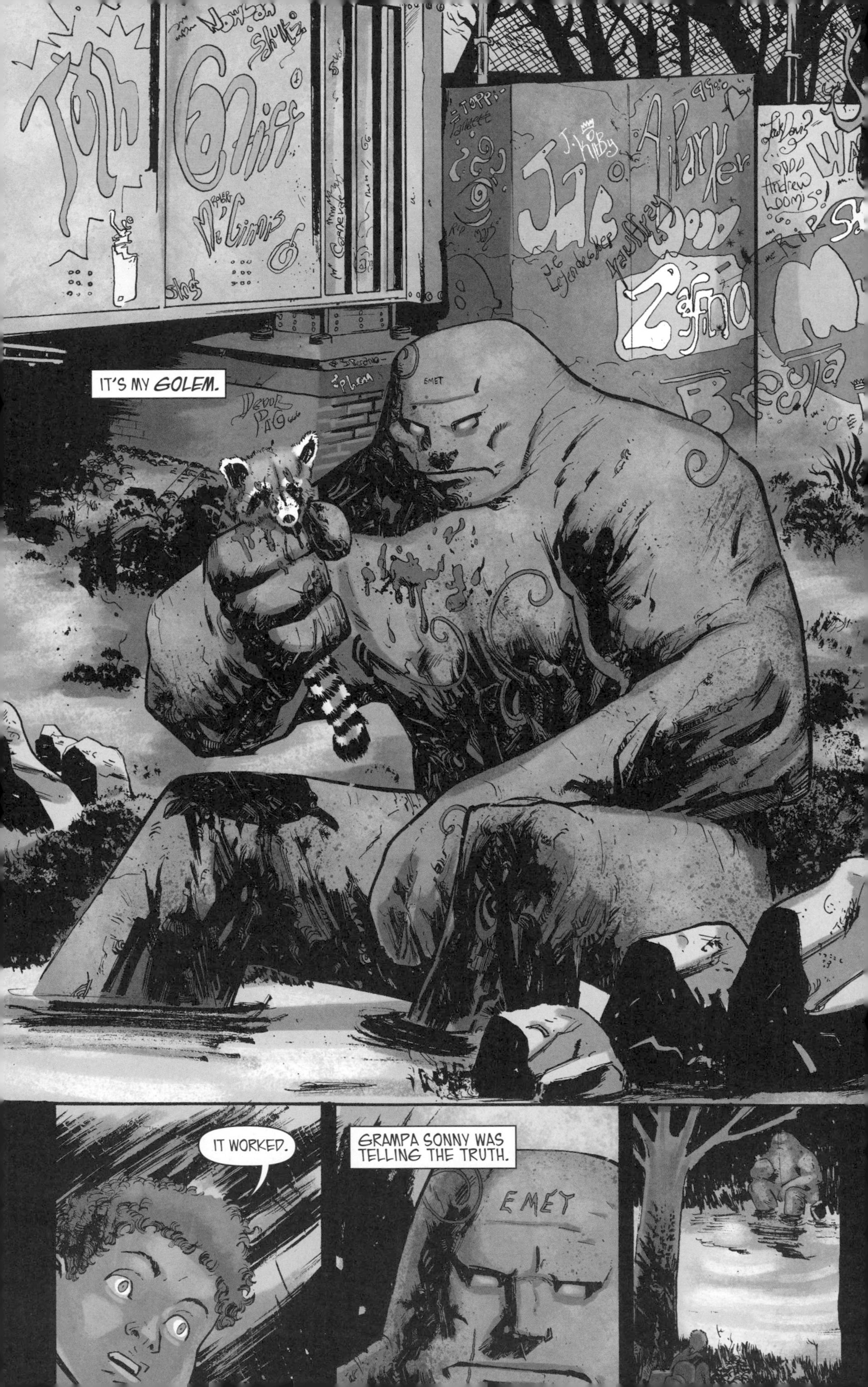
IT'S MY GOLEM.
EMET
IT WORKED.
GRAMPA SONNY WAS TELLING THE TRUTH.
EMET

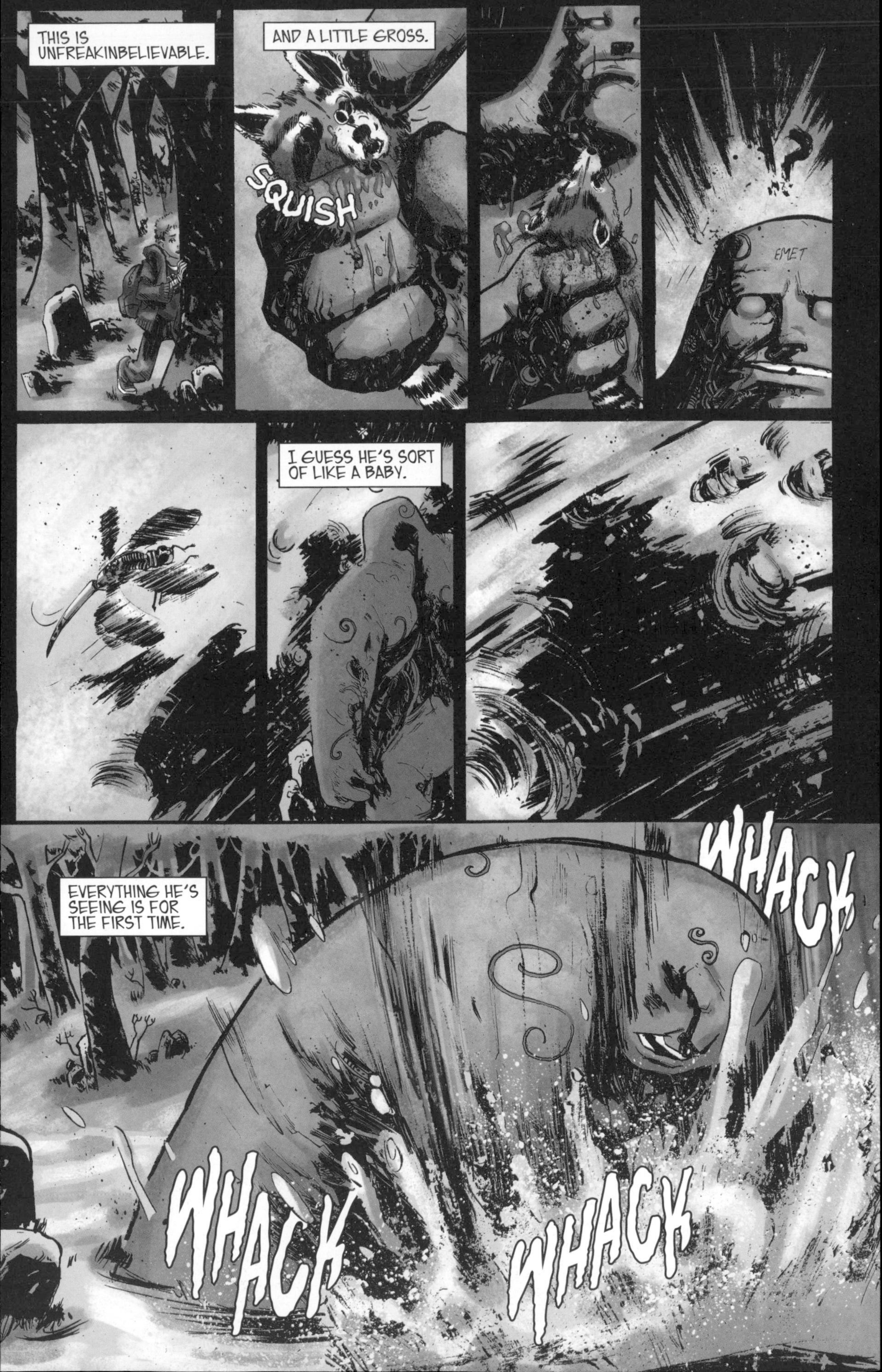
THIS IS UNFREAKINBELIEVABLE.
AND A LITTLE GROSS.
SQUISH
?
EMET
I GUESS HE'S SORT OF LIKE A BABY.
EVERYTHING HE'S SEEING IS FOR THE FIRST TIME.
WHACK
WHACK
WHACK

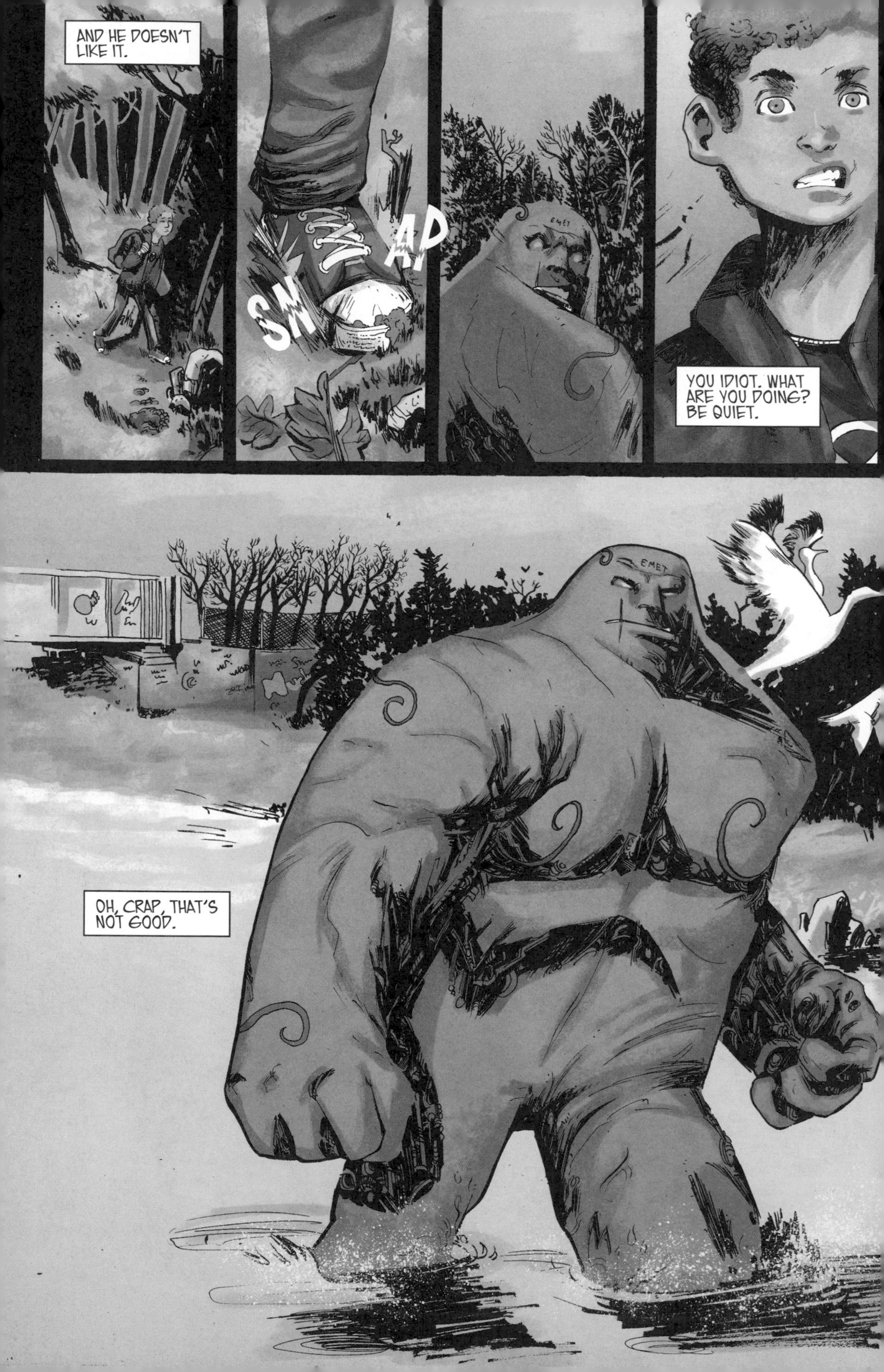
AND HE DOESN'T LIKE IT.
SNAP
YOU IDIOT. WHAT ARE YOU DOING? BE QUIET.
EMET
OH, CRAP, THAT'S NOT GOOD.

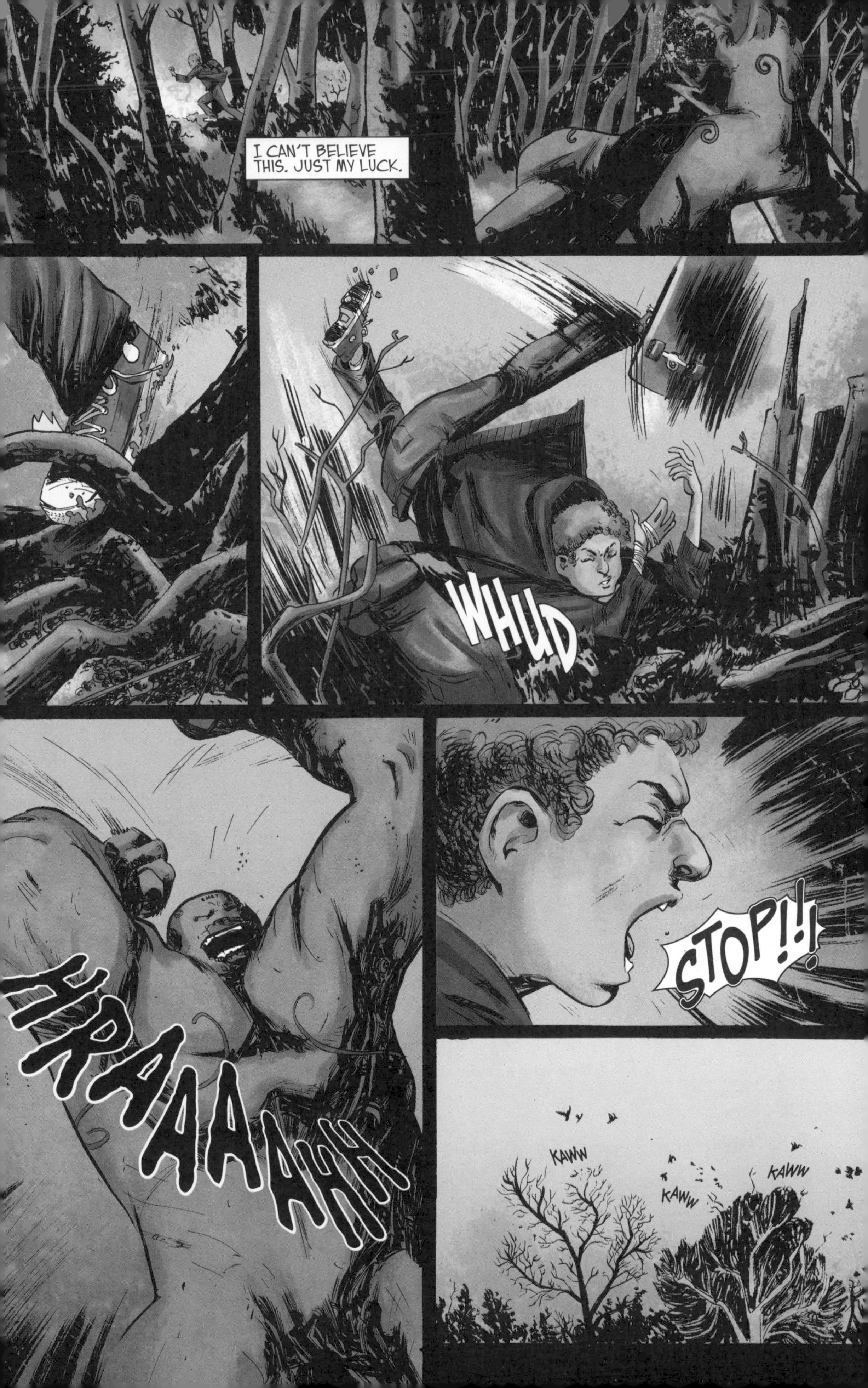
I CAN'T BELIEVE THIS. JUST MY LUCK.
WHUD
HRAAAAAHH
STOP!!!
KAWW
KAWW
KAWW

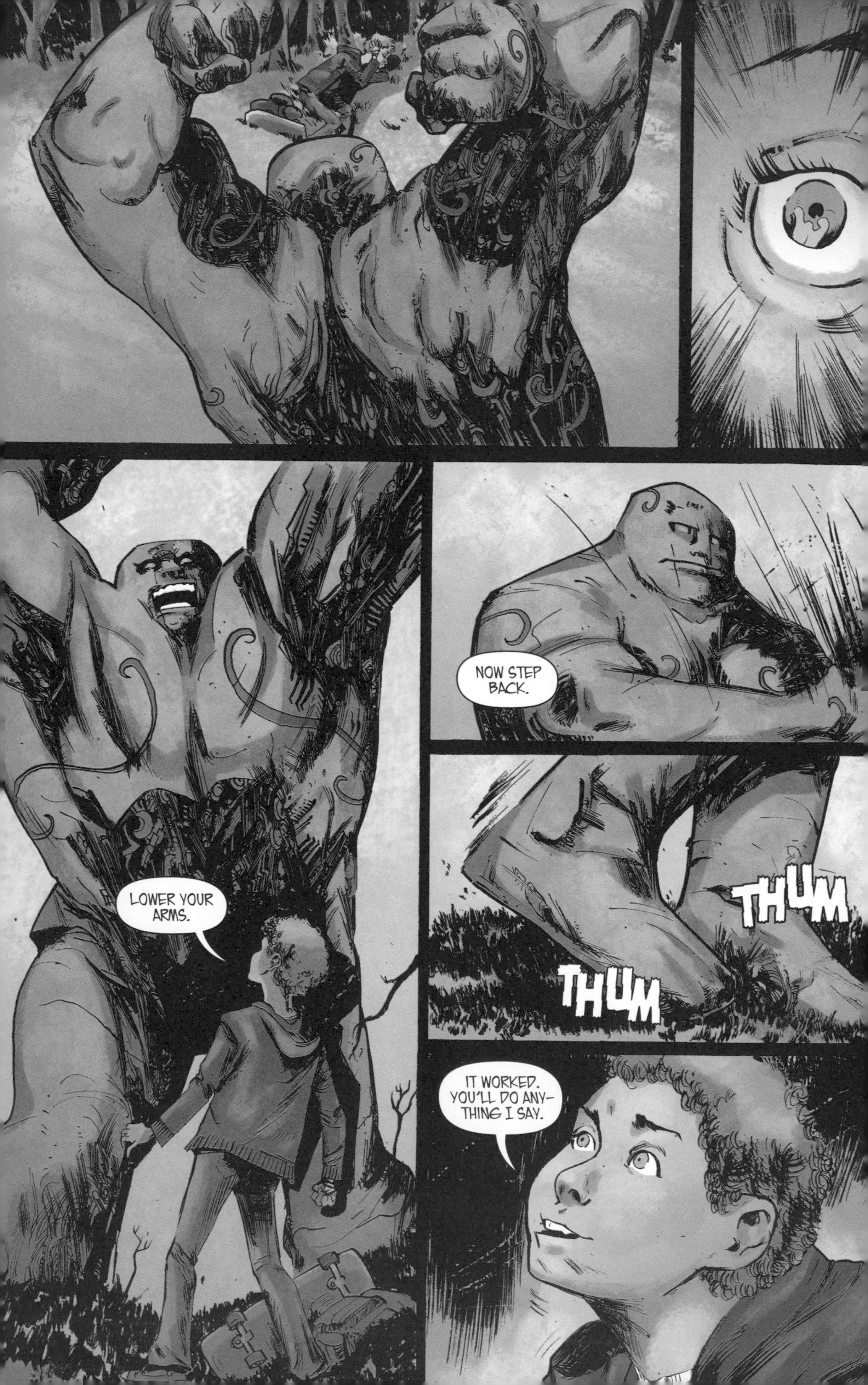
LOWER YOUR ARMS.
NOW STEP BACK.
THUM
THUM
IT WORKED. YOU'LL DO ANY-THING I SAY.

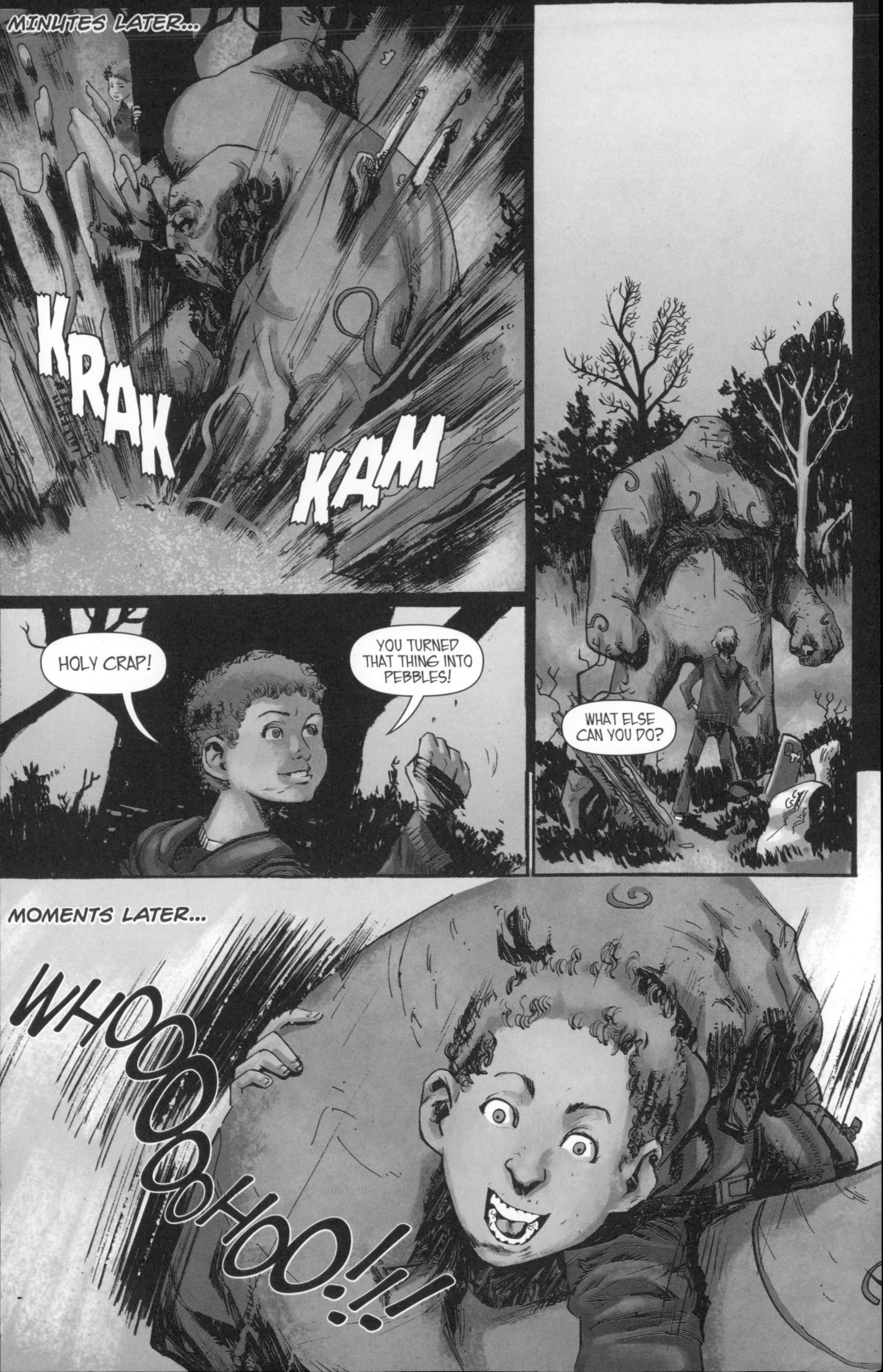
MINUTES LATER...
KRAK
KAM
HOLY CRAP!
YOU TURNED THAT THING INTO PEBBLES!
WHAT ELSE CAN YOU DO?
MOMENTS LATER...
WHOOOOOHOO!!!

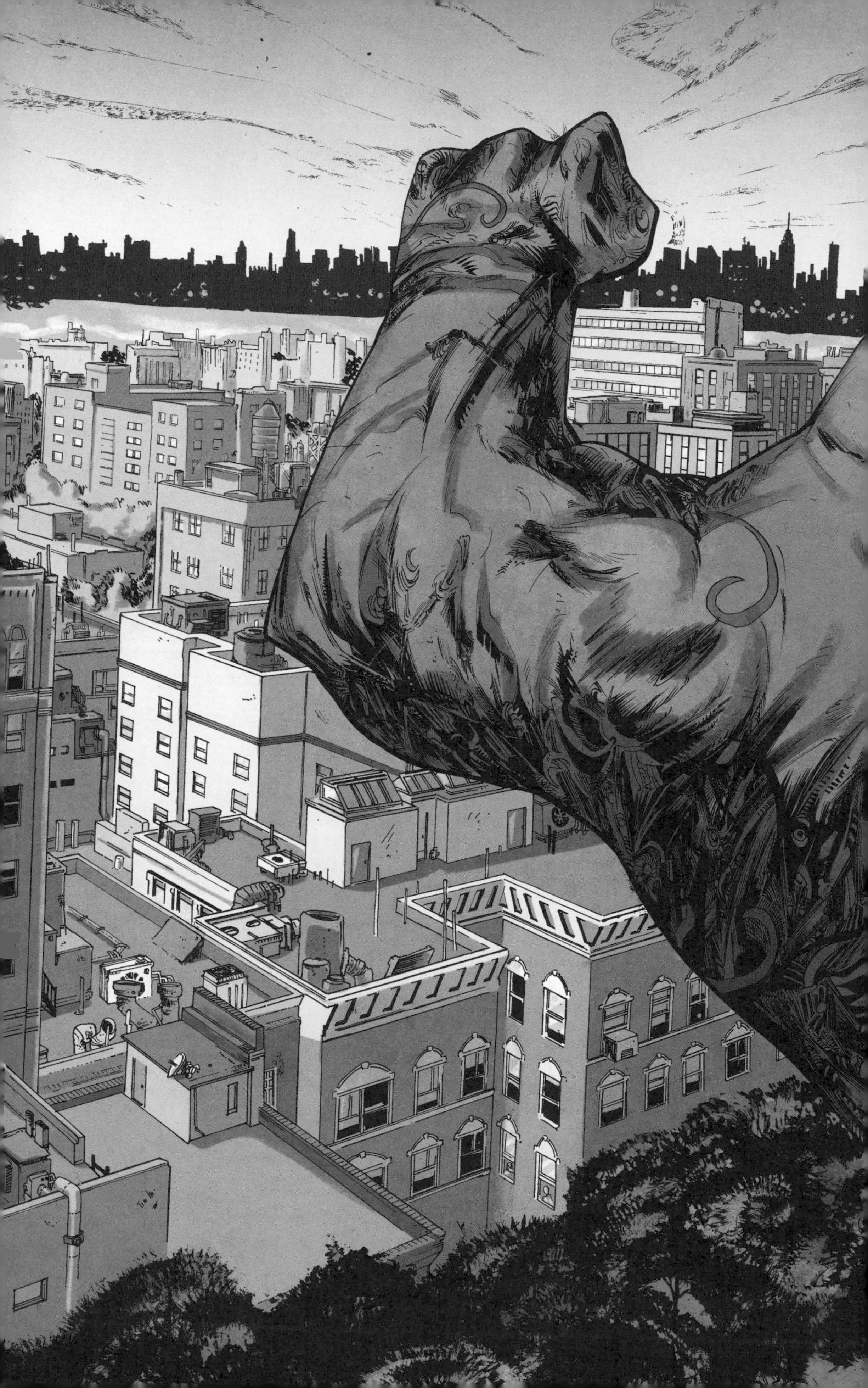

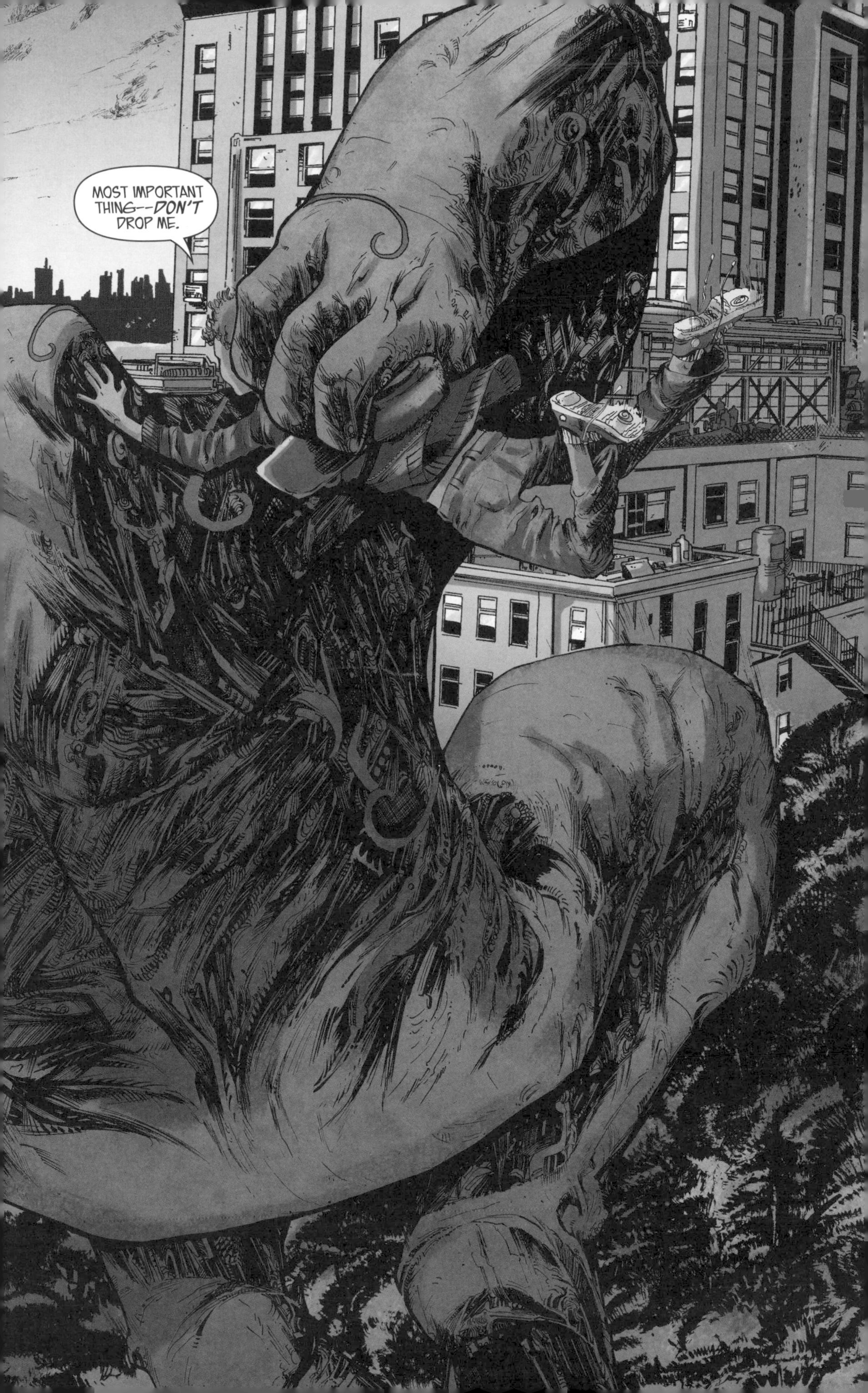
MOST IMPORTANT THING--DON'T DROP ME.

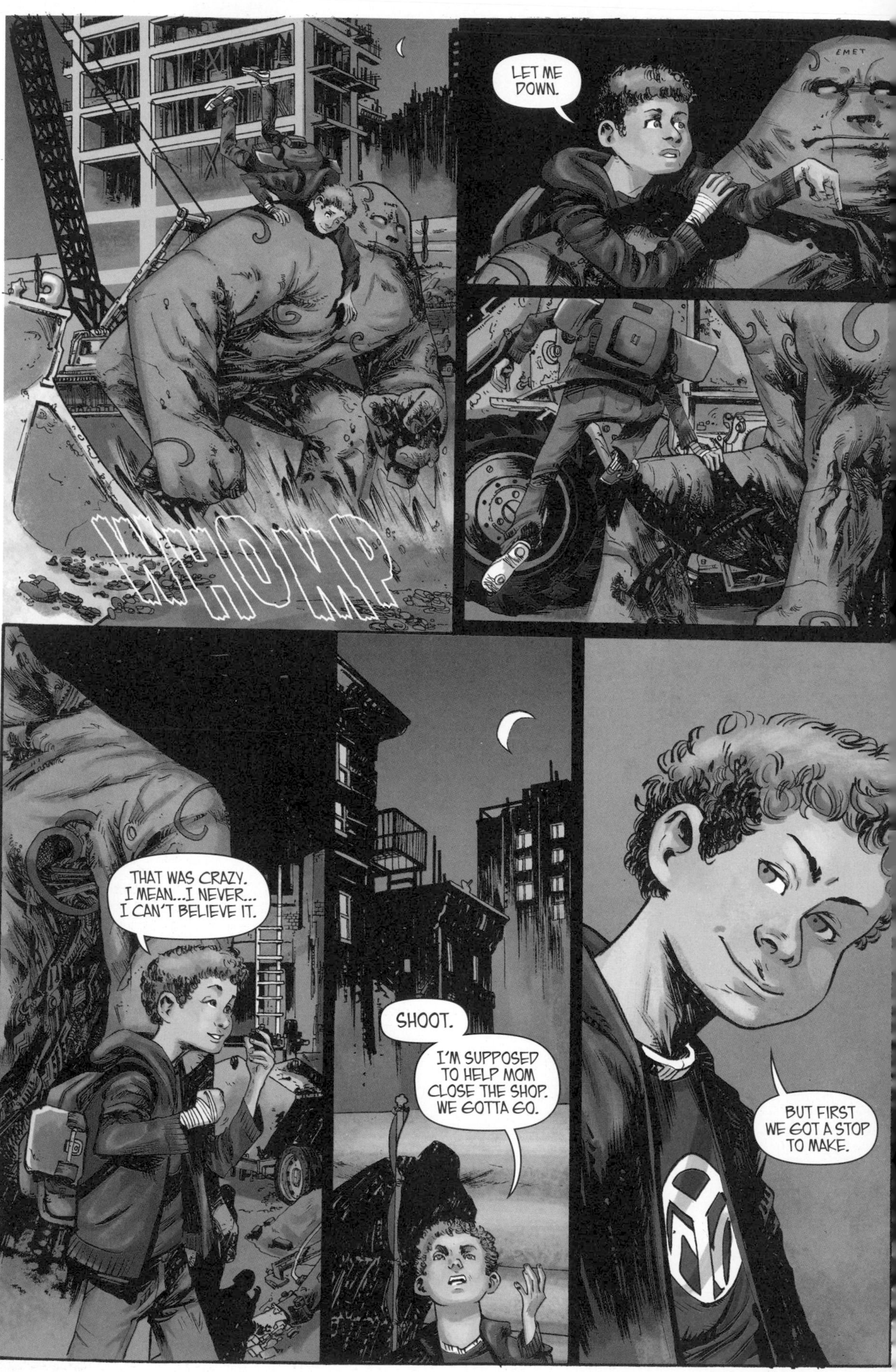
WHOMP
LET ME DOWN.
THAT WAS CRAZY. I MEAN...I NEVER... I CAN'T BELIEVE IT.
SHOOT.
I'M SUPPOSED TO HELP MOM CLOSE THE SHOP. WE GOTTA GO.
BUT FIRST WE GOT A STOP TO MAKE.

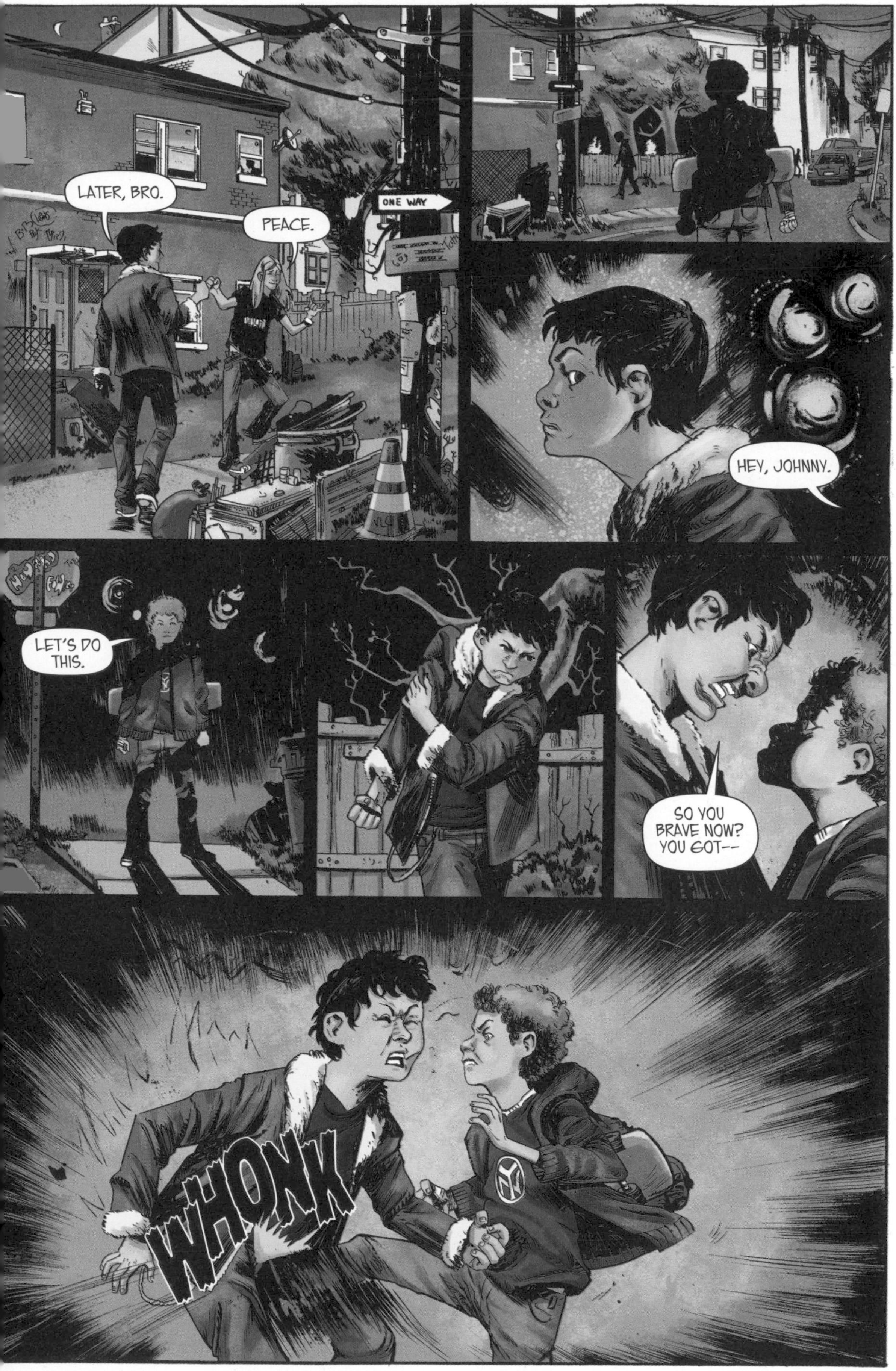
LATER, BRO.
PEACE.
ONE WAY
HEY, JOHNNY.
LET'S DO THIS.
SO YOU BRAVE NOW? YOU GOT--
WHONK

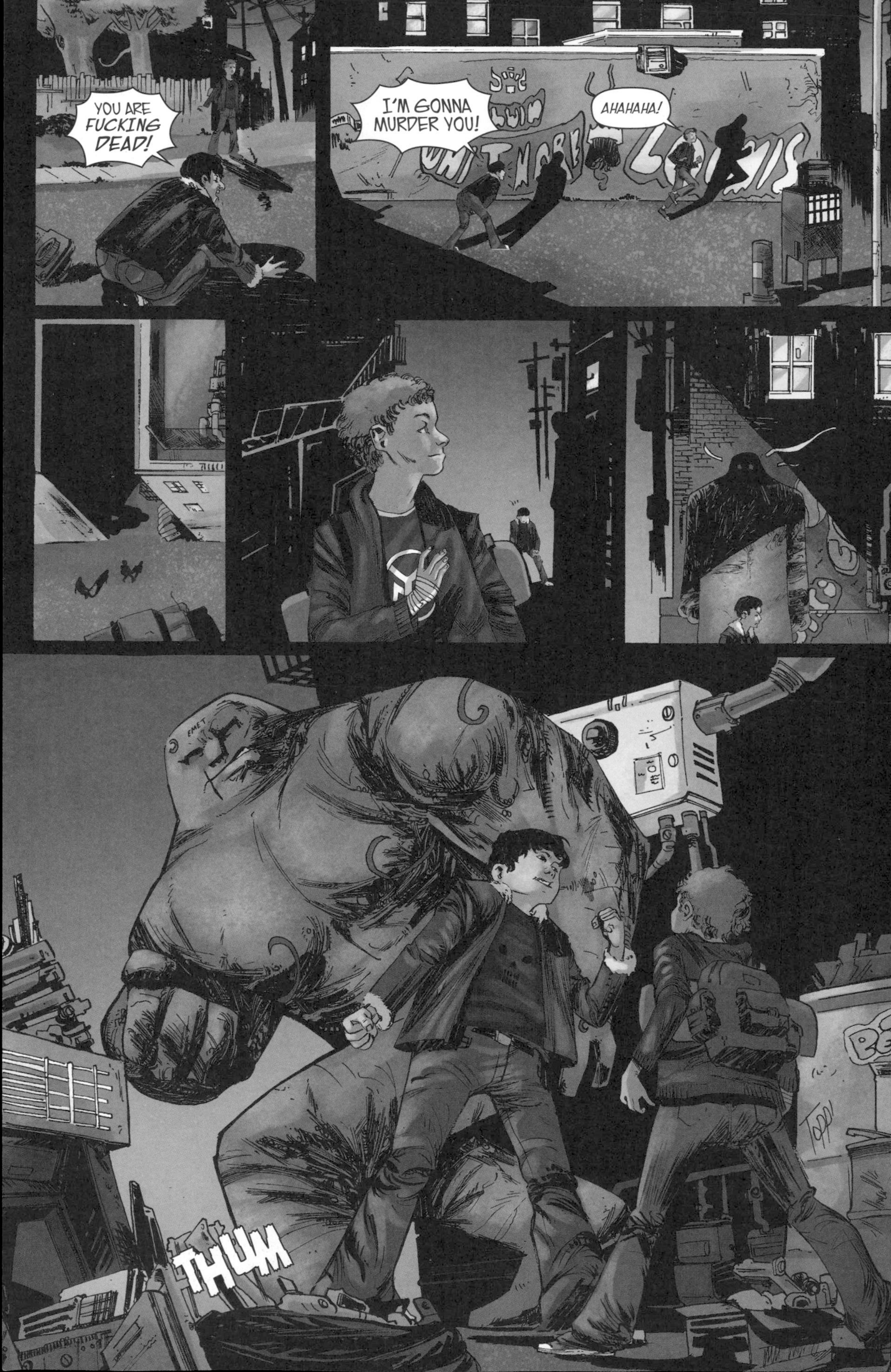
YOU ARE FUCKING DEAD!
I'M GONNA MURDER YOU!
AHAHAHA!
THUM

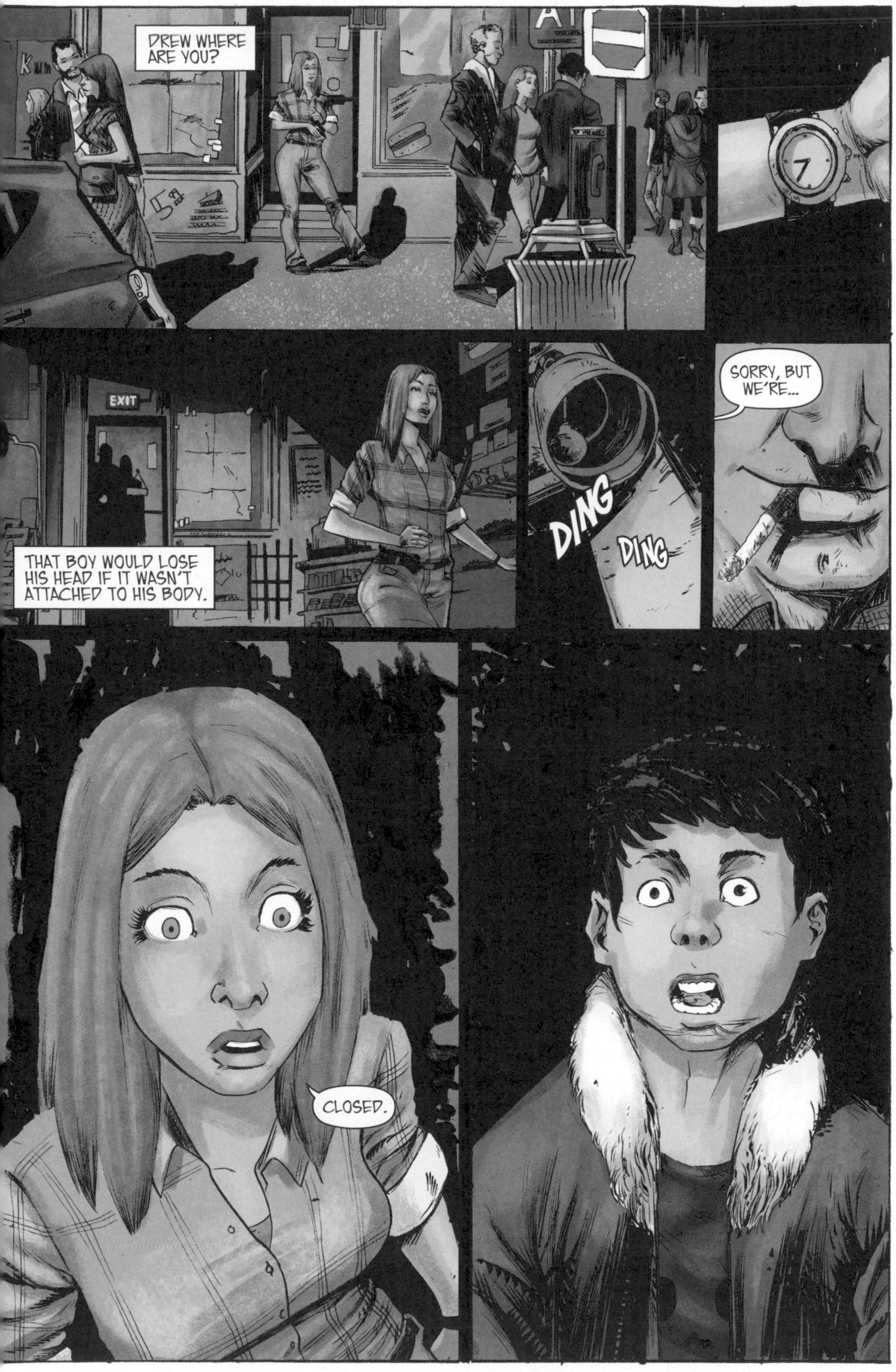
DREW WHERE ARE YOU?
THAT BOY WOULD LOSE HIS HEAD IF IT WASN'T ATTACHED TO HIS BODY.
EXIT
DING
DING
SORRY, BUT WE'RE...
CLOSED.

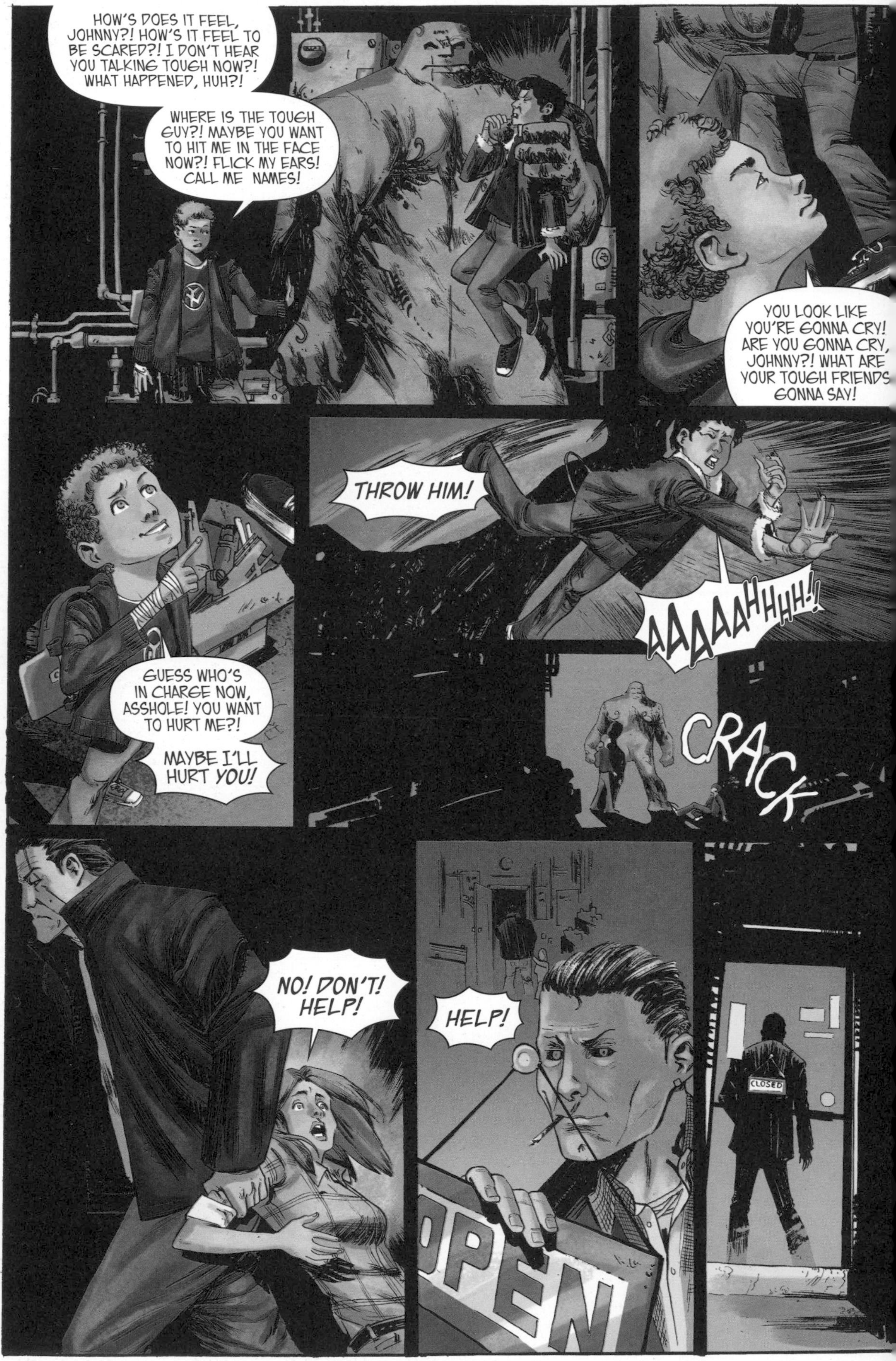
HOW'S DOES IT FEEL, JOHNNY?! HOW'S IT FEEL TO BE SCARED?! I DON'T HEAR YOU TALKING TOUGH NOW?! WHAT HAPPENED, HUH?!
WHERE IS THE TOUGH GUY?! MAYBE YOU WANT TO HIT ME IN THE FACE NOW?! FLICK MY EARS! CALL ME NAMES!
YOU LOOK LIKE YOU'RE GONNA CRY! ARE YOU GONNA CRY, JOHNNY?! WHAT ARE YOUR TOUGH FRIENDS GONNA SAY!
GUESS WHO'S IN CHARGE NOW, ASSHOLE! YOU WANT TO HURT ME?!
MAYBE I'LL HURT YOU!
THROW HIM!
AAAAAHHHH!!
CRACK
NO! DON'T! HELP!
HELP!
OPEN
CLOSED

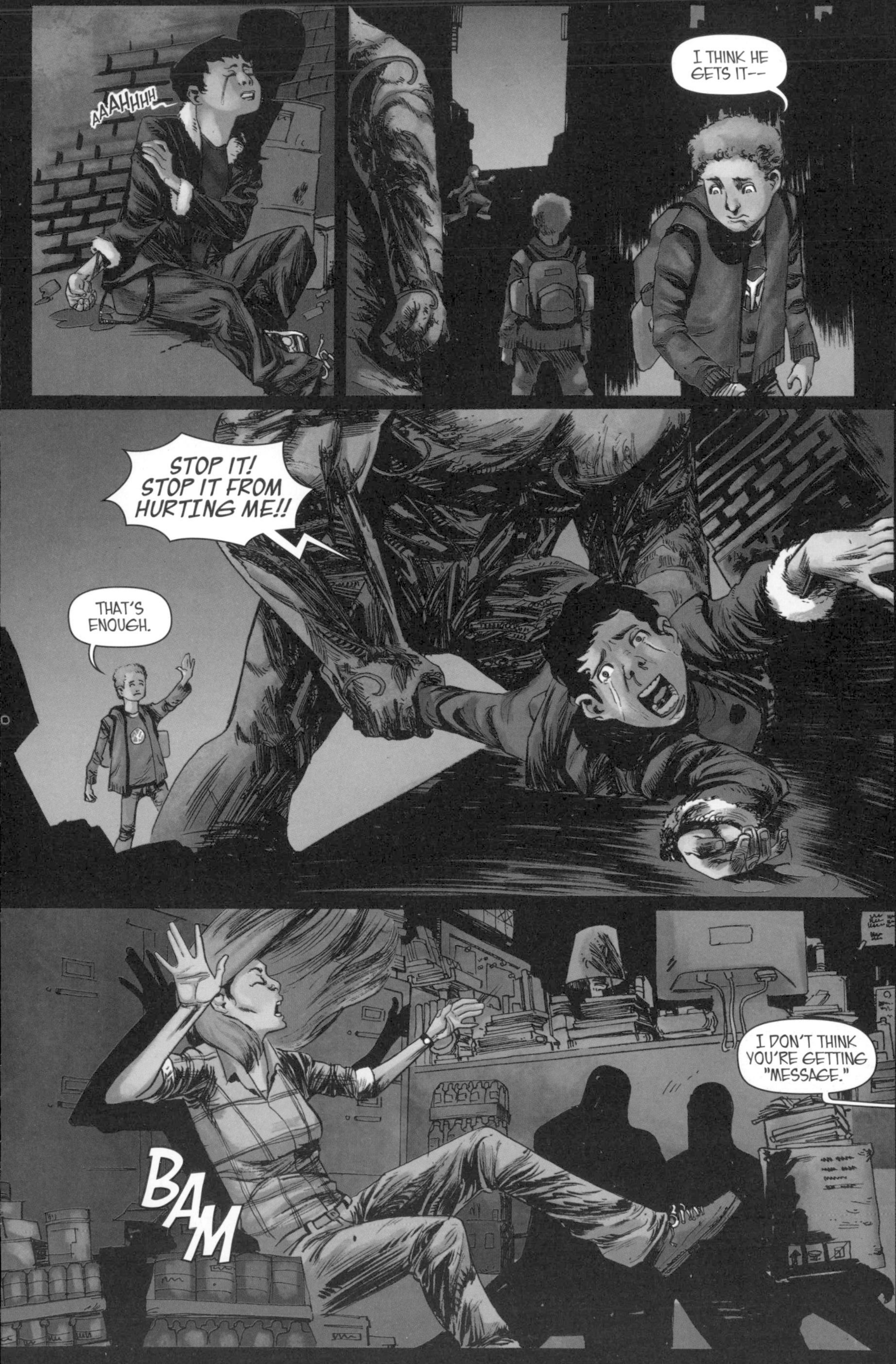
AAAHHH
I THINK HE GETS IT--
STOP IT! STOP IT FROM HURTING ME!!
THAT'S ENOUGH.
I DON'T THINK YOU'RE GETTING "MESSAGE."
BAM

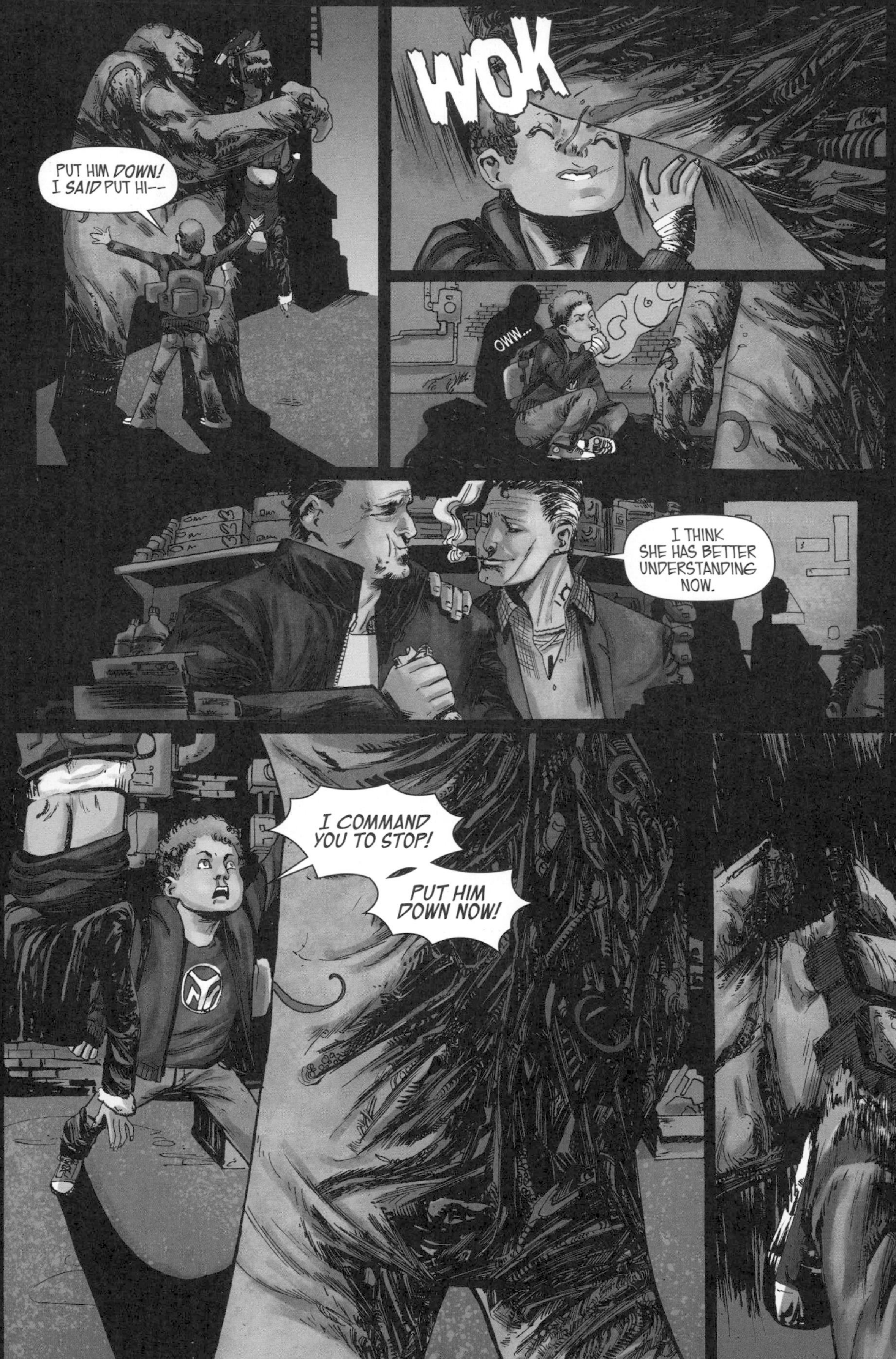
PUT HIM DOWN! I SAID PUT HI--
WOK
OWW...
I THINK SHE HAS BETTER UNDERSTANDING NOW.
I COMMAND YOU TO STOP!
PUT HIM DOWN NOW!

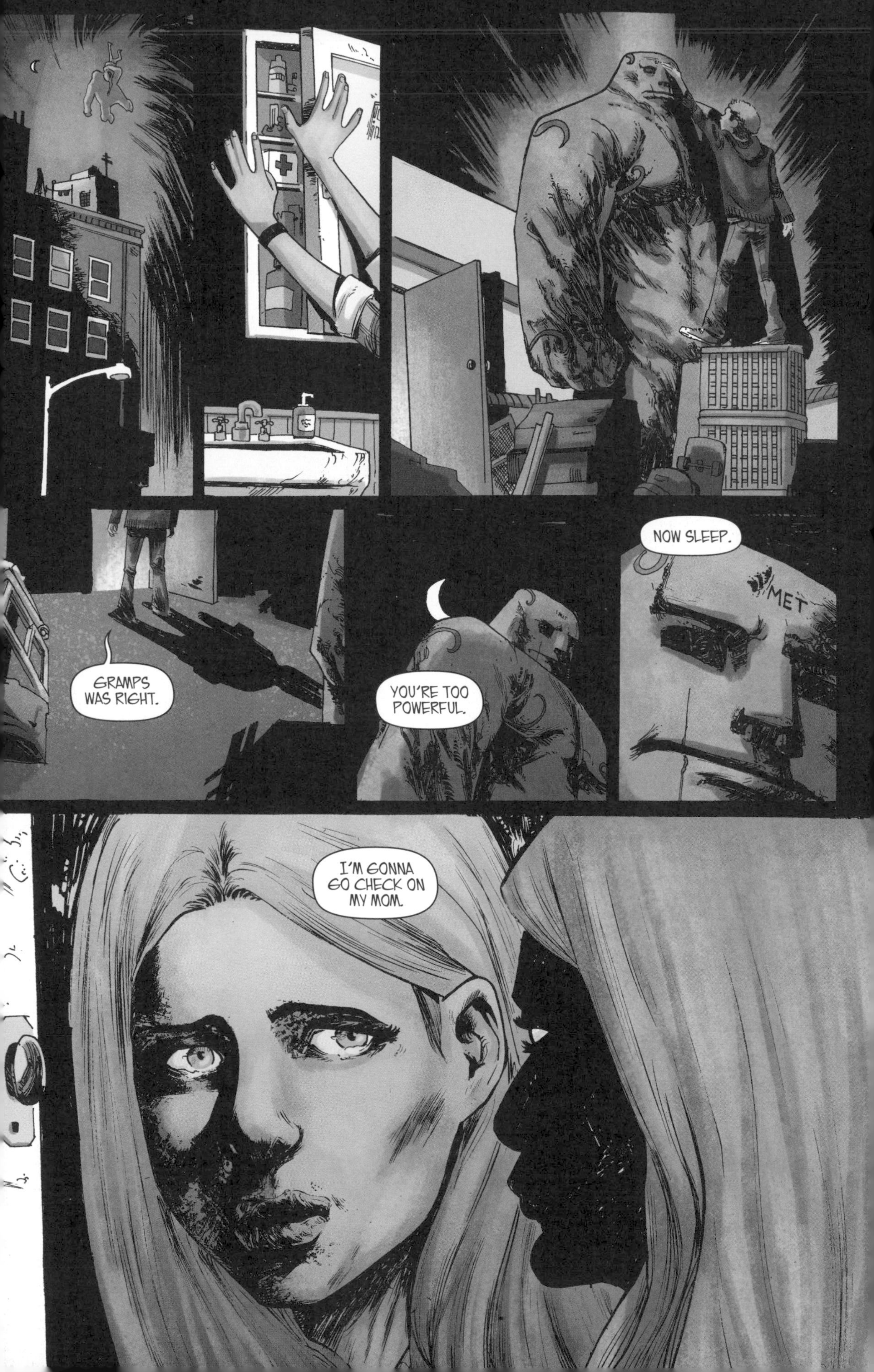
GRAMPS WAS RIGHT.
YOU'RE TOO POWERFUL.
NOW SLEEP.
MET
I'M GONNA GO CHECK ON MY MOM.

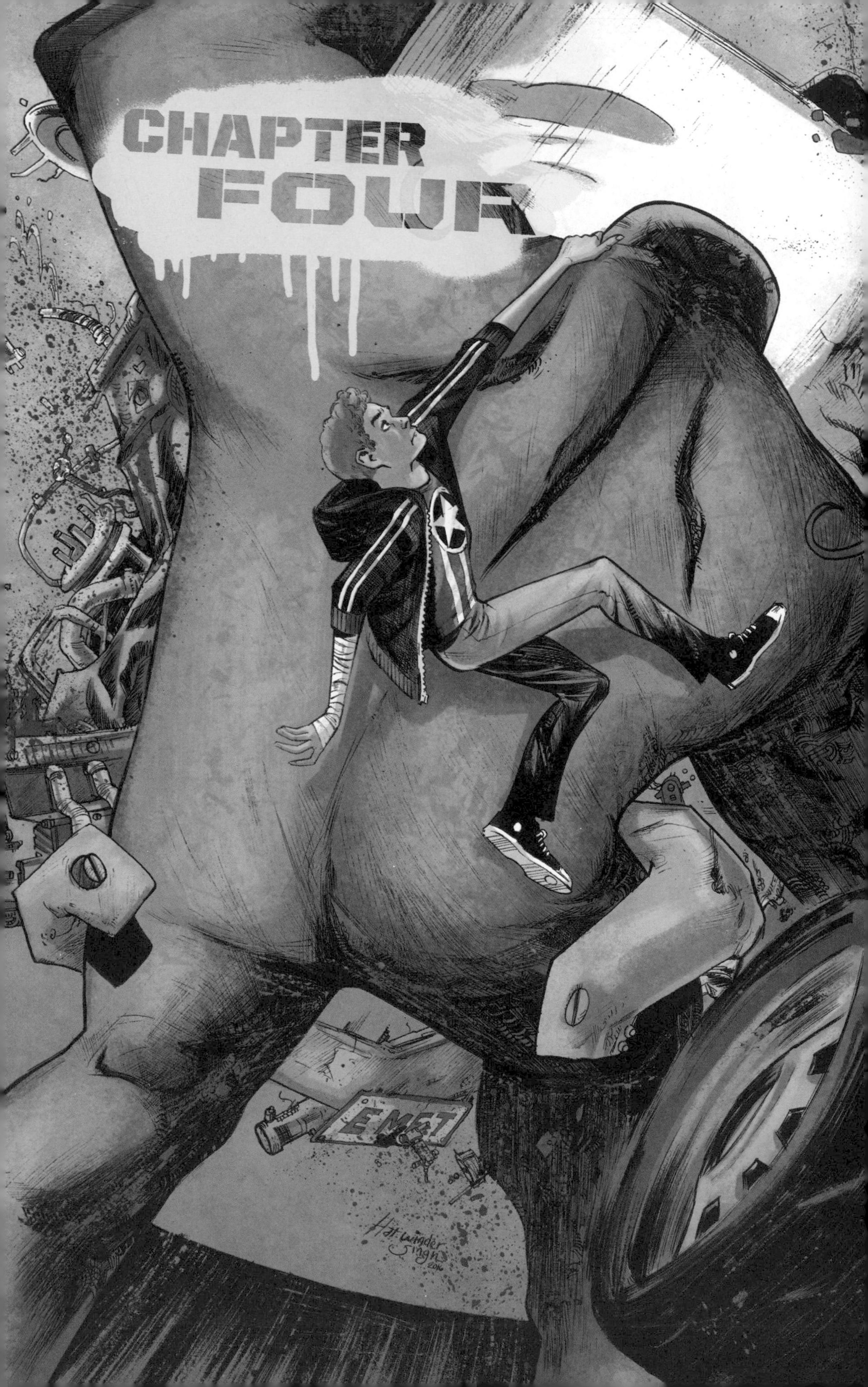
CHAPTER
FOUR
EMET

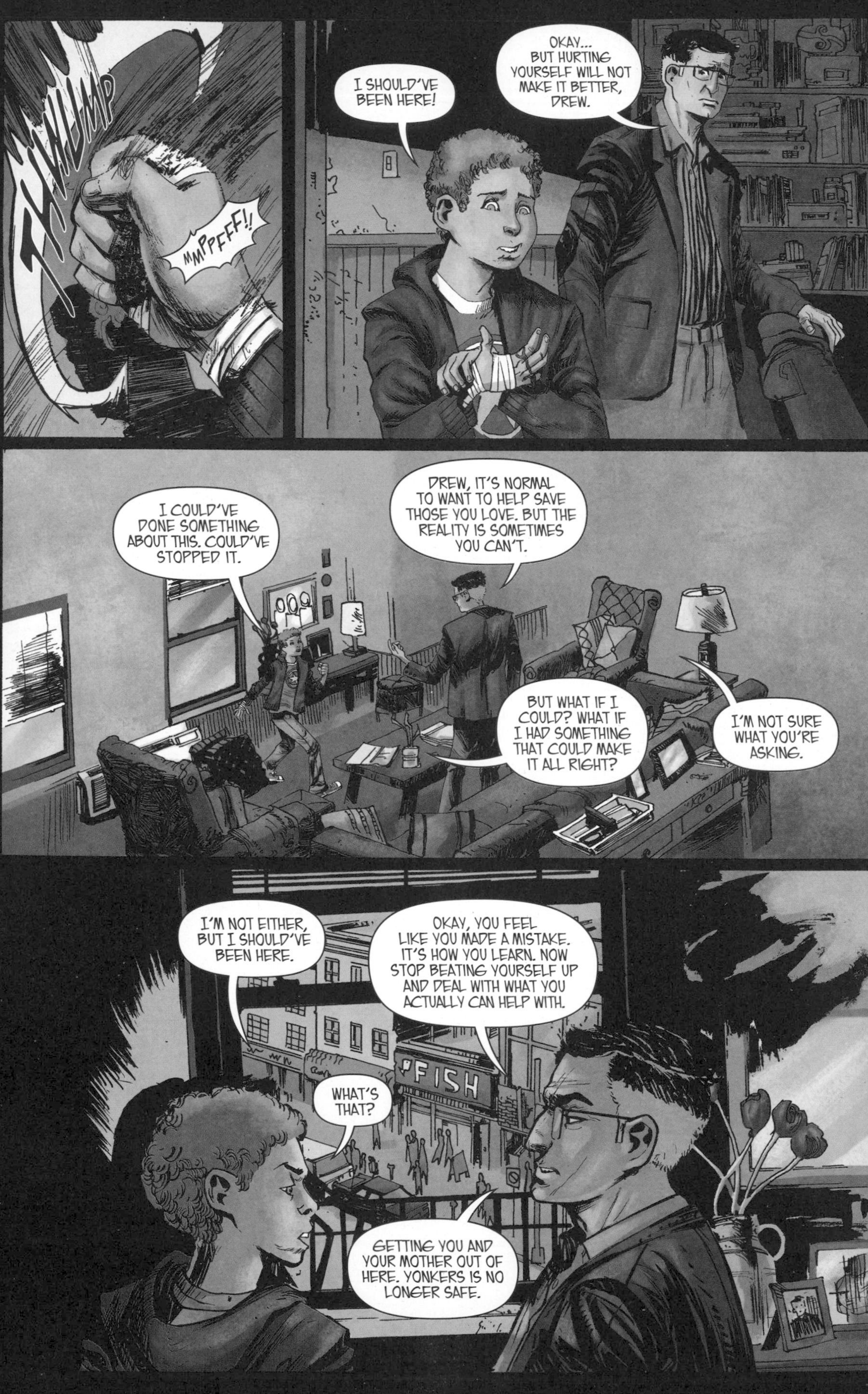
THWUMP
MMPFFF!!
I SHOULD'VE BEEN HERE!
OKAY... BUT HURTING YOURSELF WILL NOT MAKE IT BETTER, DREW.
I COULD'VE DONE SOMETHING ABOUT THIS. COULD'VE STOPPED IT.
DREW, IT'S NORMAL TO WANT TO HELP SAVE THOSE YOU LOVE. BUT THE REALITY IS SOMETIMES YOU CAN'T.
BUT WHAT IF I COULD? WHAT IF I HAD SOMETHING THAT COULD MAKE IT ALL RIGHT?
I'M NOT SURE WHAT YOU'RE ASKING.
I'M NOT EITHER, BUT I SHOULD'VE BEEN HERE.
OKAY, YOU FEEL LIKE YOU MADE A MISTAKE. IT'S HOW YOU LEARN. NOW STOP BEATING YOURSELF UP AND DEAL WITH WHAT YOU ACTUALLY CAN HELP WITH.
FISH
WHAT'S THAT?
GETTING YOU AND YOUR MOTHER OUT OF HERE. YONKERS IS NO LONGER SAFE.

AND LET THEM WIN?

THERE IS NO WINNING WITH MEN LIKE THIS.

DESYA SHOULD HAVE TO LEAVE, NOT US.

DESYA IS A PUPPET. HE DOES WHAT HE'S TOLD. HE'S NOT OUR PROBLEM.

YOU MEAN LITTLE STALIN?

IS HE EVEN REAL, DR. HIRSCH? I MEAN, NO ONE HAS EVER SEEN THIS GUY.

HE IS VERY REAL, DREW. AND SOMEONE YOU SHOULD HOPE YOU NEVER DO SEE.

WHY'S THAT?

BECAUSE IT MEANS YOU'RE PROBABLY DEAD.

WHERE DID HE COME FROM?

IT'S NOT ABOUT WHERE HE CAME FROM, BUT HOW HE CAME TO BE.

YOU'VE NEVER BEEN TO RUSSIA, SO YOU DON'T KNOW, DREW.

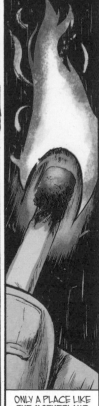

ONLY A PLACE LIKE THE MOTHERLAND CAN MAKE SOMEONE LIKE LITTLE STALIN.

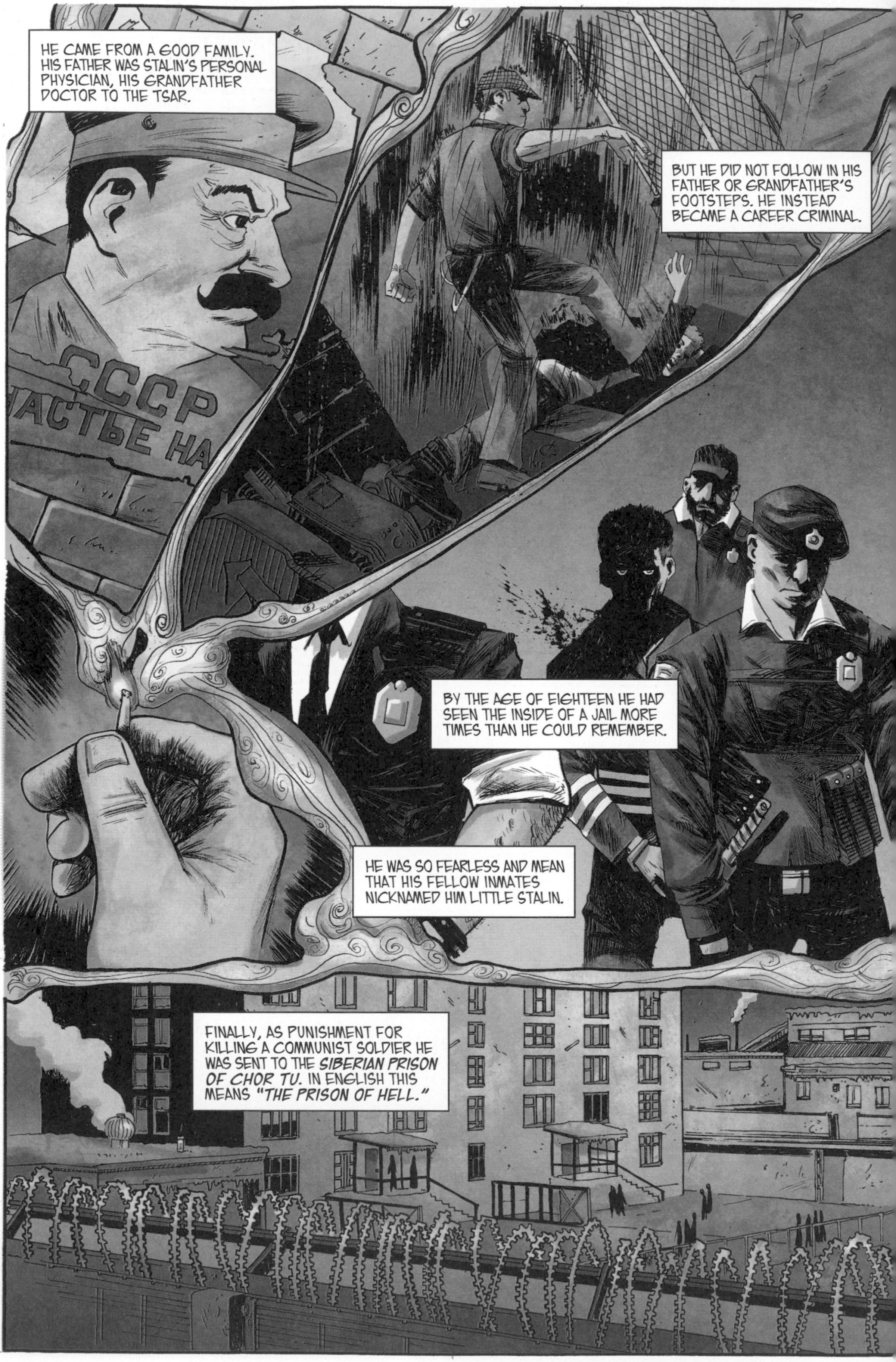
HE CAME FROM A GOOD FAMILY. HIS FATHER WAS STALIN'S PERSONAL PHYSICIAN, HIS GRANDFATHER DOCTOR TO THE TSAR.
CCCP
BUT HE DID NOT FOLLOW IN HIS FATHER OR GRANDFATHER'S FOOTSTEPS. HE INSTEAD BECAME A CAREER CRIMINAL.
BY THE AGE OF EIGHTEEN HE HAD SEEN THE INSIDE OF A JAIL MORE TIMES THAN HE COULD REMEMBER.
HE WAS SO FEARLESS AND MEAN THAT HIS FELLOW INMATES NICKNAMED HIM LITTLE STALIN.
FINALLY, AS PUNISHMENT FOR KILLING A COMMUNIST SOLDIER HE WAS SENT TO THE *SIBERIAN PRISON OF CHOR TU*. IN ENGLISH THIS MEANS *"THE PRISON OF HELL."*

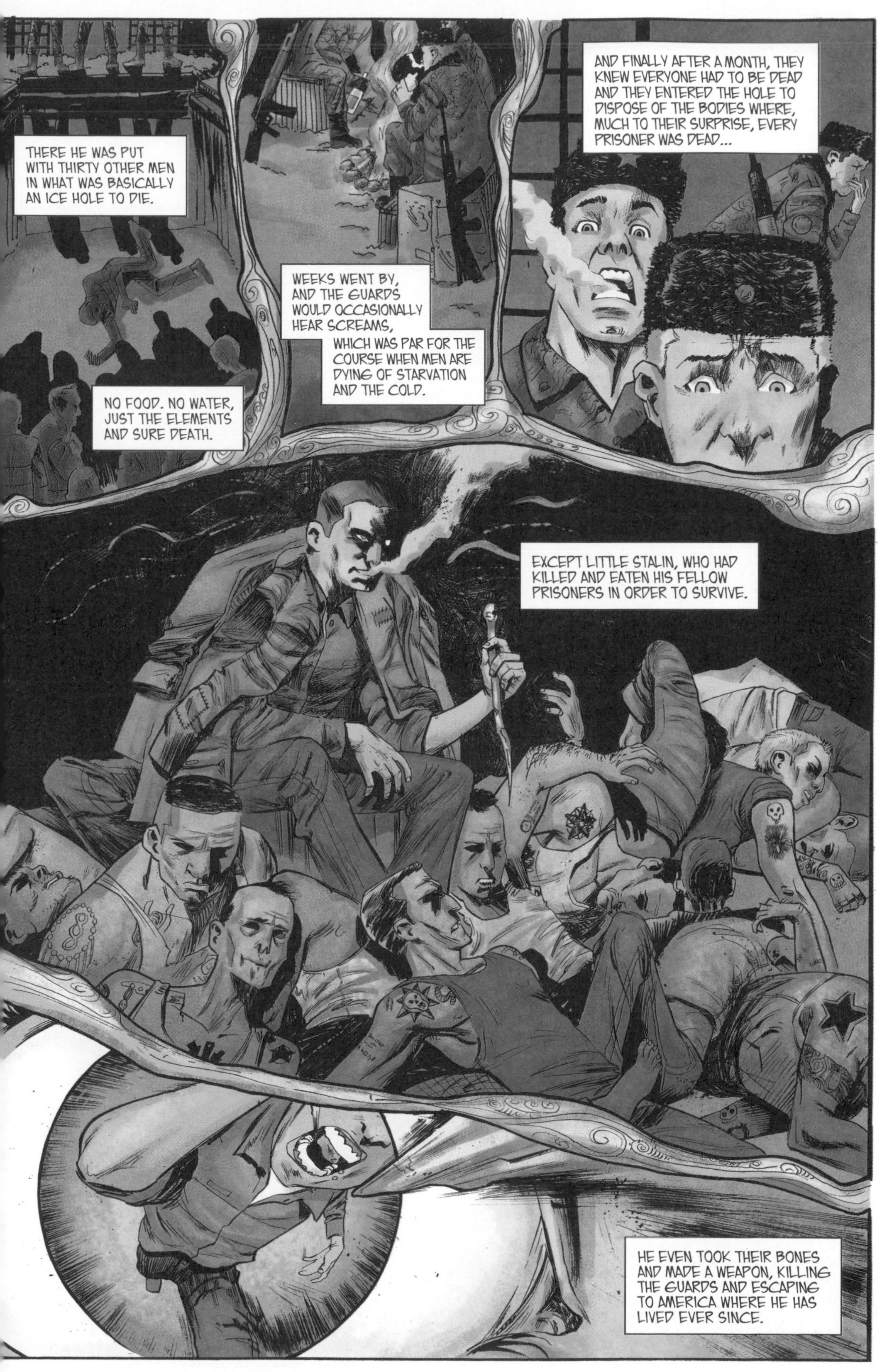
THERE HE WAS PUT WITH THIRTY OTHER MEN IN WHAT WAS BASICALLY AN ICE HOLE TO DIE.
NO FOOD. NO WATER, JUST THE ELEMENTS AND SURE DEATH.
WEEKS WENT BY, AND THE GUARDS WOULD OCCASIONALLY HEAR SCREAMS,
WHICH WAS PAR FOR THE COURSE WHEN MEN ARE DYING OF STARVATION AND THE COLD.
AND FINALLY AFTER A MONTH, THEY KNEW EVERYONE HAD TO BE DEAD AND THEY ENTERED THE HOLE TO DISPOSE OF THE BODIES WHERE, MUCH TO THEIR SURPRISE, EVERY PRISONER WAS DEAD...
EXCEPT LITTLE STALIN, WHO HAD KILLED AND EATEN HIS FELLOW PRISONERS IN ORDER TO SURVIVE.
HE EVEN TOOK THEIR BONES AND MADE A WEAPON, KILLING THE GUARDS AND ESCAPING TO AMERICA WHERE HE HAS LIVED EVER SINCE.

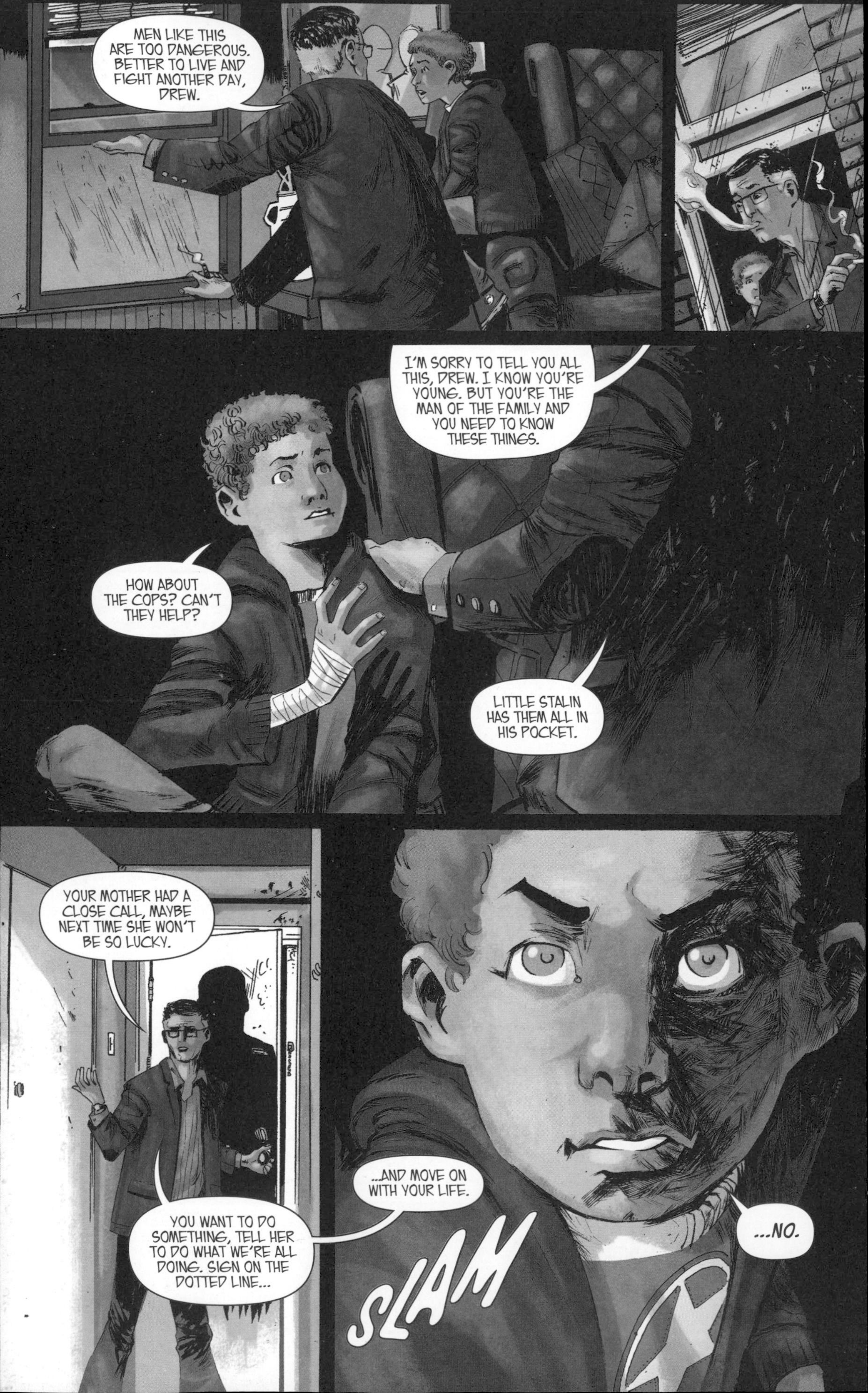
MEN LIKE THIS ARE TOO DANGEROUS. BETTER TO LIVE AND FIGHT ANOTHER DAY, DREW.
I'M SORRY TO TELL YOU ALL THIS, DREW. I KNOW YOU'RE YOUNG. BUT YOU'RE THE MAN OF THE FAMILY AND YOU NEED TO KNOW THESE THINGS.
HOW ABOUT THE COPS? CAN'T THEY HELP?
LITTLE STALIN HAS THEM ALL IN HIS POCKET.
YOUR MOTHER HAD A CLOSE CALL, MAYBE NEXT TIME SHE WON'T BE SO LUCKY.
YOU WANT TO DO SOMETHING, TELL HER TO DO WHAT WE'RE ALL DOING. SIGN ON THE DOTTED LINE...
...AND MOVE ON WITH YOUR LIFE.
...NO.
SLAM

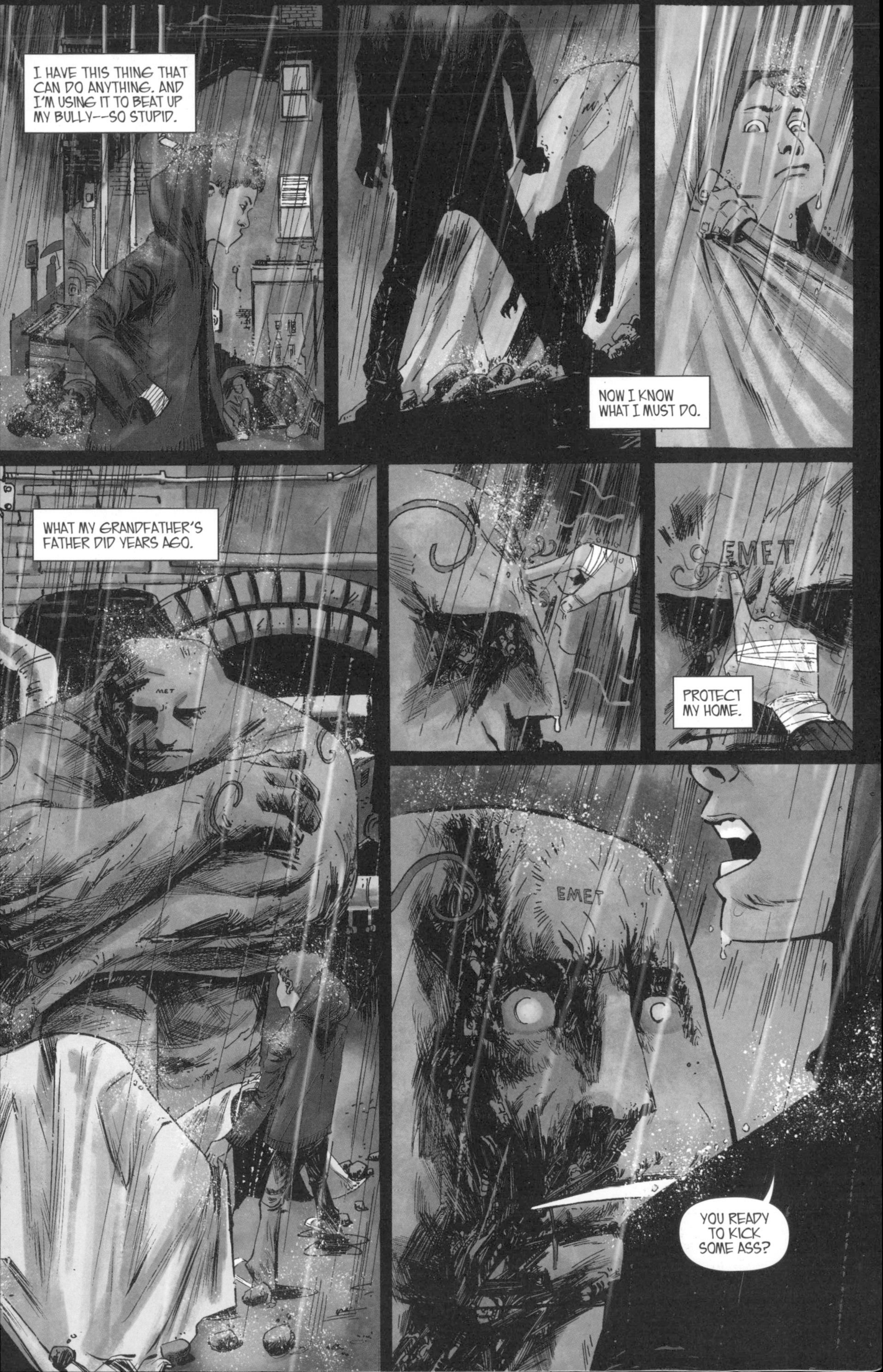
I HAVE THIS THING THAT CAN DO ANYTHING. AND I'M USING IT TO BEAT UP MY BULLY--SO STUPID.
NOW I KNOW WHAT I MUST DO.
WHAT MY GRANDFATHER'S FATHER DID YEARS AGO.
EMET
PROTECT MY HOME.
EMET
YOU READY TO KICK SOME ASS?

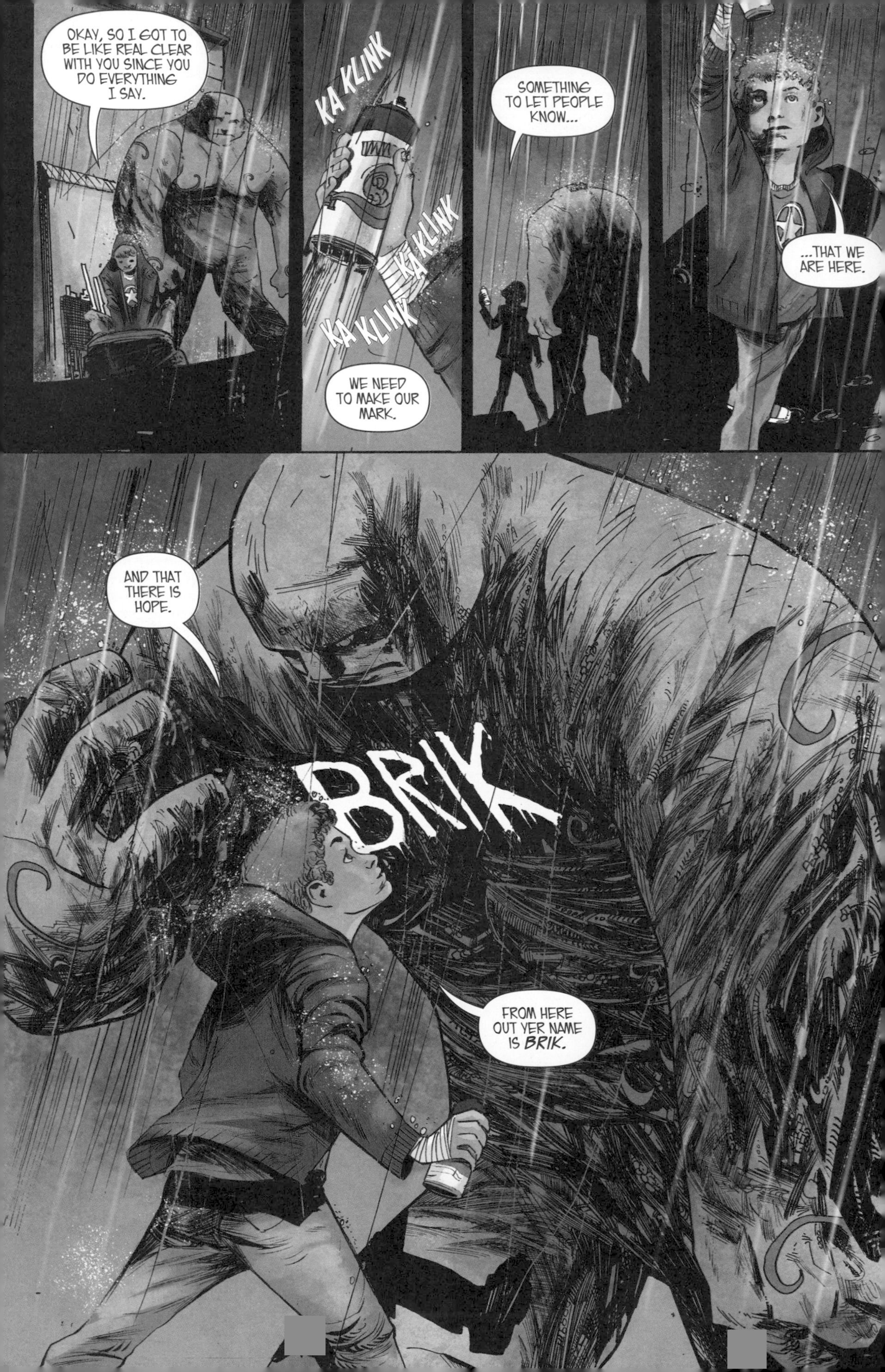

OKAY, SO I GOT TO BE LIKE REAL CLEAR WITH YOU SINCE YOU DO EVERYTHING I SAY.
KA KLINK
KA KLINK
KA KLINK
WE NEED TO MAKE OUR MARK.
SOMETHING TO LET PEOPLE KNOW...
...THAT WE ARE HERE.
AND THAT THERE IS HOPE.
BRIK
FROM HERE OUT YER NAME IS *BRIK.*

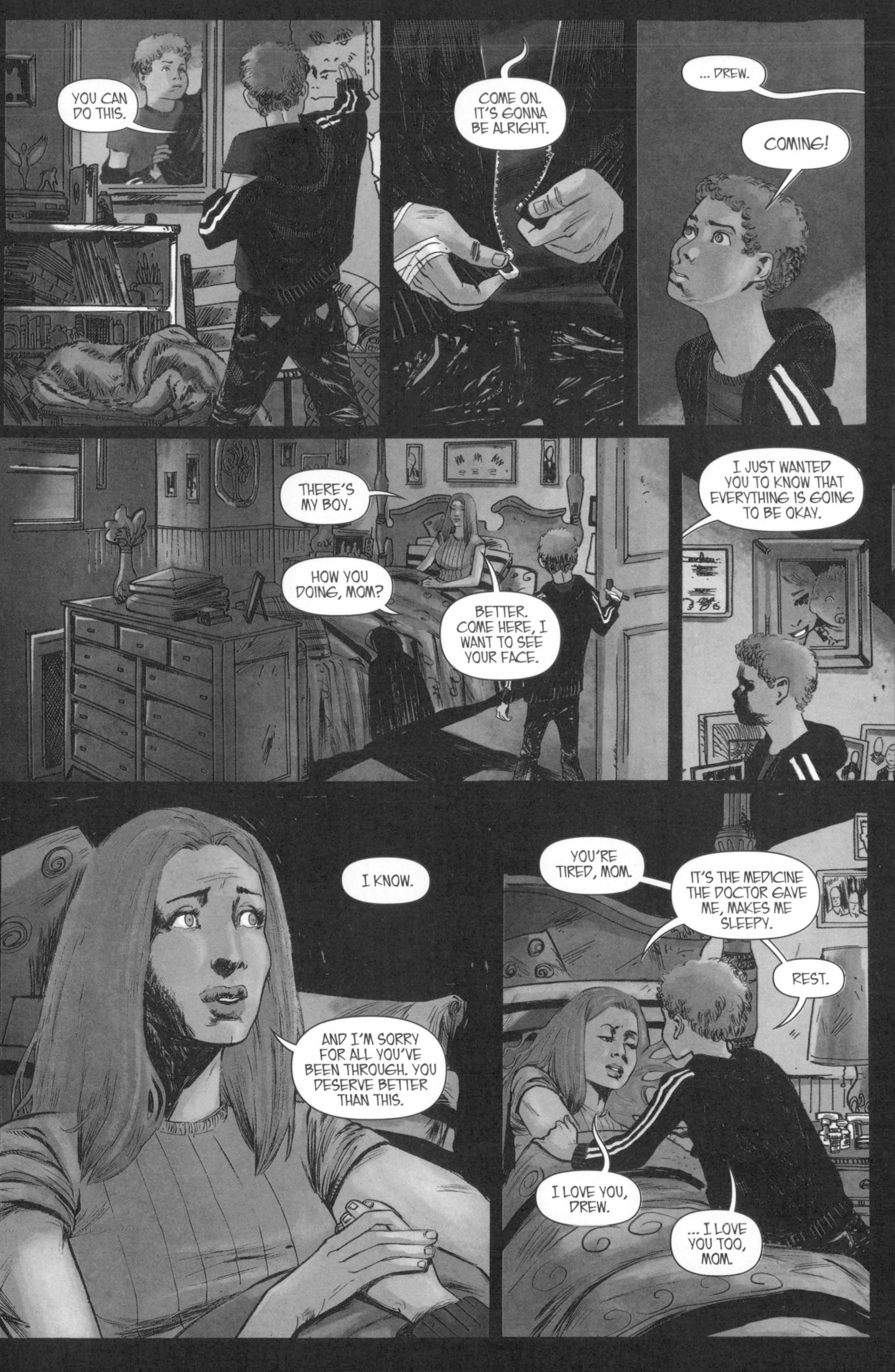
YOU CAN DO THIS.
COME ON. IT'S GONNA BE ALRIGHT.
... DREW.
COMING!
THERE'S MY BOY.
HOW YOU DOING, MOM?
BETTER. COME HERE, I WANT TO SEE YOUR FACE.
I JUST WANTED YOU TO KNOW THAT EVERYTHING IS GOING TO BE OKAY.
I KNOW.
AND I'M SORRY FOR ALL YOU'VE BEEN THROUGH. YOU DESERVE BETTER THAN THIS.
YOU'RE TIRED, MOM.
IT'S THE MEDICINE THE DOCTOR GAVE ME, MAKES ME SLEEPY.
REST.
I LOVE YOU, DREW.
... I LOVE YOU TOO, MOM.

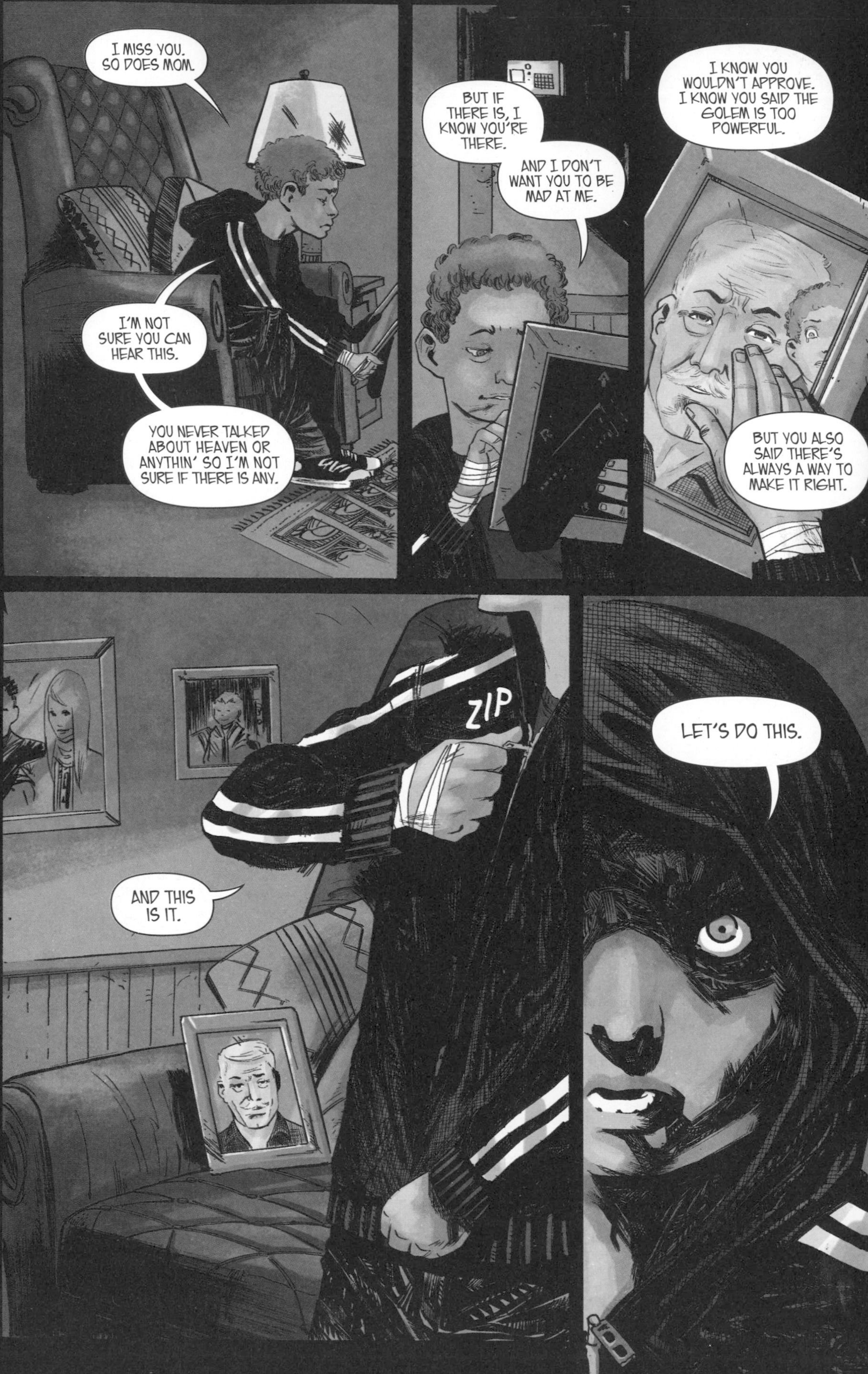
I MISS YOU. SO DOES MOM.
I'M NOT SURE YOU CAN HEAR THIS.
YOU NEVER TALKED ABOUT HEAVEN OR ANYTHIN' SO I'M NOT SURE IF THERE IS ANY.
BUT IF THERE IS, I KNOW YOU'RE THERE.
AND I DON'T WANT YOU TO BE MAD AT ME.
I KNOW YOU WOULDN'T APPROVE. I KNOW YOU SAID THE GOLEM IS TOO POWERFUL.
BUT YOU ALSO SAID THERE'S ALWAYS A WAY TO MAKE IT RIGHT.
ZIP
AND THIS IS IT.
LET'S DO THIS.

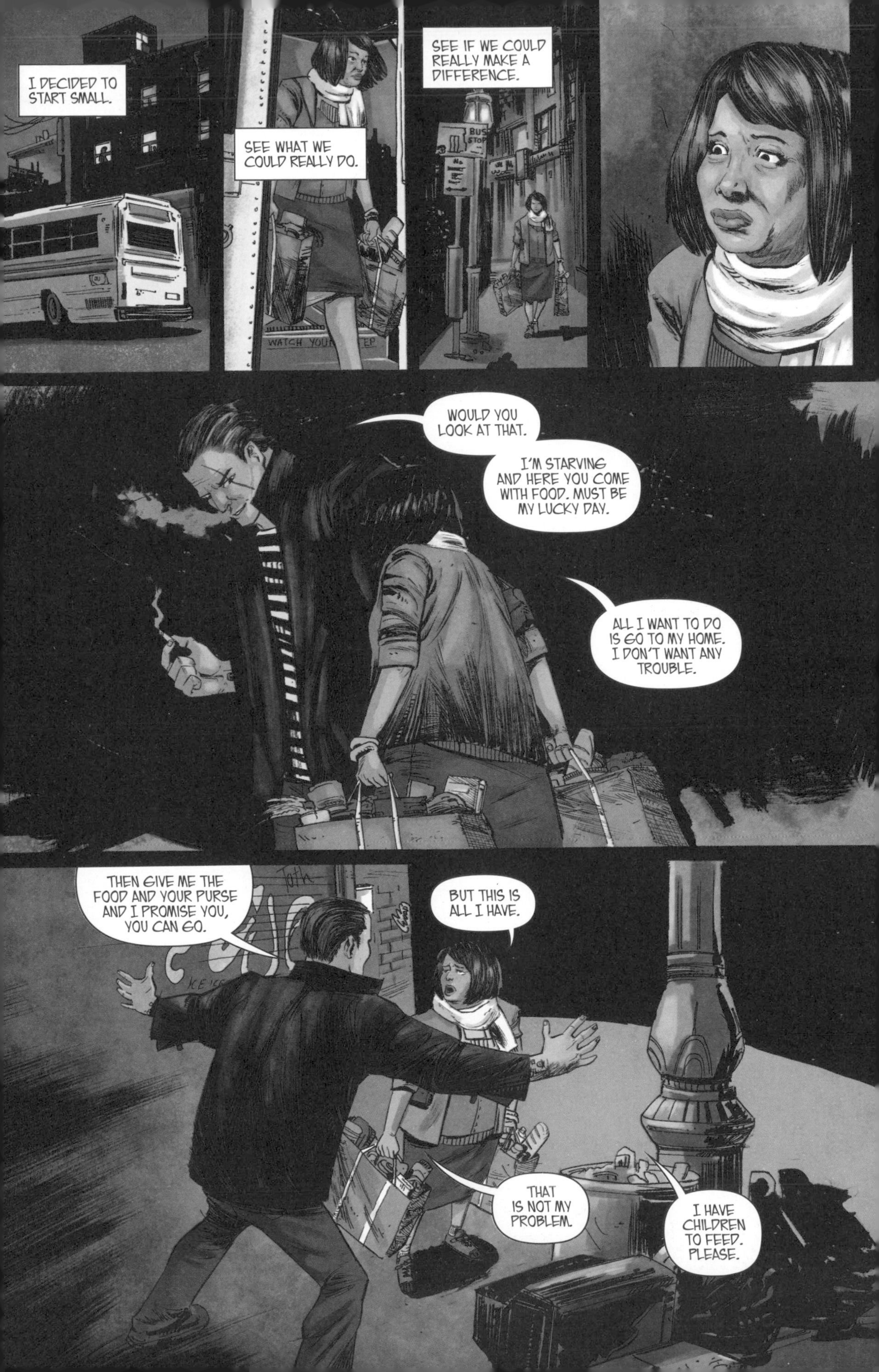
I DECIDED TO START SMALL.
SEE WHAT WE COULD REALLY DO.
WATCH YOUR STEP
SEE IF WE COULD REALLY MAKE A DIFFERENCE.
BUS STOP
WOULD YOU LOOK AT THAT.
I'M STARVING AND HERE YOU COME WITH FOOD. MUST BE MY LUCKY DAY.
ALL I WANT TO DO IS GO TO MY HOME. I DON'T WANT ANY TROUBLE.
THEN GIVE ME THE FOOD AND YOUR PURSE AND I PROMISE YOU, YOU CAN GO.
BUT THIS IS ALL I HAVE.
THAT IS NOT MY PROBLEM.
I HAVE CHILDREN TO FEED. PLEASE.

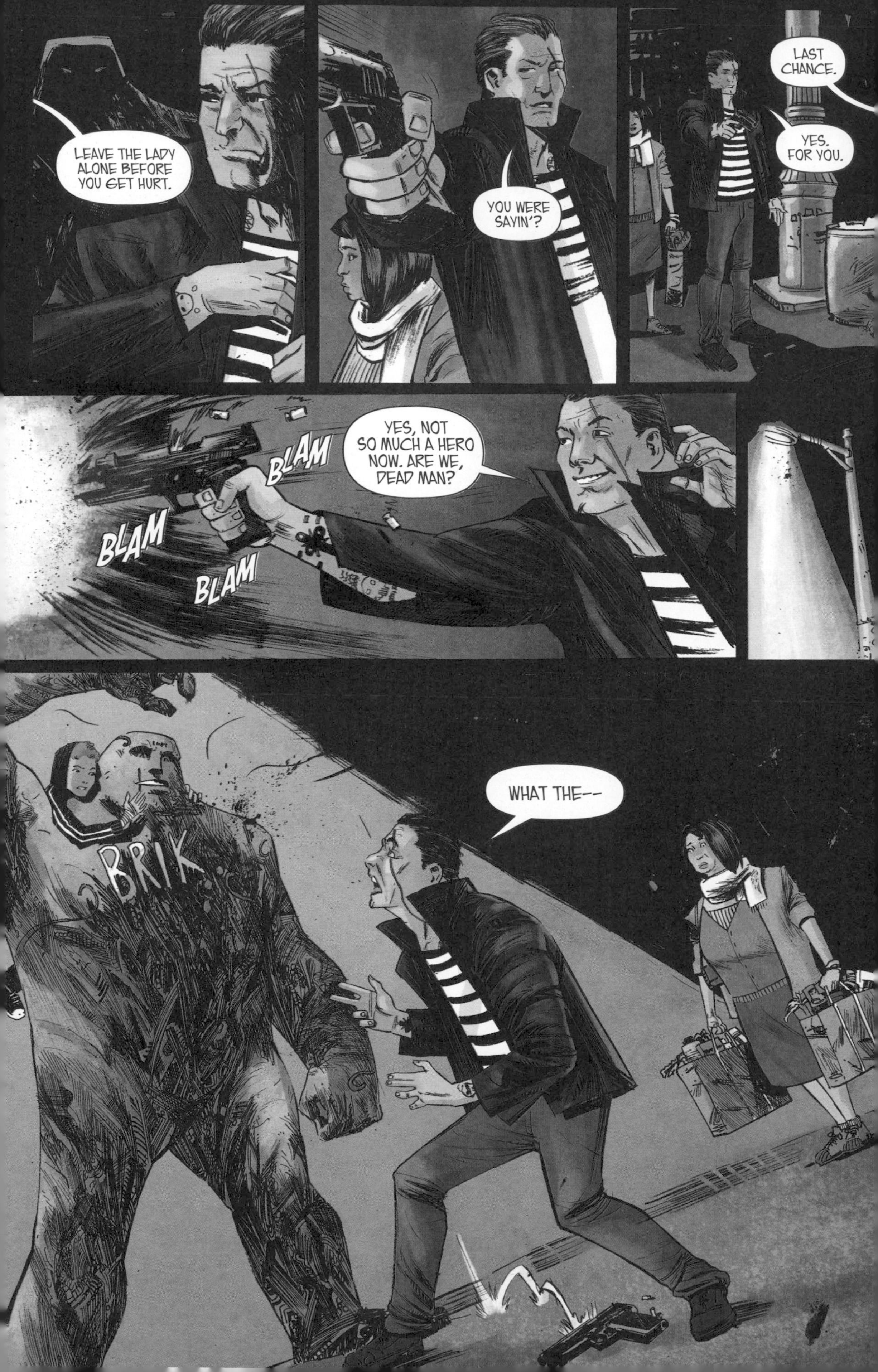
LEAVE THE LADY ALONE BEFORE YOU GET HURT.
YOU WERE SAYIN'?
LAST CHANCE.
YES. FOR YOU.
YES, NOT SO MUCH A HERO NOW. ARE WE, DEAD MAN?
BLAM
BLAM
BLAM
BLAM
BRIK
WHAT THE--

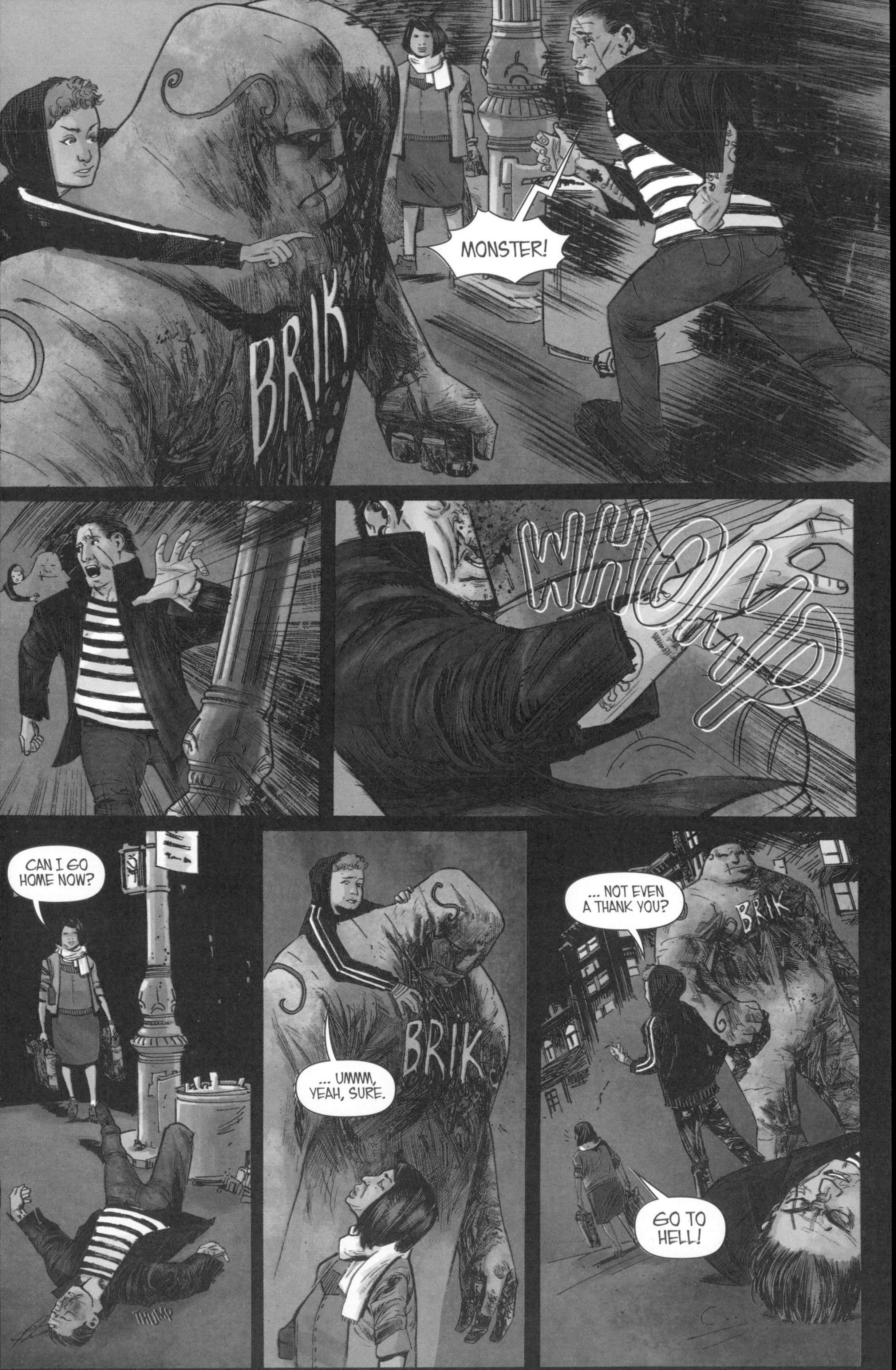
MONSTER!
BRIK
WHOMP
CAN I GO HOME NOW?
THUMP
... UMMM, YEAH, SURE.
BRIK
... NOT EVEN A THANK YOU?
BRIK
GO TO HELL!

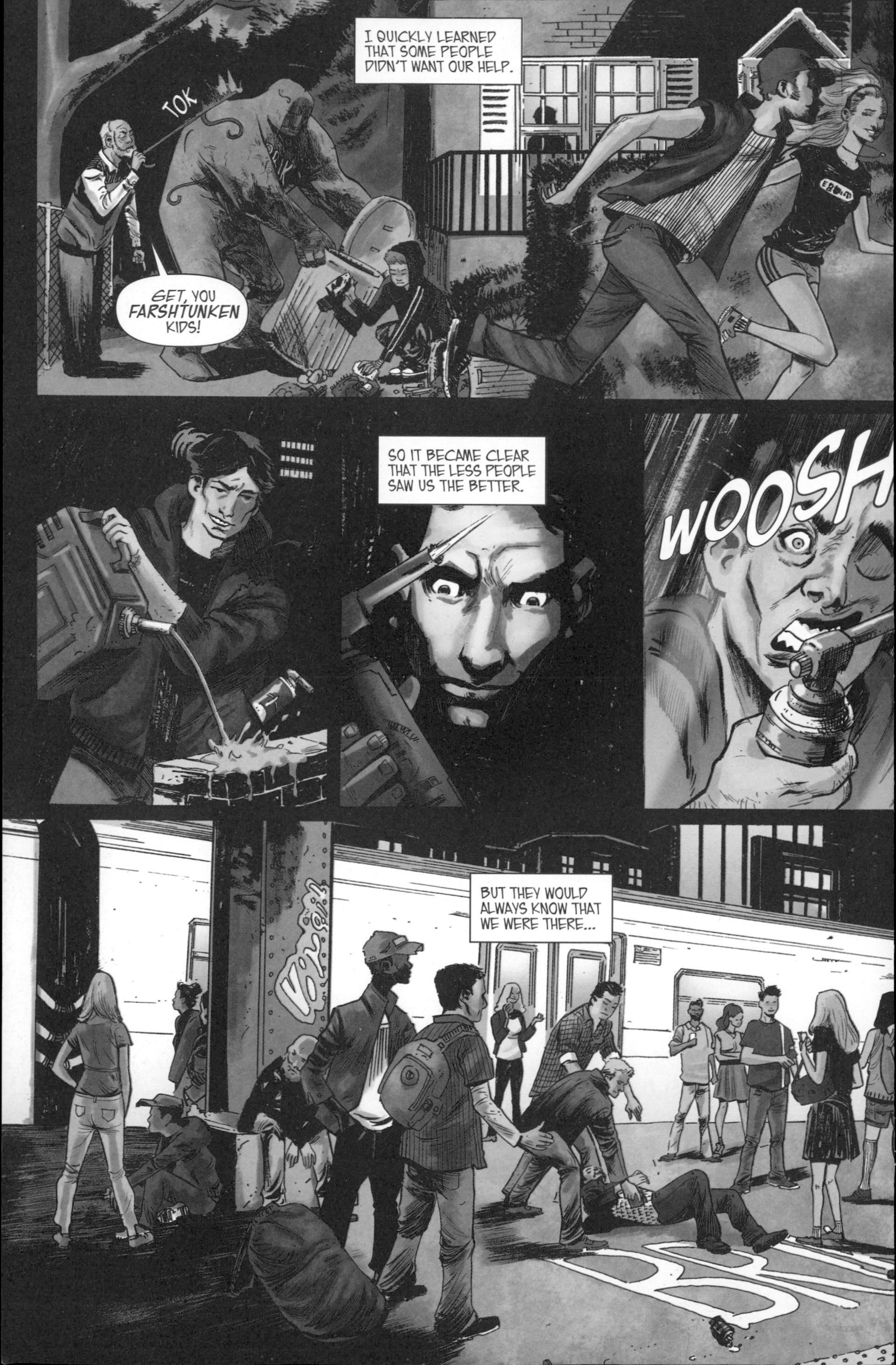

I QUICKLY LEARNED THAT SOME PEOPLE DIDN'T WANT OUR HELP.
TOK
GET, YOU FARSHTUNKEN KIDS!
SO IT BECAME CLEAR THAT THE LESS PEOPLE SAW US THE BETTER.
WOOSH
BUT THEY WOULD ALWAYS KNOW THAT WE WERE THERE...

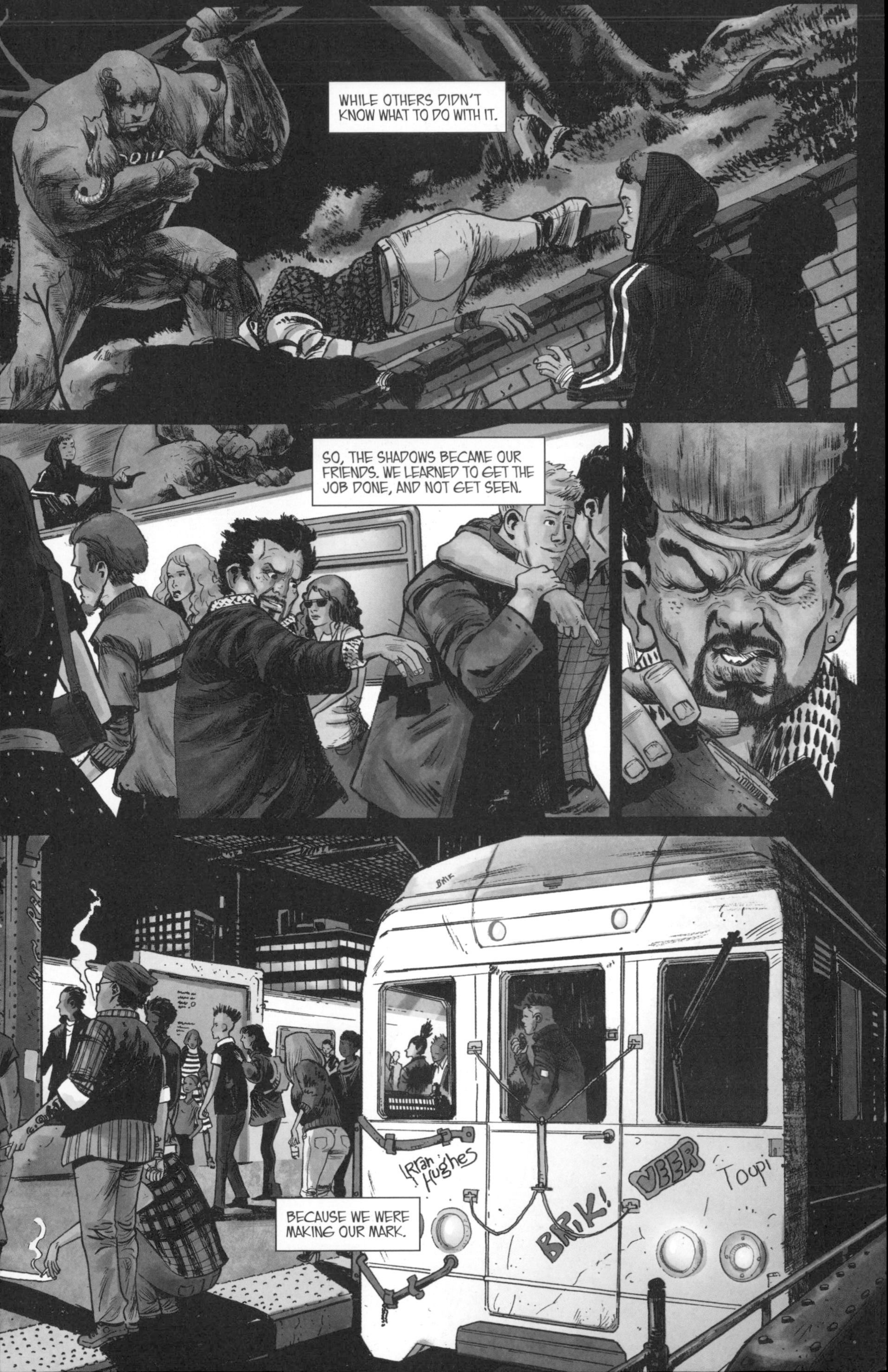
WHILE OTHERS DIDN'T KNOW WHAT TO DO WITH IT.
SO, THE SHADOWS BECAME OUR FRIENDS. WE LEARNED TO GET THE JOB DONE, AND NOT GET SEEN.
BECAUSE WE WERE MAKING OUR MARK.

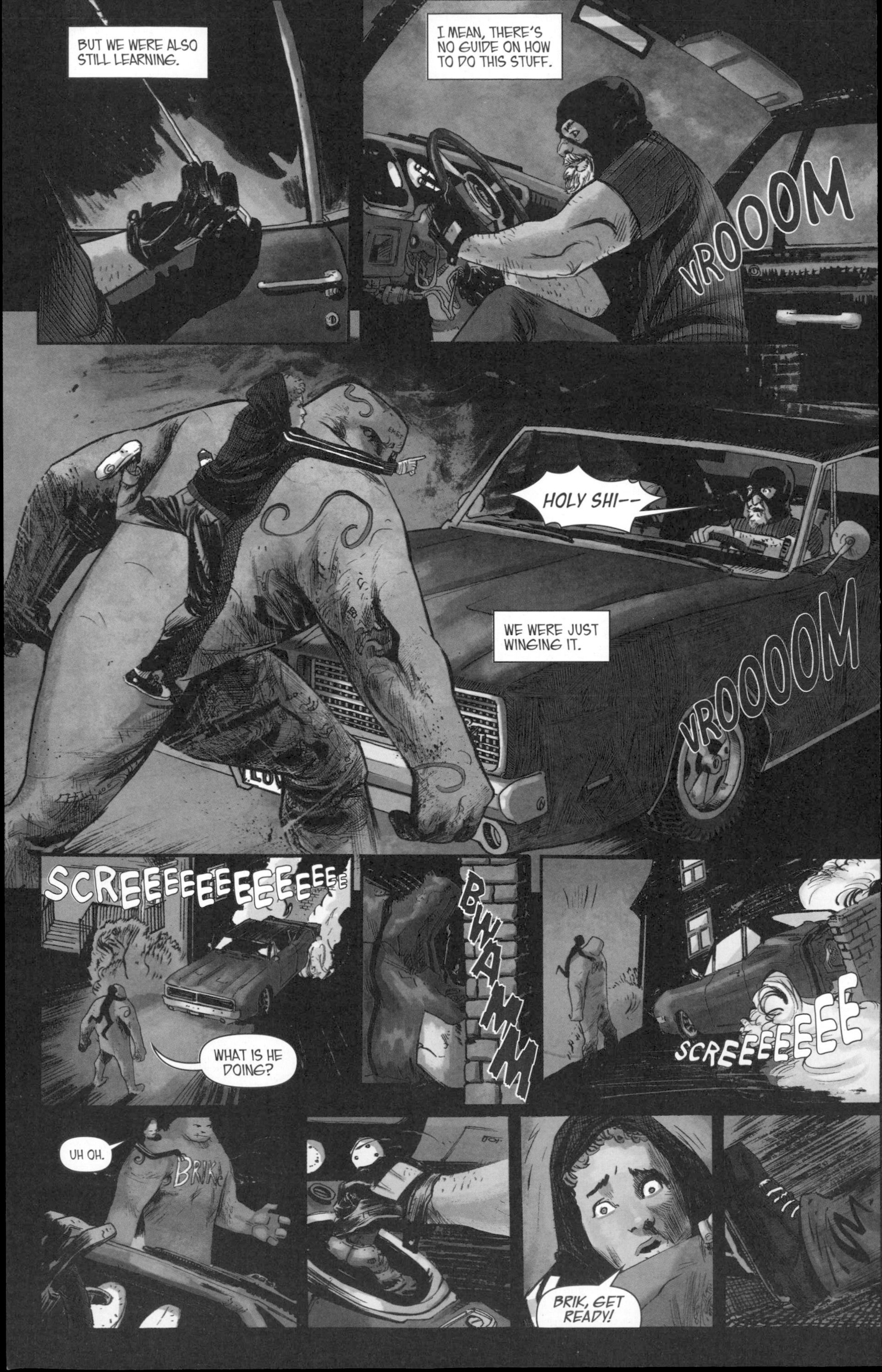

BUT WE WERE ALSO STILL LEARNING.
I MEAN, THERE'S NO GUIDE ON HOW TO DO THIS STUFF.
VROOOM
HOLY SHI--
WE WERE JUST WINGING IT.
VROOOOM
SCREEEEEEEEEEEEEE
WHAT IS HE DOING?
BWAMM
SCREEEEEEEE
UH OH.
BRIK
BRIK, GET READY!

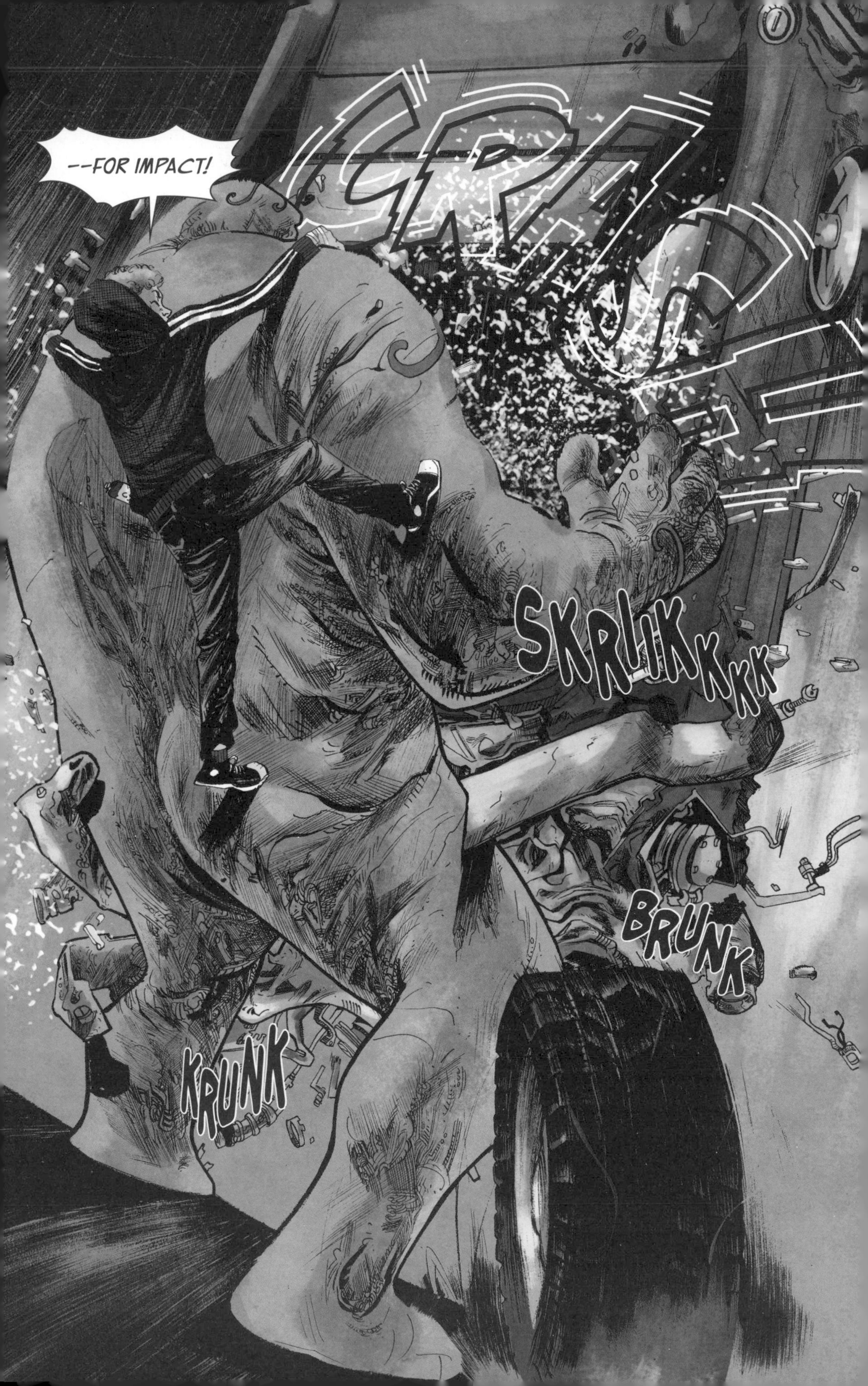
--FOR IMPACT!
CRASH
SKRIIKKKK
BRUNK
KRUNK

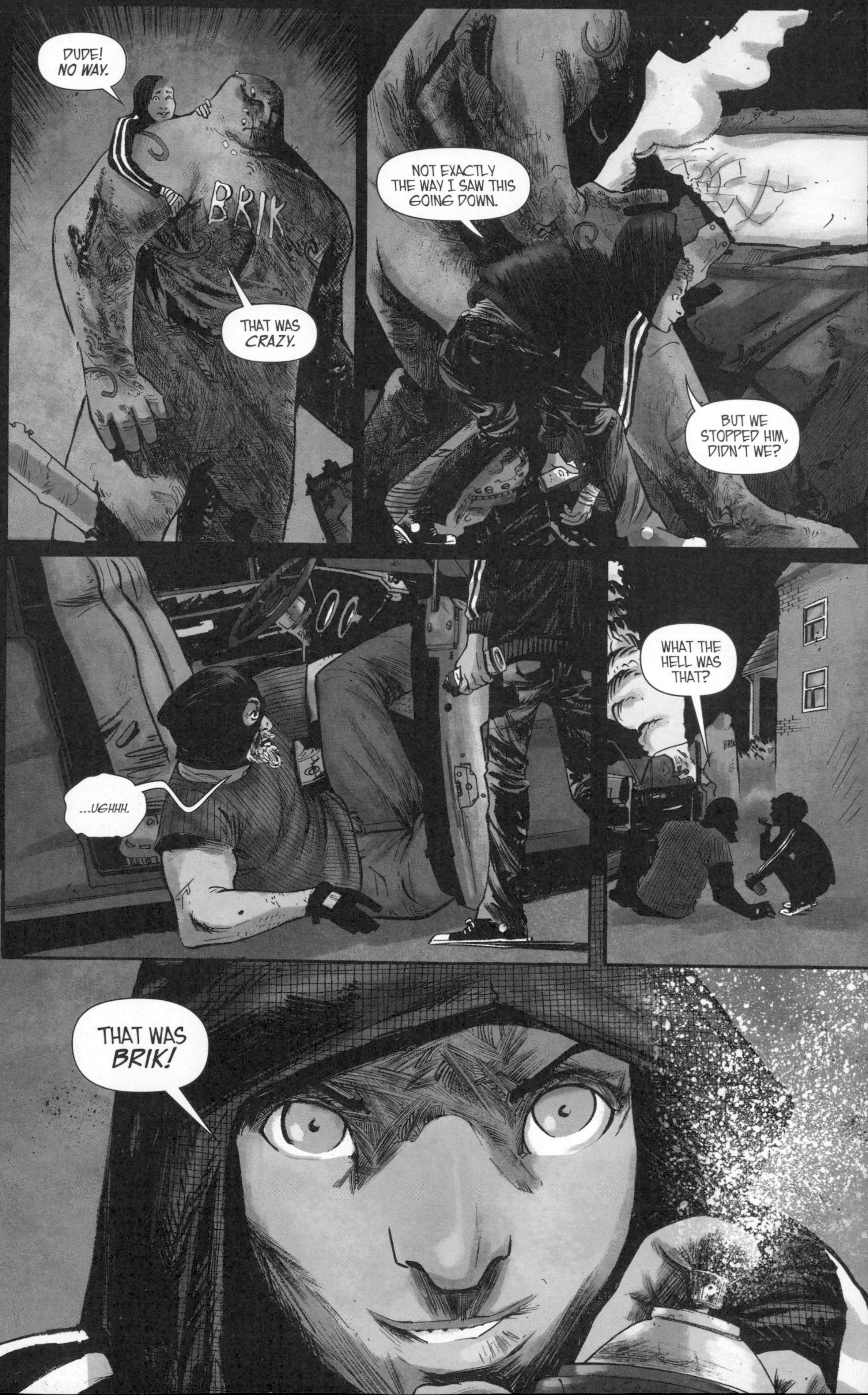
DUDE! NO WAY.
THAT WAS CRAZY.
NOT EXACTLY THE WAY I SAW THIS GOING DOWN.
BUT WE STOPPED HIM, DIDN'T WE?
...UGHHH.
WHAT THE HELL WAS THAT?
THAT WAS BRIK!

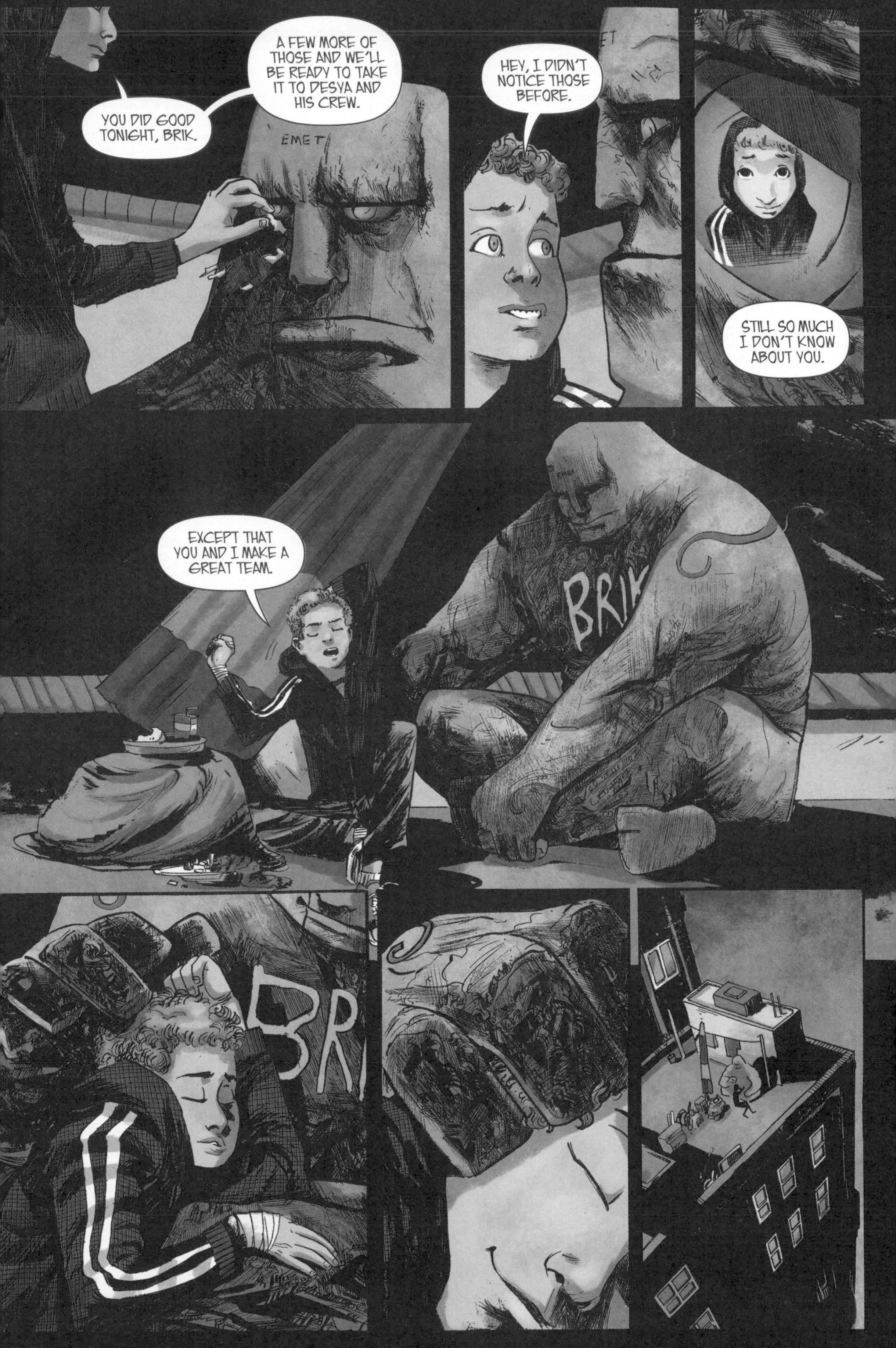
YOU DID GOOD TONIGHT, BRIK.
A FEW MORE OF THOSE AND WE'LL BE READY TO TAKE IT TO DESYA AND HIS CREW.
EMET
HEY, I DIDN'T NOTICE THOSE BEFORE.
STILL SO MUCH I DON'T KNOW ABOUT YOU.
EXCEPT THAT YOU AND I MAKE A GREAT TEAM.
BRIK

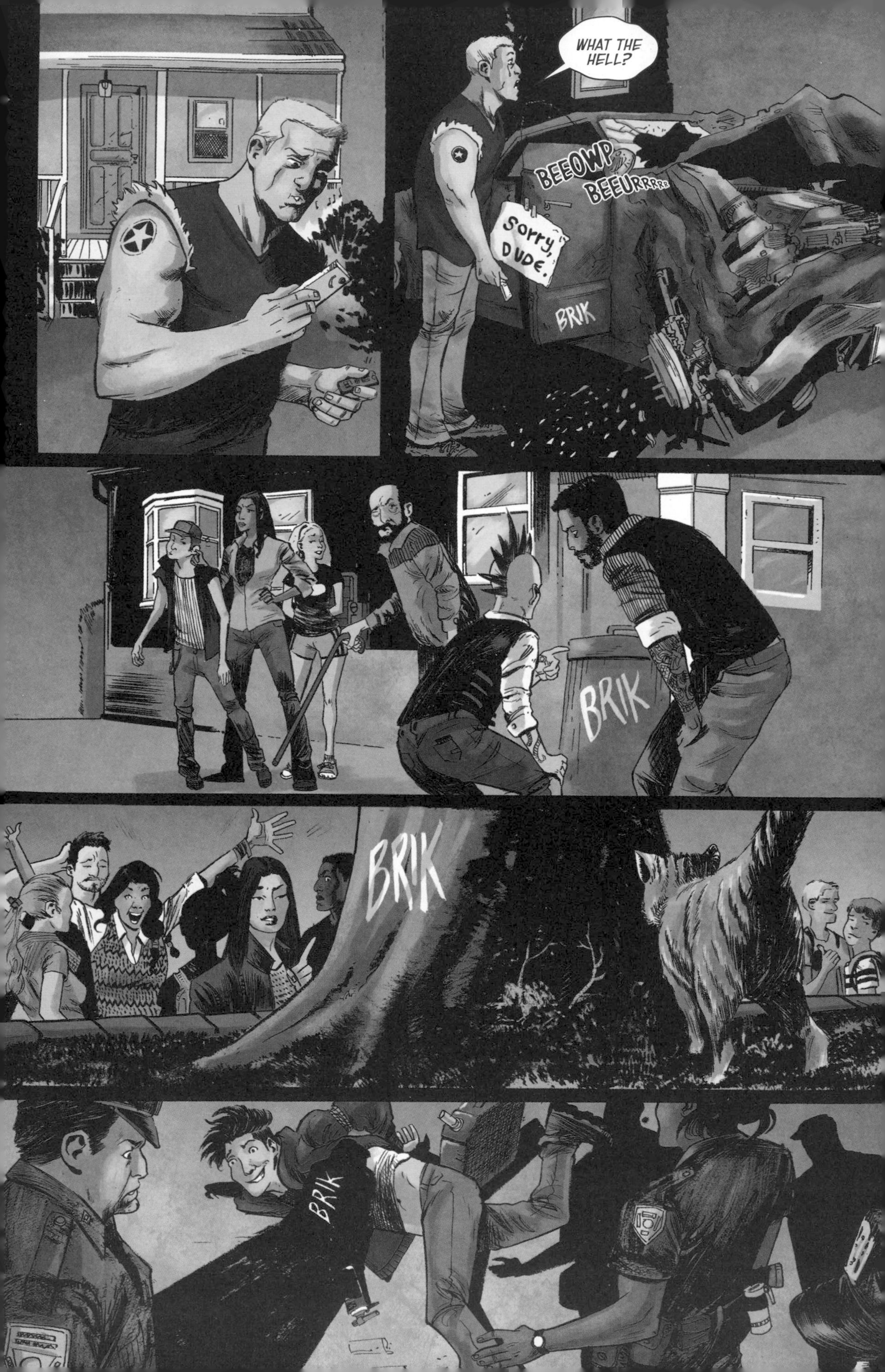

WHAT THE HELL?
BEEOWP
BEEURRRRR
Sorry, DUDE.
BRIK
BRIK
BRIK
BRIK

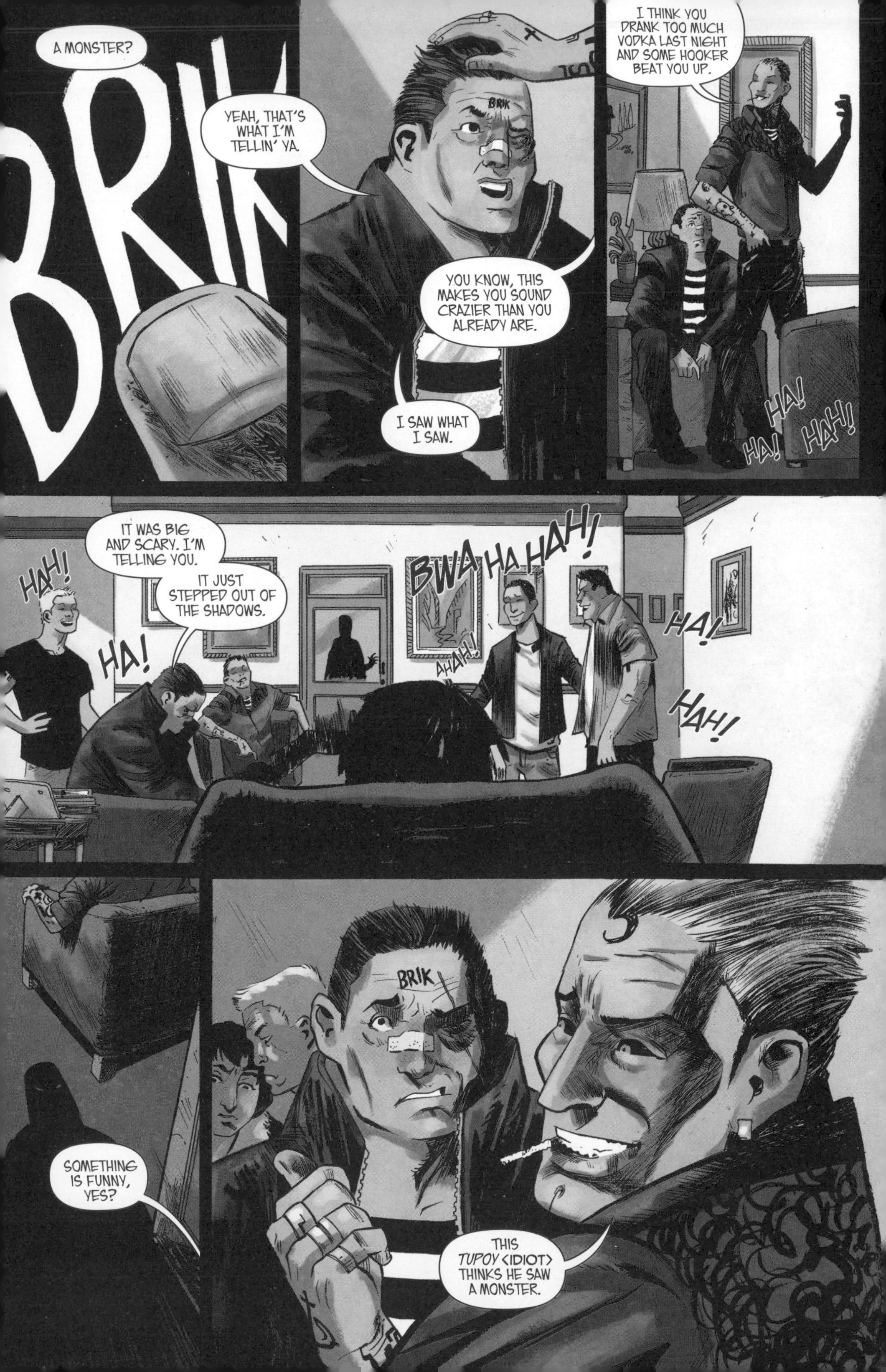
A MONSTER?
BRIK
YEAH, THAT'S WHAT I'M TELLIN' YA.
BRIK
YOU KNOW, THIS MAKES YOU SOUND CRAZIER THAN YOU ALREADY ARE.
I SAW WHAT I SAW.
I THINK YOU DRANK TOO MUCH VODKA LAST NIGHT AND SOME HOOKER BEAT YOU UP.
HA! HA! HAH!
IT WAS BIG AND SCARY. I'M TELLING YOU.
IT JUST STEPPED OUT OF THE SHADOWS.
HAH!
HA!
BWA HA HAH!
AHAH!
HA!
HAH!
BRIK
SOMETHING IS FUNNY, YES?
THIS *TUPOY* <IDIOT> THINKS HE SAW A MONSTER.

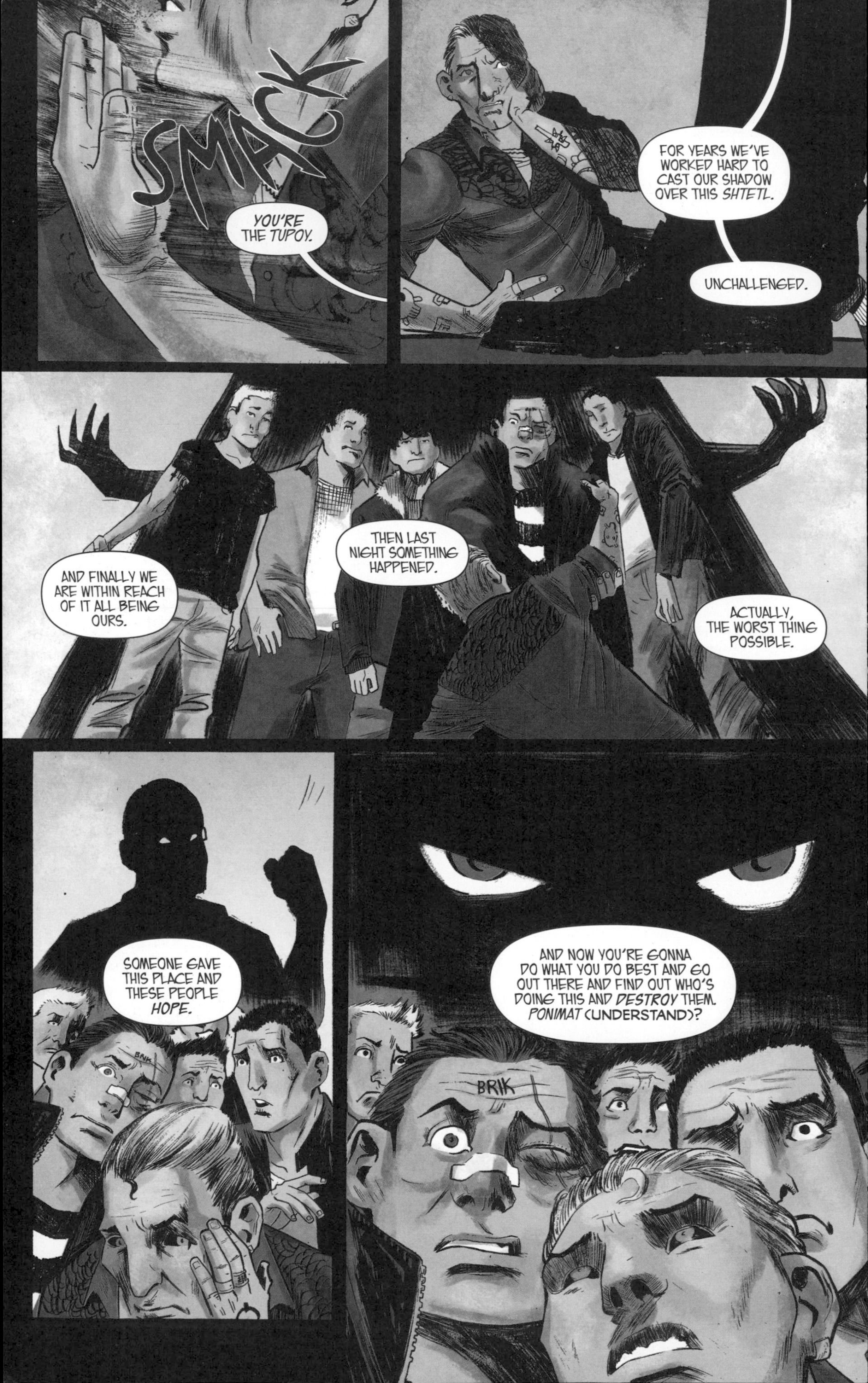
SMACK
YOU'RE THE TUPOY.
FOR YEARS WE'VE WORKED HARD TO CAST OUR SHADOW OVER THIS SHTETL.
UNCHALLENGED.
AND FINALLY WE ARE WITHIN REACH OF IT ALL BEING OURS.
THEN LAST NIGHT SOMETHING HAPPENED.
ACTUALLY, THE WORST THING POSSIBLE.
SOMEONE GAVE THIS PLACE AND THESE PEOPLE HOPE.
AND NOW YOU'RE GONNA DO WHAT YOU DO BEST AND GO OUT THERE AND FIND OUT WHO'S DOING THIS AND DESTROY THEM. PONIMAT (UNDERSTAND)?
BRIK

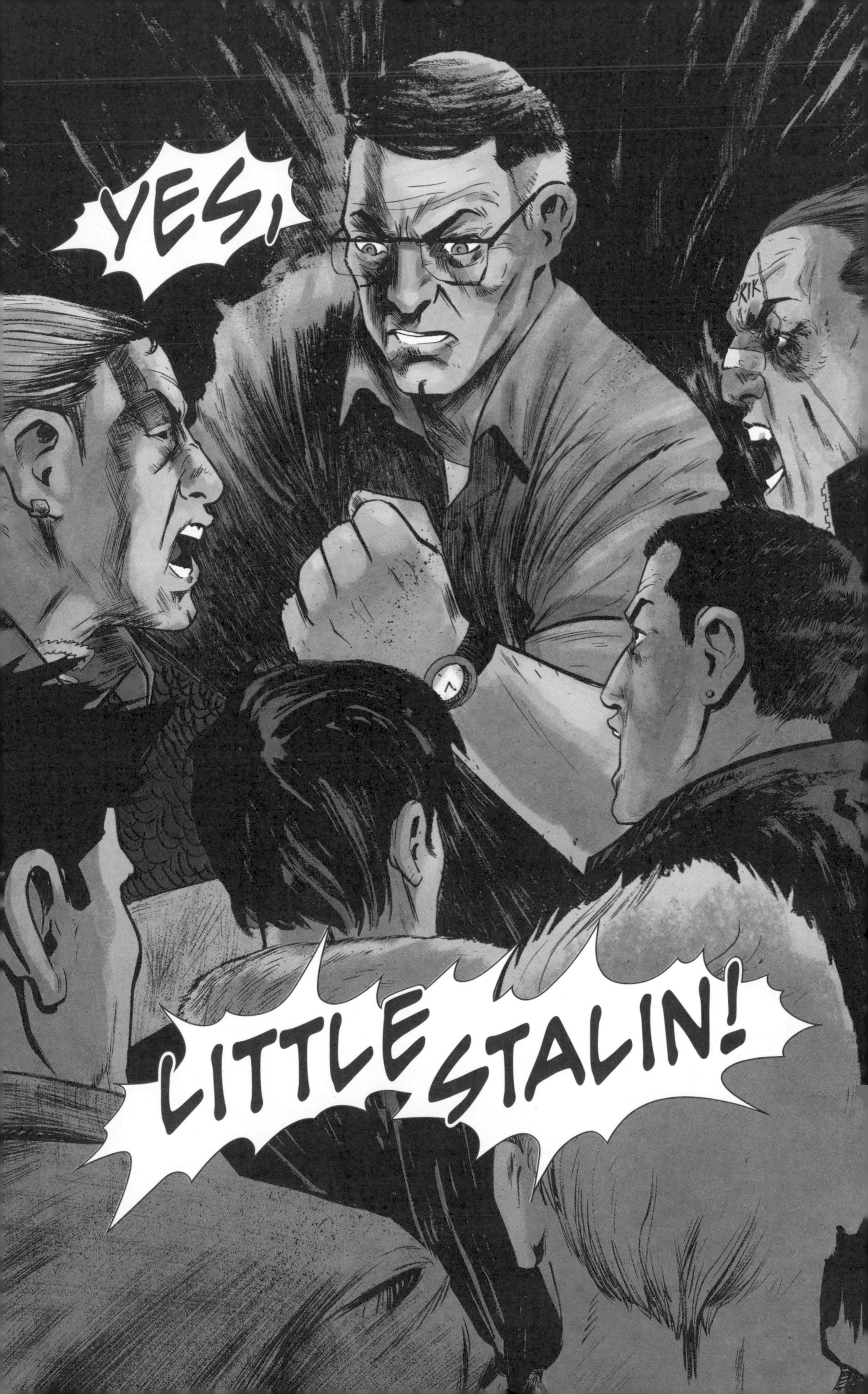
YES,
LITTLE STALIN!

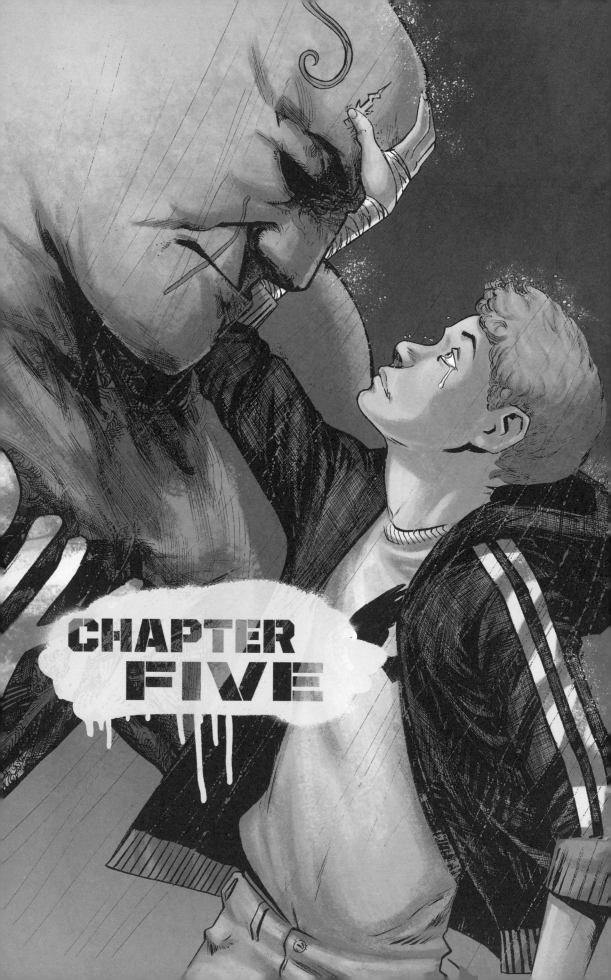

CHAPTER
FIVE

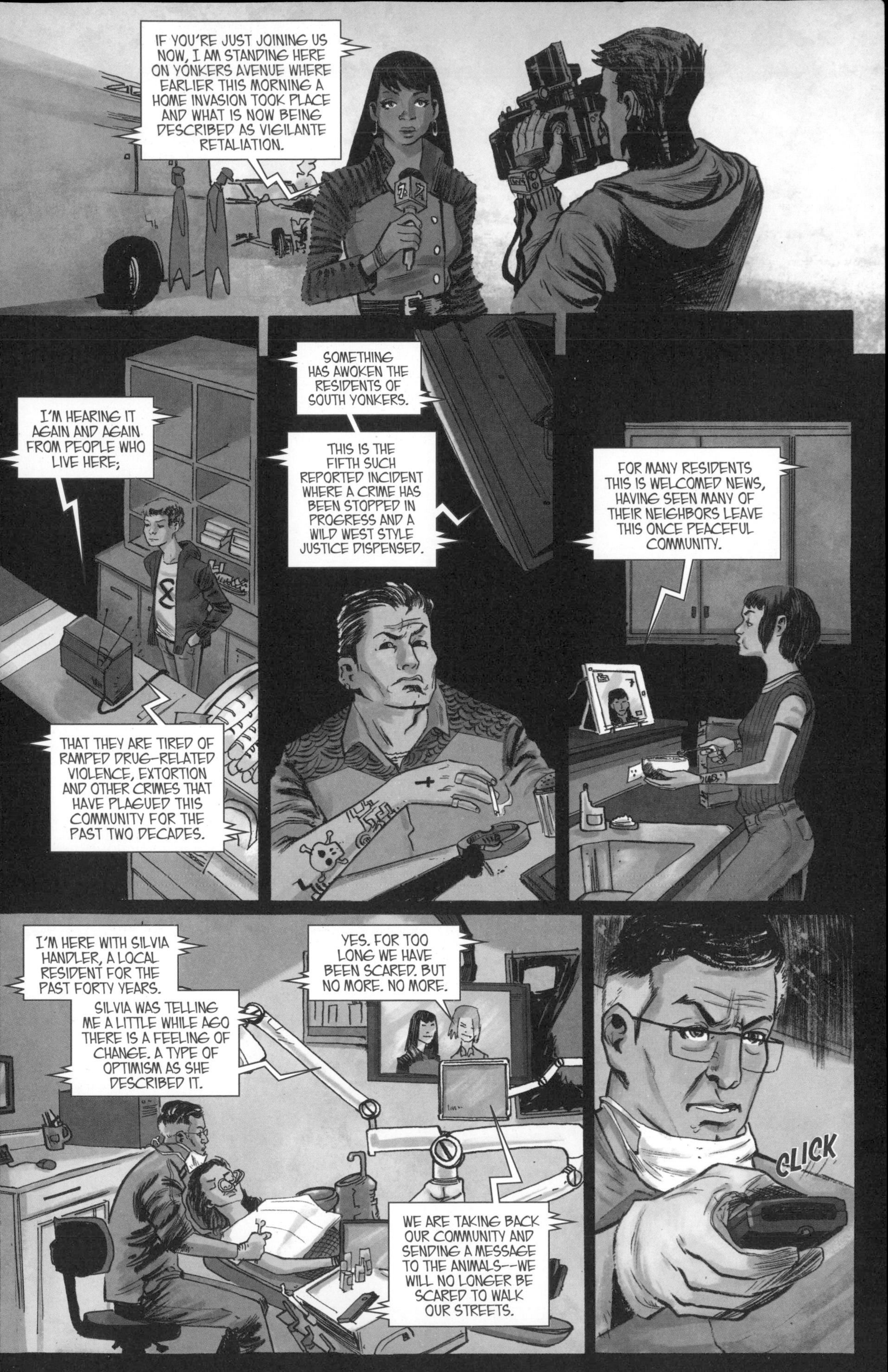

IF YOU'RE JUST JOINING US NOW, I AM STANDING HERE ON YONKERS AVENUE WHERE EARLIER THIS MORNING A HOME INVASION TOOK PLACE AND WHAT IS NOW BEING DESCRIBED AS VIGILANTE RETALIATION.
I'M HEARING IT AGAIN AND AGAIN FROM PEOPLE WHO LIVE HERE;
THAT THEY ARE TIRED OF RAMPED DRUG-RELATED VIOLENCE, EXTORTION AND OTHER CRIMES THAT HAVE PLAGUED THIS COMMUNITY FOR THE PAST TWO DECADES.
SOMETHING HAS AWOKEN THE RESIDENTS OF SOUTH YONKERS.
THIS IS THE FIFTH SUCH REPORTED INCIDENT WHERE A CRIME HAS BEEN STOPPED IN PROGRESS AND A WILD WEST STYLE JUSTICE DISPENSED.
FOR MANY RESIDENTS THIS IS WELCOMED NEWS, HAVING SEEN MANY OF THEIR NEIGHBORS LEAVE THIS ONCE PEACEFUL COMMUNITY.
I'M HERE WITH SILVIA HANDLER, A LOCAL RESIDENT FOR THE PAST FORTY YEARS.
SILVIA WAS TELLING ME A LITTLE WHILE AGO THERE IS A FEELING OF CHANGE. A TYPE OF OPTIMISM AS SHE DESCRIBED IT.
YES. FOR TOO LONG WE HAVE BEEN SCARED. BUT NO MORE. NO MORE.
WE ARE TAKING BACK OUR COMMUNITY AND SENDING A MESSAGE TO THE ANIMALS--WE WILL NO LONGER BE SCARED TO WALK OUR STREETS.
CLICK

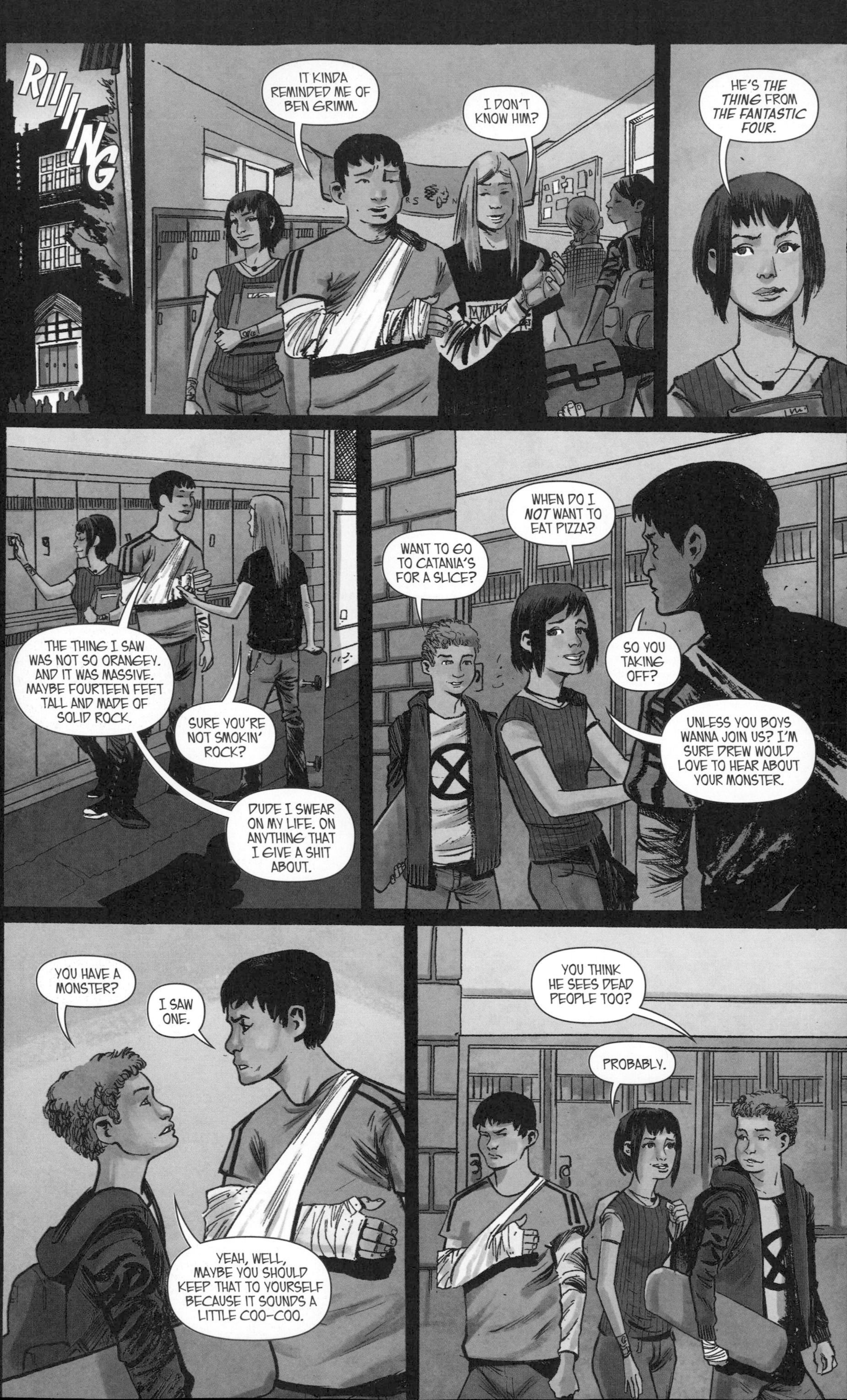
RIIIING
IT KINDA REMINDED ME OF BEN GRIMM.
I DON'T KNOW HIM?
HE'S *THE THING* FROM *THE FANTASTIC FOUR*.
THE THING I SAW WAS NOT SO ORANGEY. AND IT WAS MASSIVE. MAYBE FOURTEEN FEET TALL AND MADE OF SOLID ROCK.
SURE YOU'RE NOT SMOKIN' ROCK?
DUDE I SWEAR ON MY LIFE. ON ANYTHING THAT I GIVE A SHIT ABOUT.
WANT TO GO TO CATANIA'S FOR A SLICE?
WHEN DO I *NOT* WANT TO EAT PIZZA?
SO YOU TAKING OFF?
UNLESS YOU BOYS WANNA JOIN US? I'M SURE DREW WOULD LOVE TO HEAR ABOUT YOUR MONSTER.
YOU HAVE A MONSTER?
I SAW ONE.
YEAH, WELL, MAYBE YOU SHOULD KEEP THAT TO YOURSELF BECAUSE IT SOUNDS A LITTLE COO-COO.
YOU THINK HE SEES DEAD PEOPLE TOO?
PROBABLY.

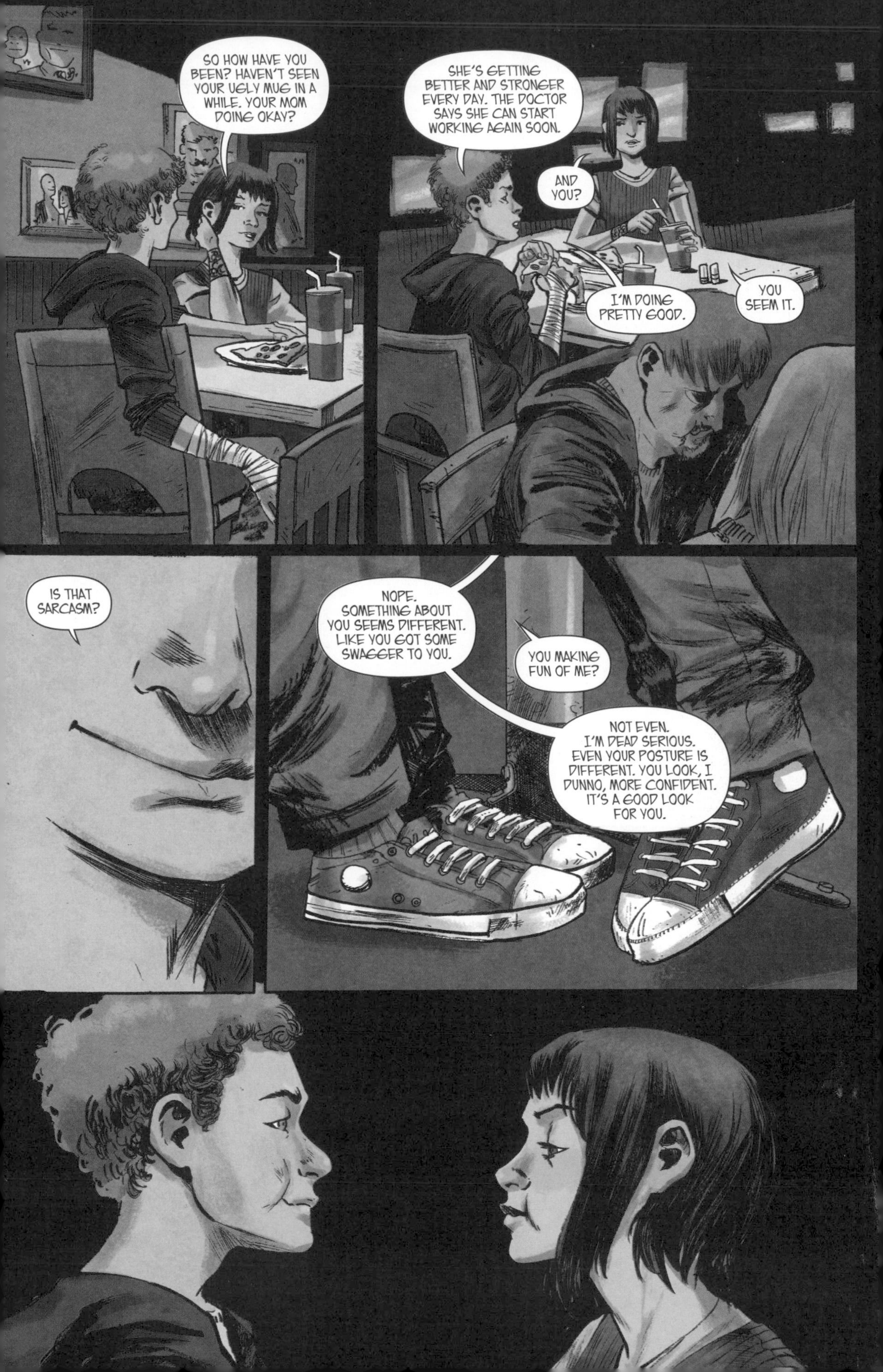
SO HOW HAVE YOU BEEN? HAVEN'T SEEN YOUR UGLY MUG IN A WHILE. YOUR MOM DOING OKAY?
SHE'S GETTING BETTER AND STRONGER EVERY DAY. THE DOCTOR SAYS SHE CAN START WORKING AGAIN SOON.
AND YOU?
I'M DOING PRETTY GOOD.
YOU SEEM IT.
IS THAT SARCASM?
NOPE. SOMETHING ABOUT YOU SEEMS DIFFERENT. LIKE YOU GOT SOME SWAGGER TO YOU.
YOU MAKING FUN OF ME?
NOT EVEN. I'M DEAD SERIOUS. EVEN YOUR POSTURE IS DIFFERENT. YOU LOOK, I DUNNO, MORE CONFIDENT. IT'S A GOOD LOOK FOR YOU.

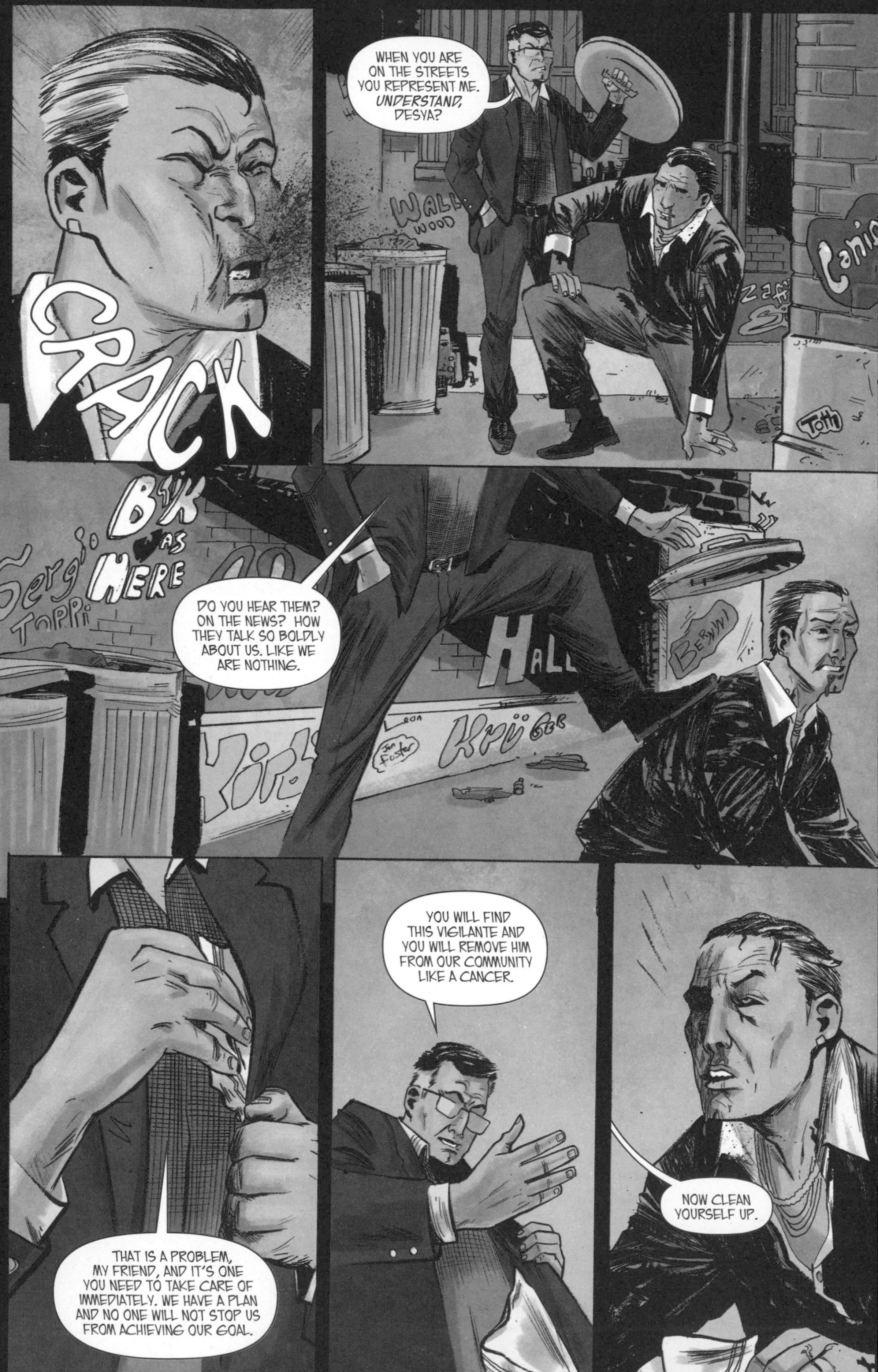
CRACK
WHEN YOU ARE ON THE STREETS YOU REPRESENT ME. UNDERSTAND, DESYA?
DO YOU HEAR THEM? ON THE NEWS? HOW THEY TALK SO BOLDLY ABOUT US. LIKE WE ARE NOTHING.
THAT IS A PROBLEM, MY FRIEND, AND IT'S ONE YOU NEED TO TAKE CARE OF IMMEDIATELY. WE HAVE A PLAN AND NO ONE WILL NOT STOP US FROM ACHIEVING OUR GOAL.
YOU WILL FIND THIS VIGILANTE AND YOU WILL REMOVE HIM FROM OUR COMMUNITY LIKE A CANCER.
NOW CLEAN YOURSELF UP.

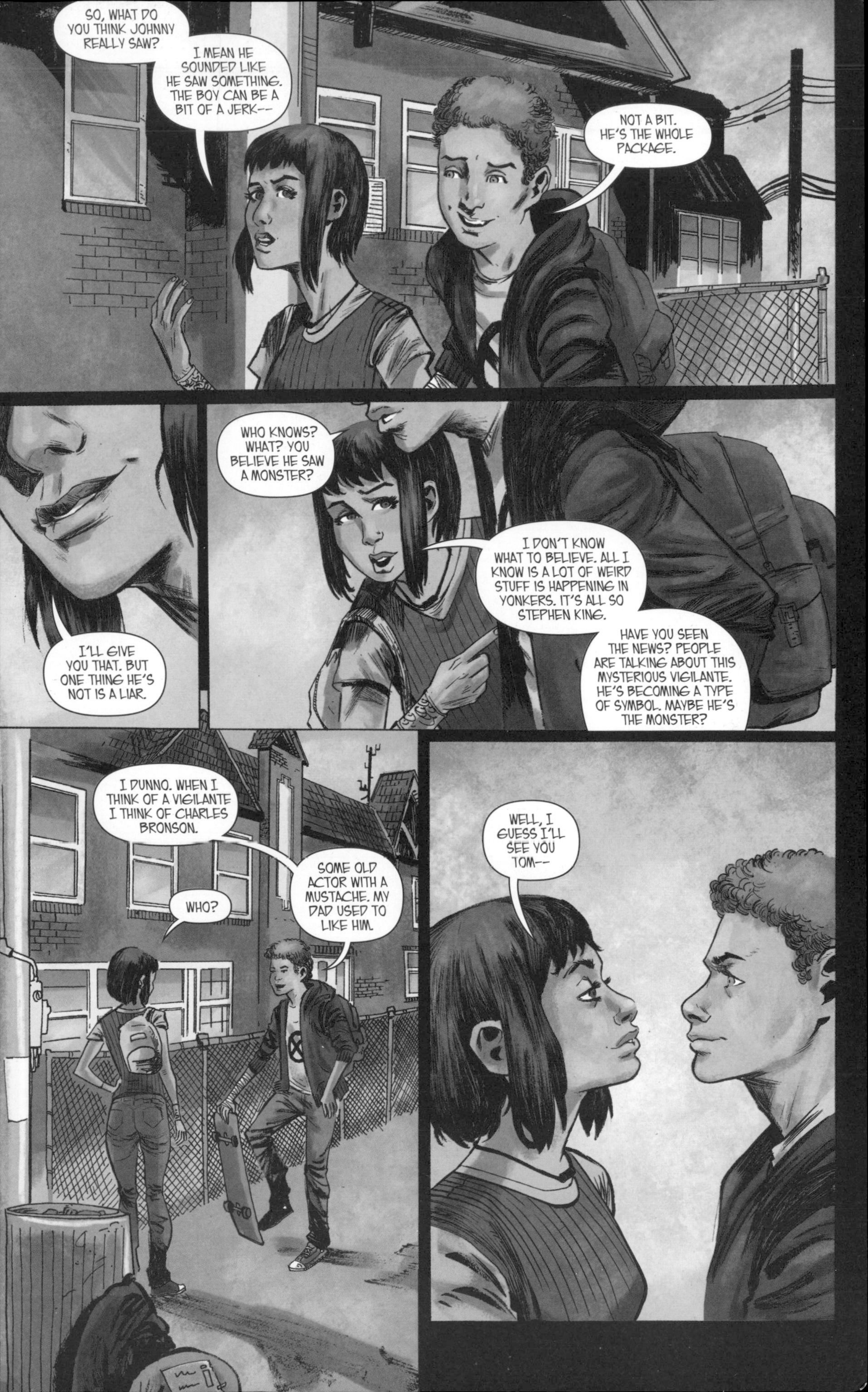
SO, WHAT DO YOU THINK JOHNNY REALLY SAW?
I MEAN HE SOUNDED LIKE HE SAW SOMETHING. THE BOY CAN BE A BIT OF A JERK--
NOT A BIT. HE'S THE WHOLE PACKAGE.
I'LL GIVE YOU THAT. BUT ONE THING HE'S NOT IS A LIAR.
WHO KNOWS? WHAT? YOU BELIEVE HE SAW A MONSTER?
I DON'T KNOW WHAT TO BELIEVE. ALL I KNOW IS A LOT OF WEIRD STUFF IS HAPPENING IN YONKERS. IT'S ALL SO STEPHEN KING.
HAVE YOU SEEN THE NEWS? PEOPLE ARE TALKING ABOUT THIS MYSTERIOUS VIGILANTE. HE'S BECOMING A TYPE OF SYMBOL. MAYBE HE'S THE MONSTER?
I DUNNO. WHEN I THINK OF A VIGILANTE I THINK OF CHARLES BRONSON.
WHO?
SOME OLD ACTOR WITH A MUSTACHE. MY DAD USED TO LIKE HIM.
WELL, I GUESS I'LL SEE YOU TOM--

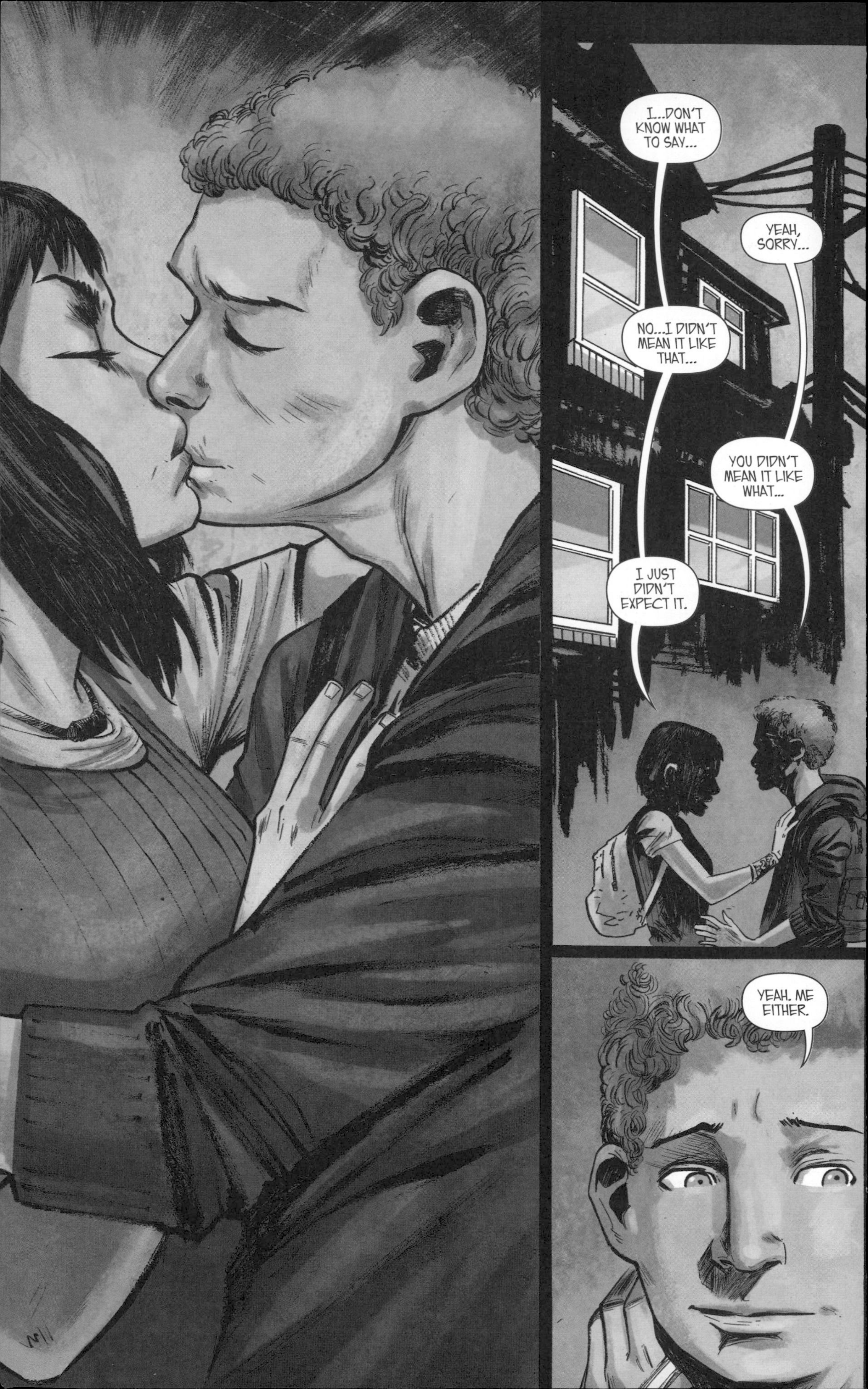
I...DON'T KNOW WHAT TO SAY...
YEAH, SORRY...
NO...I DIDN'T MEAN IT LIKE THAT...
YOU DIDN'T MEAN IT LIKE WHAT...
I JUST DIDN'T EXPECT IT.
YEAH. ME EITHER.

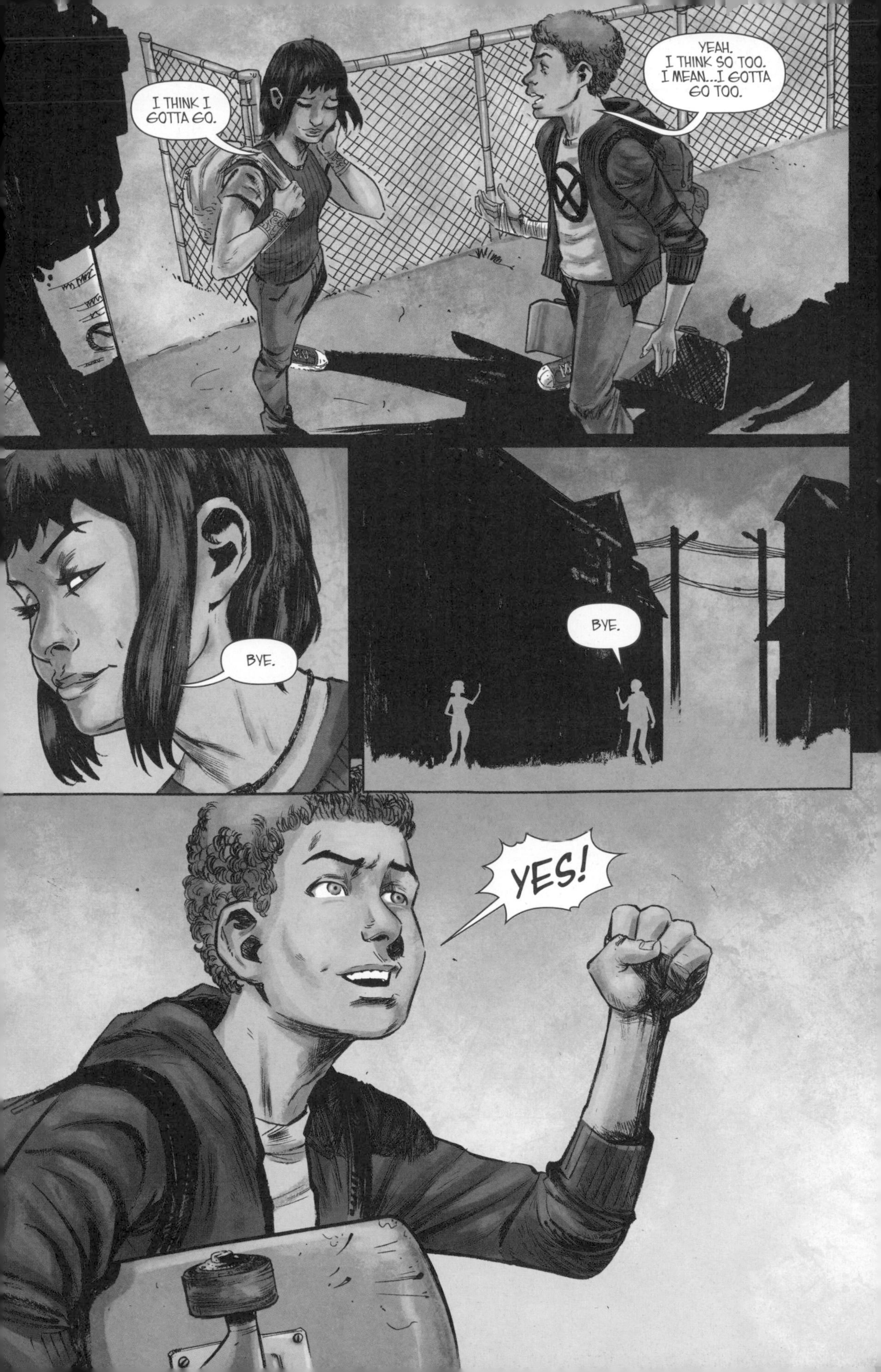
I THINK I GOTTA GO.
YEAH. I THINK SO TOO. I MEAN...I GOTTA GO TOO.
BYE.
BYE.
YES!

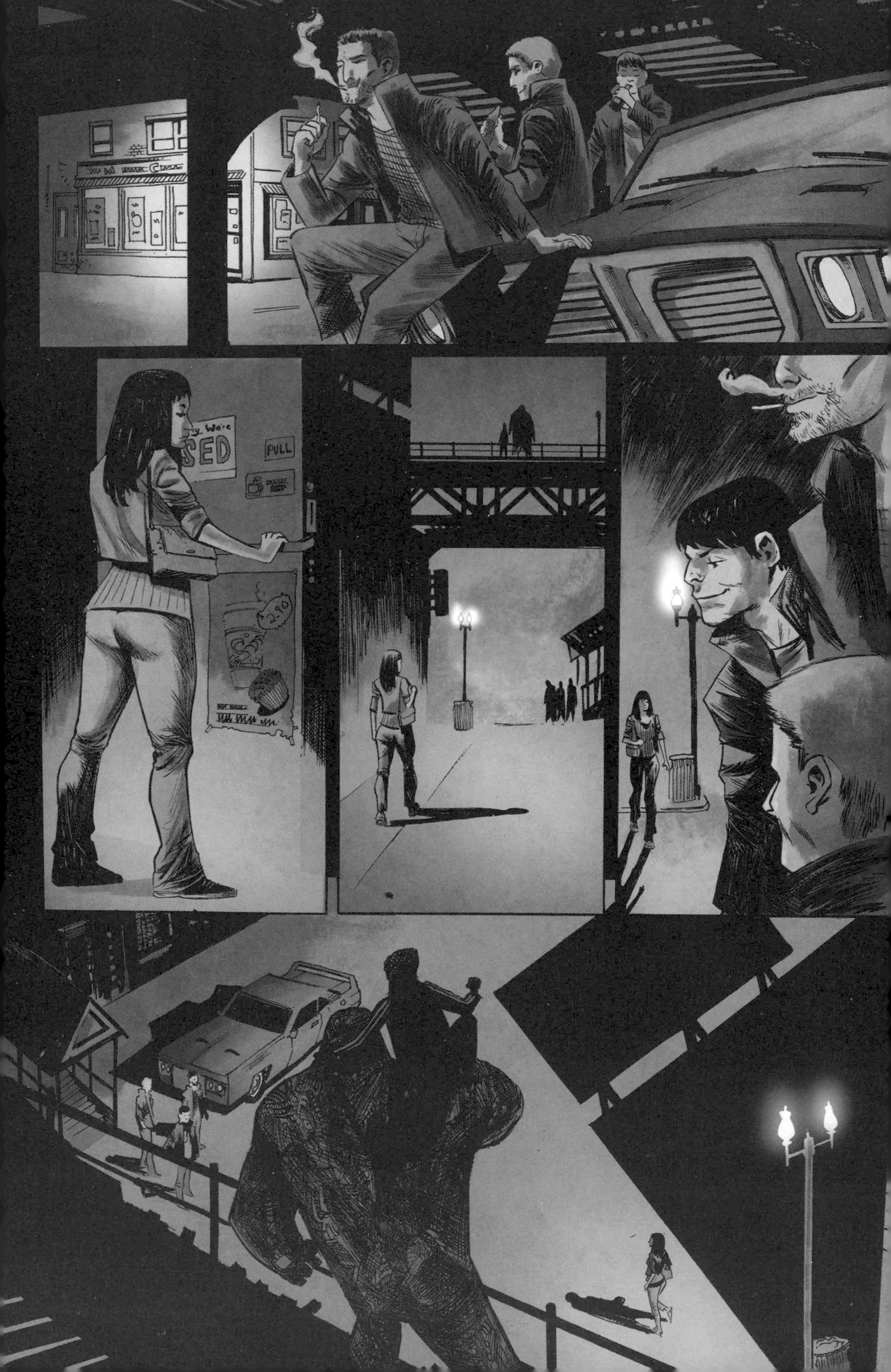
We're
PULL
2.90

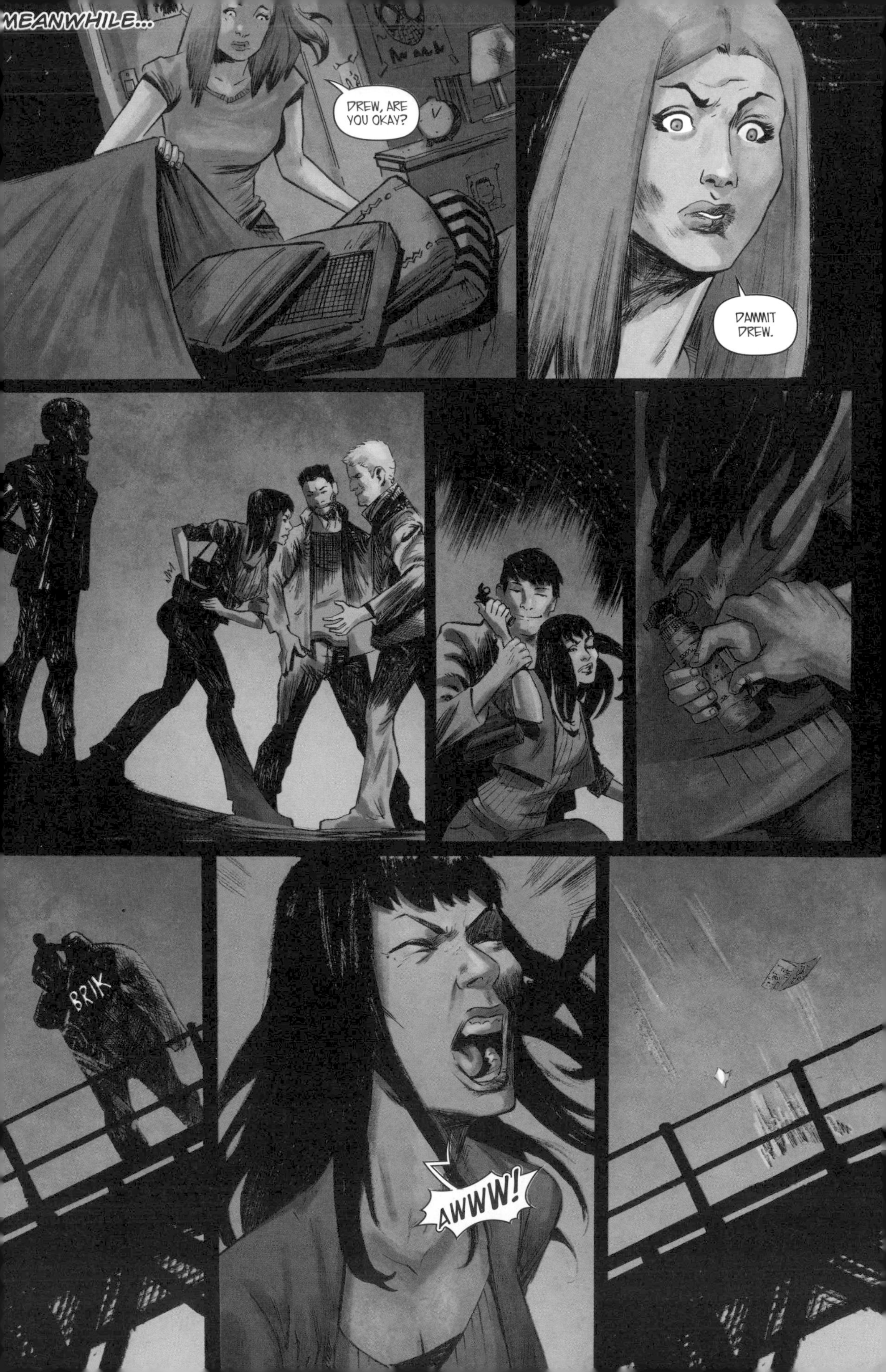

MEANWHILE...
DREW, ARE YOU OKAY?
DAMMIT DREW.
BRIK
AWWW!

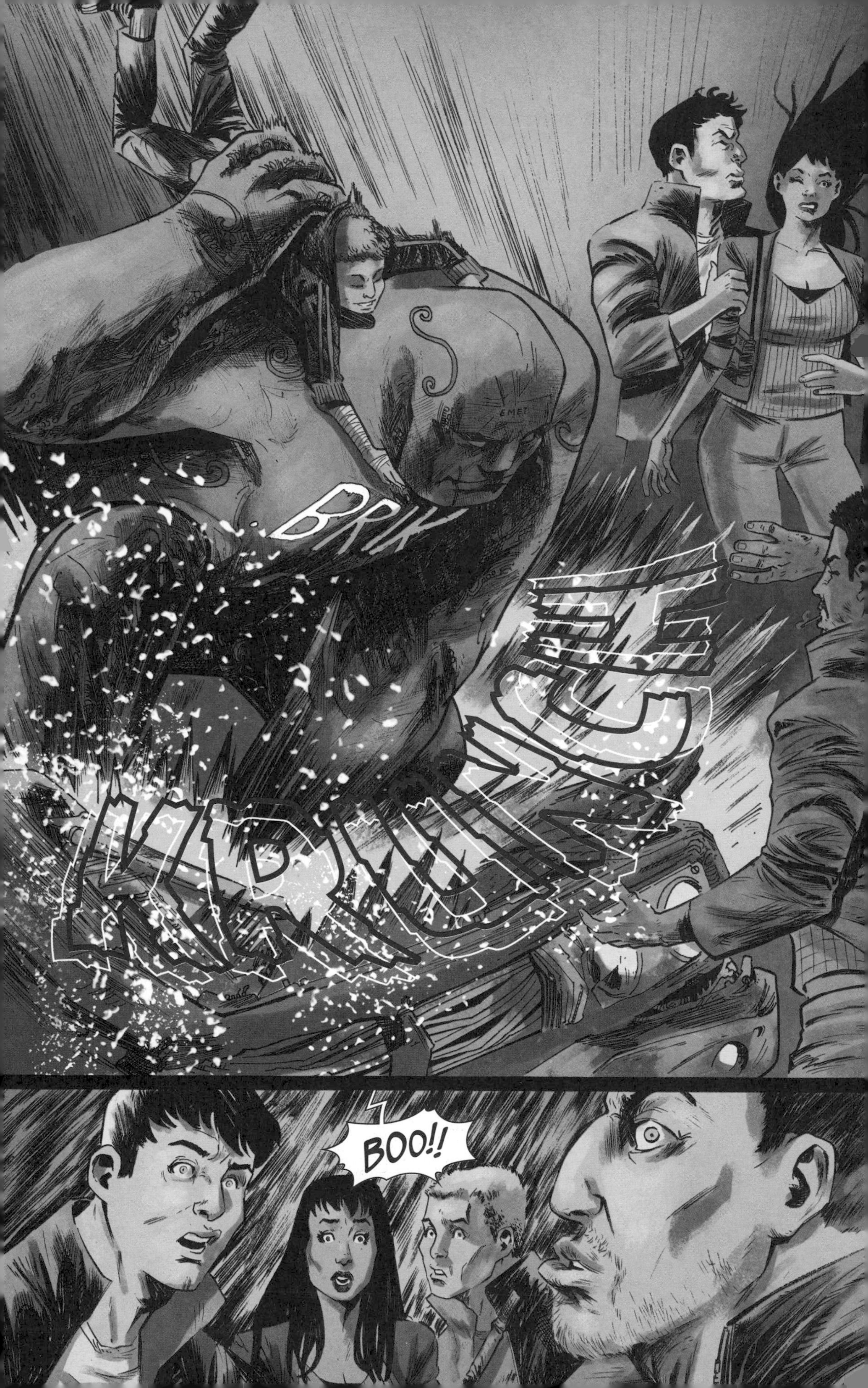
EMET
BRIK
KRUNCH
BOO!!

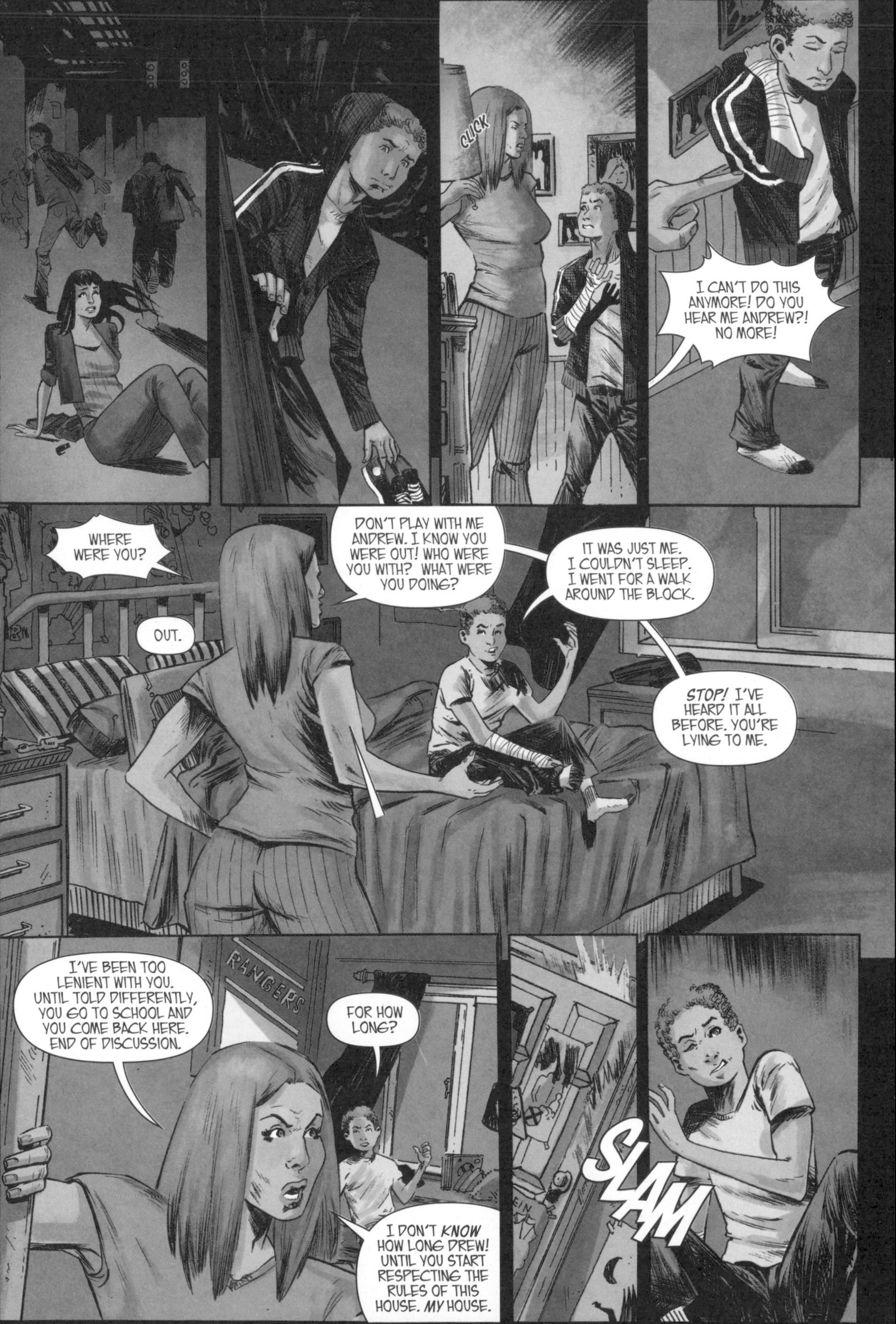
CLICK
I CAN'T DO THIS ANYMORE! DO YOU HEAR ME ANDREW?! NO MORE!
WHERE WERE YOU?
OUT.
DON'T PLAY WITH ME ANDREW. I KNOW YOU WERE OUT! WHO WERE YOU WITH? WHAT WERE YOU DOING?
IT WAS JUST ME. I COULDN'T SLEEP. I WENT FOR A WALK AROUND THE BLOCK.
STOP! I'VE HEARD IT ALL BEFORE. YOU'RE LYING TO ME.
RANGERS
I'VE BEEN TOO LENIENT WITH YOU. UNTIL TOLD DIFFERENTLY, YOU GO TO SCHOOL AND YOU COME BACK HERE. END OF DISCUSSION.
FOR HOW LONG?
I DON'T KNOW HOW LONG DREW! UNTIL YOU START RESPECTING THE RULES OF THIS HOUSE. MY HOUSE.
SLAM

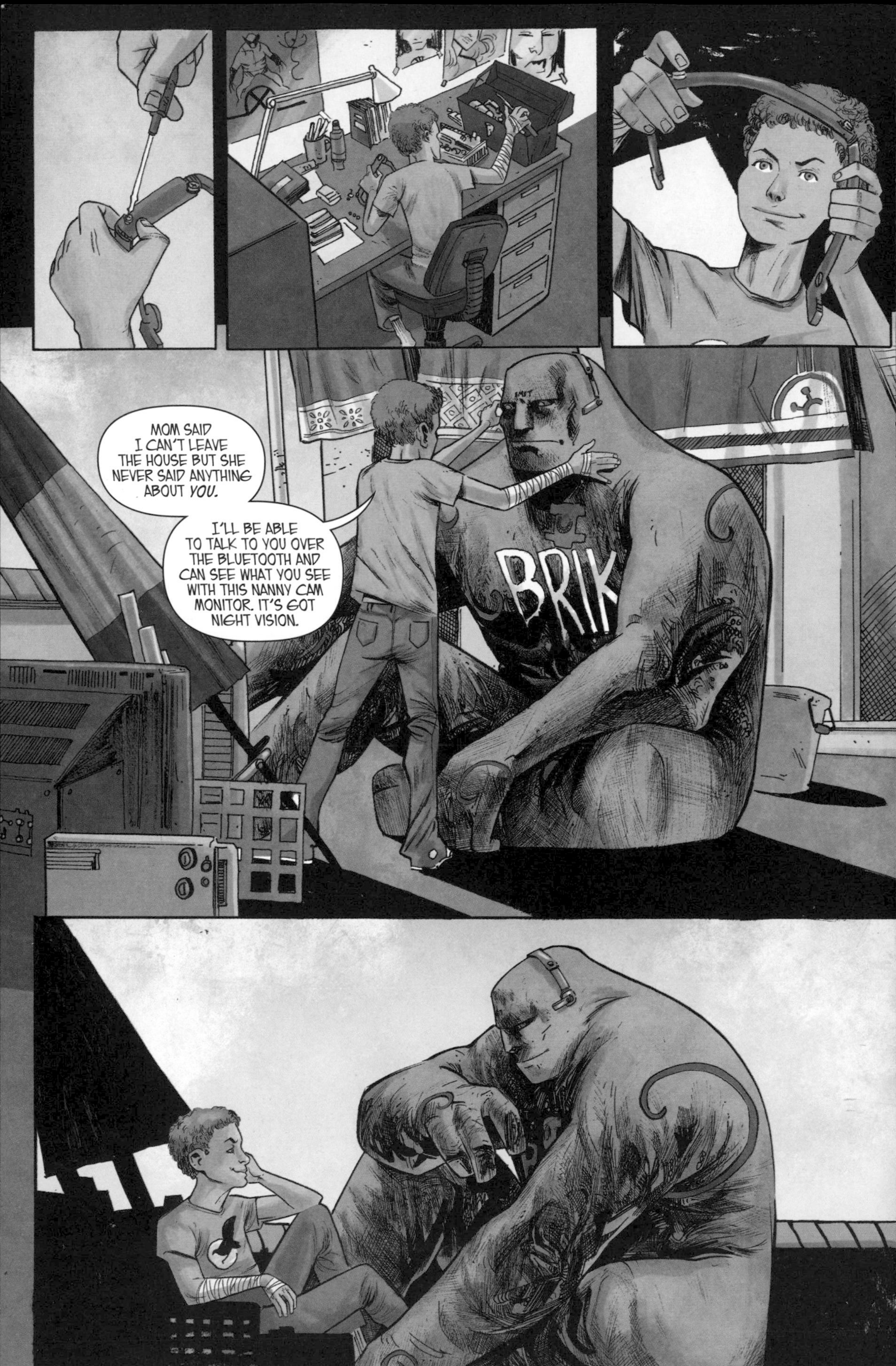
MOM SAID I CAN'T LEAVE THE HOUSE BUT SHE NEVER SAID ANYTHING ABOUT *YOU.*
I'LL BE ABLE TO TALK TO YOU OVER THE BLUETOOTH AND CAN SEE WHAT YOU SEE WITH THIS NANNY CAM MONITOR. IT'S GOT NIGHT VISION.
BRIK

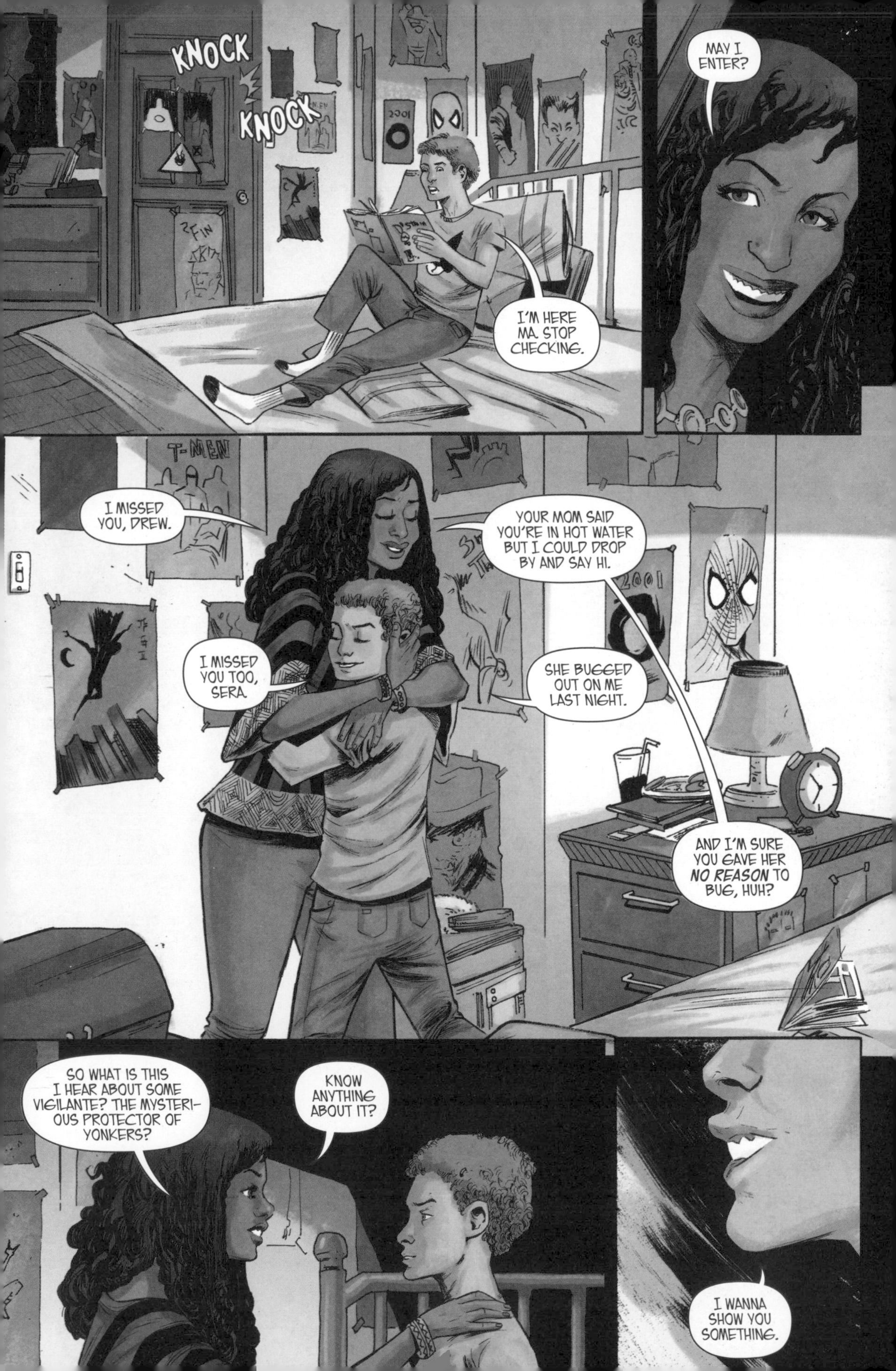
KNOCK
KNOCK
I'M HERE MA. STOP CHECKING.
MAY I ENTER?
I MISSED YOU, DREW.
YOUR MOM SAID YOU'RE IN HOT WATER BUT I COULD DROP BY AND SAY HI.
I MISSED YOU TOO, SERA.
SHE BUGGED OUT ON ME LAST NIGHT.
AND I'M SURE YOU GAVE HER *NO REASON* TO BUG, HUH?
SO WHAT IS THIS I HEAR ABOUT SOME VIGILANTE? THE MYSTERIOUS PROTECTOR OF YONKERS?
KNOW ANYTHING ABOUT IT?
I WANNA SHOW YOU SOMETHING.

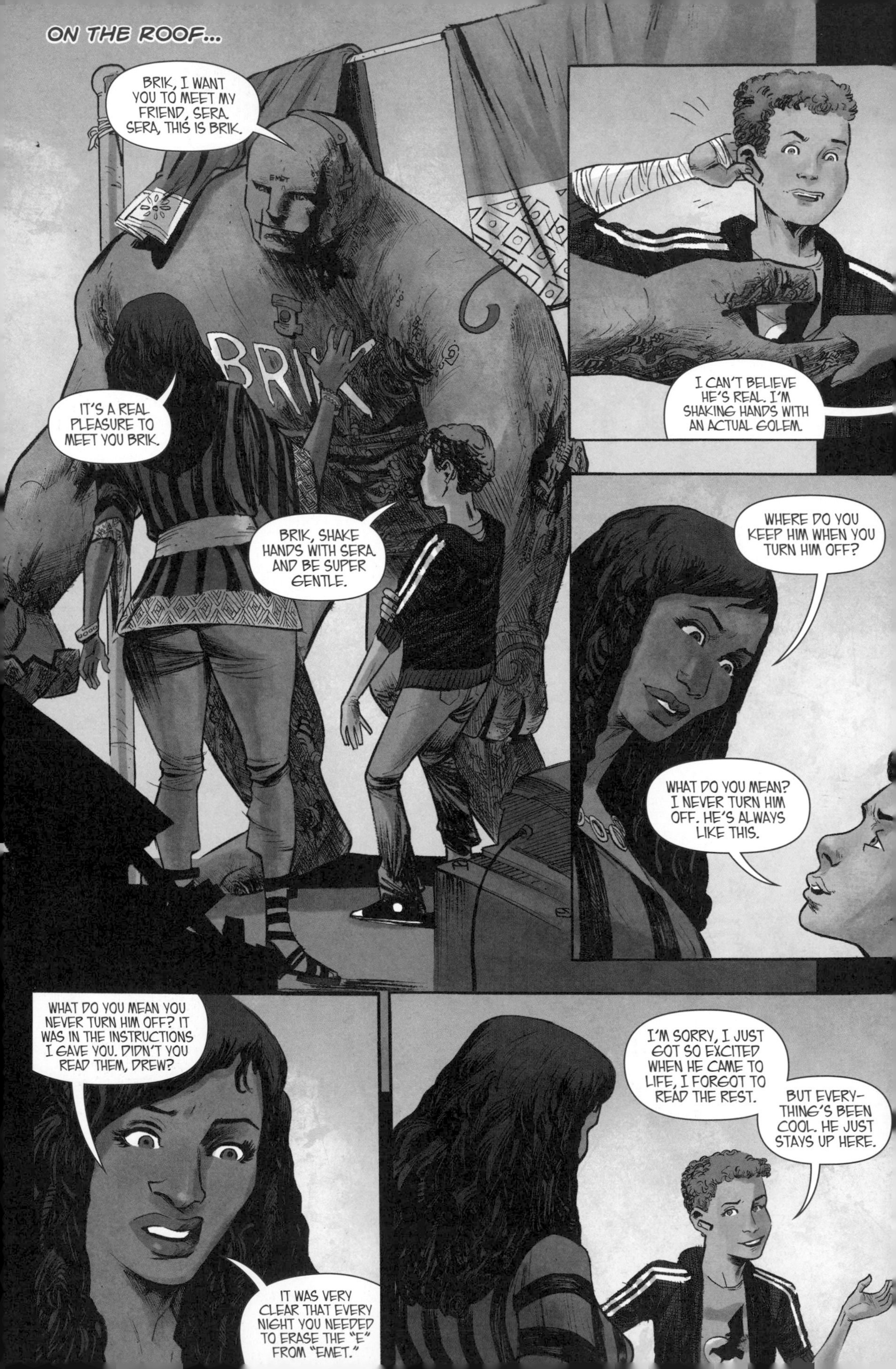
ON THE ROOF...
BRIK, I WANT YOU TO MEET MY FRIEND, SERA. SERA, THIS IS BRIK.
BRIK
IT'S A REAL PLEASURE TO MEET YOU BRIK.
BRIK, SHAKE HANDS WITH SERA AND BE SUPER GENTLE.
I CAN'T BELIEVE HE'S REAL. I'M SHAKING HANDS WITH AN ACTUAL GOLEM.
WHERE DO YOU KEEP HIM WHEN YOU TURN HIM OFF?
WHAT DO YOU MEAN? I NEVER TURN HIM OFF. HE'S ALWAYS LIKE THIS.
WHAT DO YOU MEAN YOU NEVER TURN HIM OFF? IT WAS IN THE INSTRUCTIONS I GAVE YOU. DIDN'T YOU READ THEM, DREW?
IT WAS VERY CLEAR THAT EVERY NIGHT YOU NEEDED TO ERASE THE "E" FROM "EMET."
I'M SORRY, I JUST GOT SO EXCITED WHEN HE CAME TO LIFE, I FORGOT TO READ THE REST.
BUT EVERY-THING'S BEEN COOL. HE JUST STAYS UP HERE.

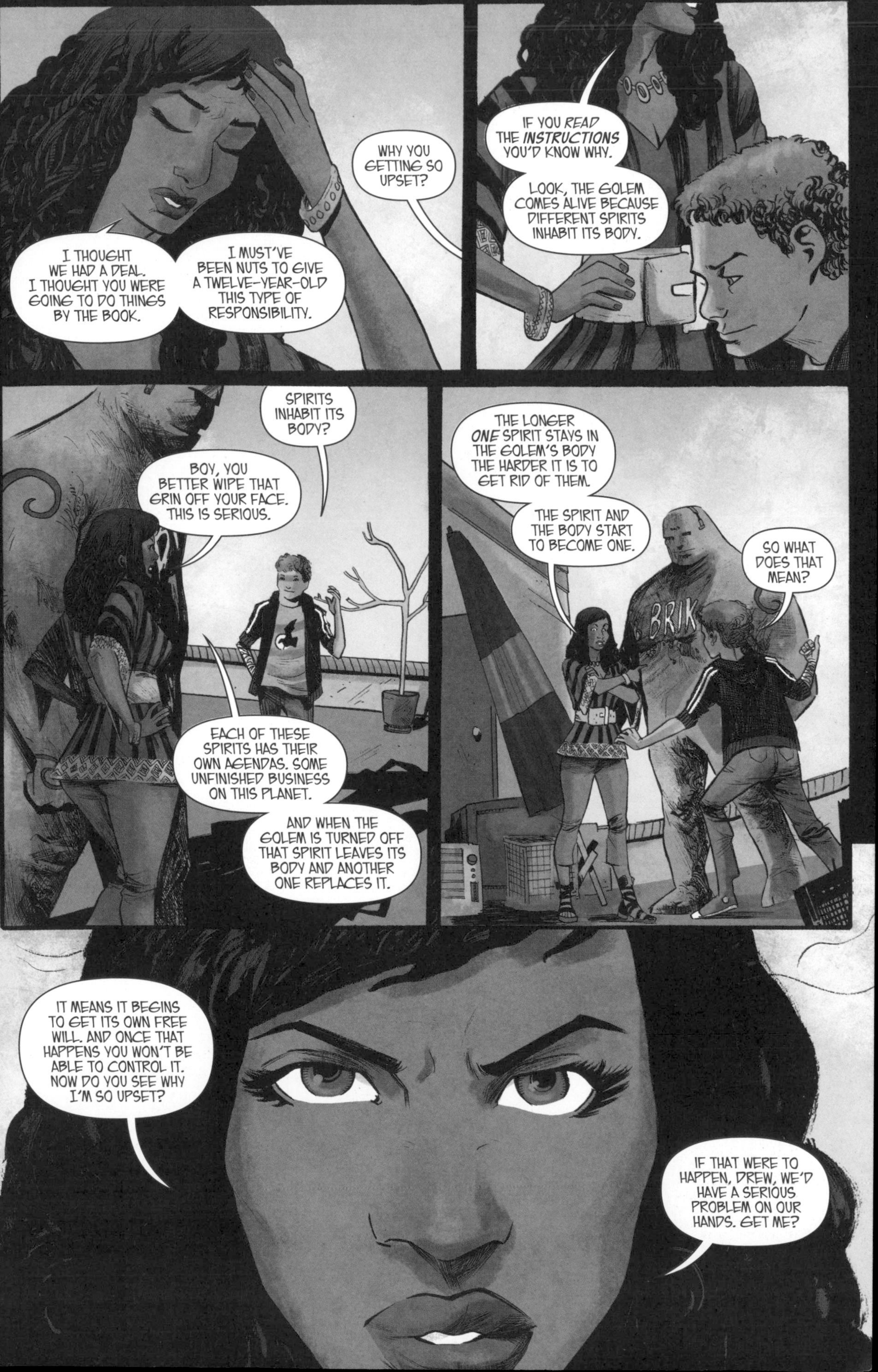
I THOUGHT WE HAD A DEAL. I THOUGHT YOU WERE GOING TO DO THINGS BY THE BOOK.
I MUST'VE BEEN NUTS TO GIVE A TWELVE-YEAR-OLD THIS TYPE OF RESPONSIBILITY.
WHY YOU GETTING SO UPSET?
IF YOU *READ* THE ***INSTRUCTIONS*** YOU'D KNOW WHY.
LOOK, THE GOLEM COMES ALIVE BECAUSE DIFFERENT SPIRITS INHABIT ITS BODY.
SPIRITS INHABIT ITS BODY?
BOY, YOU BETTER WIPE THAT GRIN OFF YOUR FACE. THIS IS SERIOUS.
EACH OF THESE SPIRITS HAS THEIR OWN AGENDAS. SOME UNFINISHED BUSINESS ON THIS PLANET.
AND WHEN THE GOLEM IS TURNED OFF THAT SPIRIT LEAVES ITS BODY AND ANOTHER ONE REPLACES IT.
THE LONGER *ONE* SPIRIT STAYS IN THE GOLEM'S BODY THE HARDER IT IS TO GET RID OF THEM.
THE SPIRIT AND THE BODY START TO BECOME ONE.
BRIK
SO WHAT DOES THAT MEAN?
IT MEANS IT BEGINS TO GET ITS OWN FREE WILL. AND ONCE THAT HAPPENS YOU WON'T BE ABLE TO CONTROL IT. NOW DO YOU SEE WHY I'M SO UPSET?
IF THAT WERE TO HAPPEN, DREW, WE'D HAVE A SERIOUS PROBLEM ON OUR HANDS. GET ME?

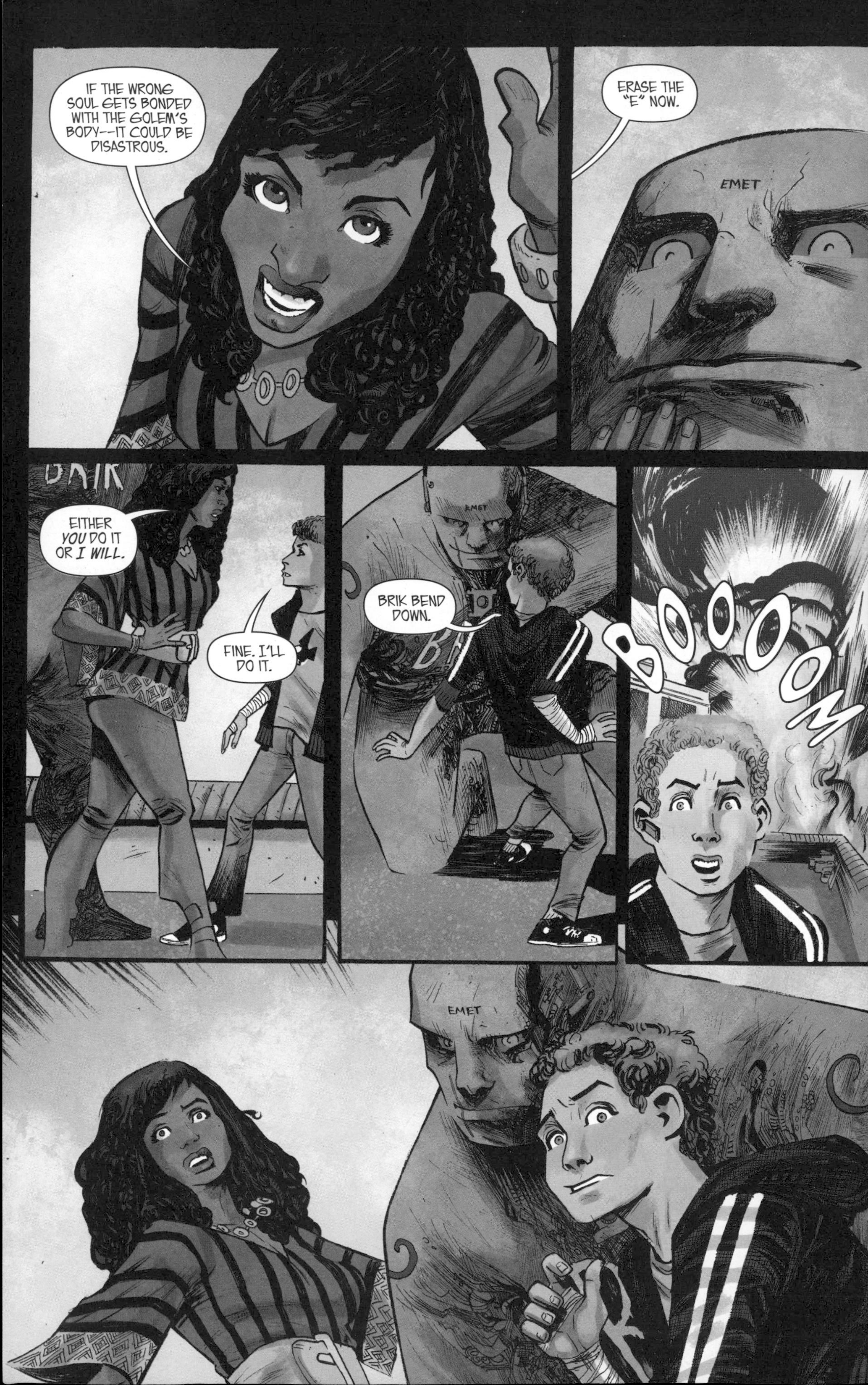
IF THE WRONG SOUL GETS BONDED WITH THE GOLEM'S BODY--IT COULD BE DISASTROUS.
ERASE THE "E" NOW.
EMET
EITHER *YOU* DO IT OR *I WILL*.
FINE. I'LL DO IT.
EMET
BRIK BEND DOWN.
BOOOOOM
EMET

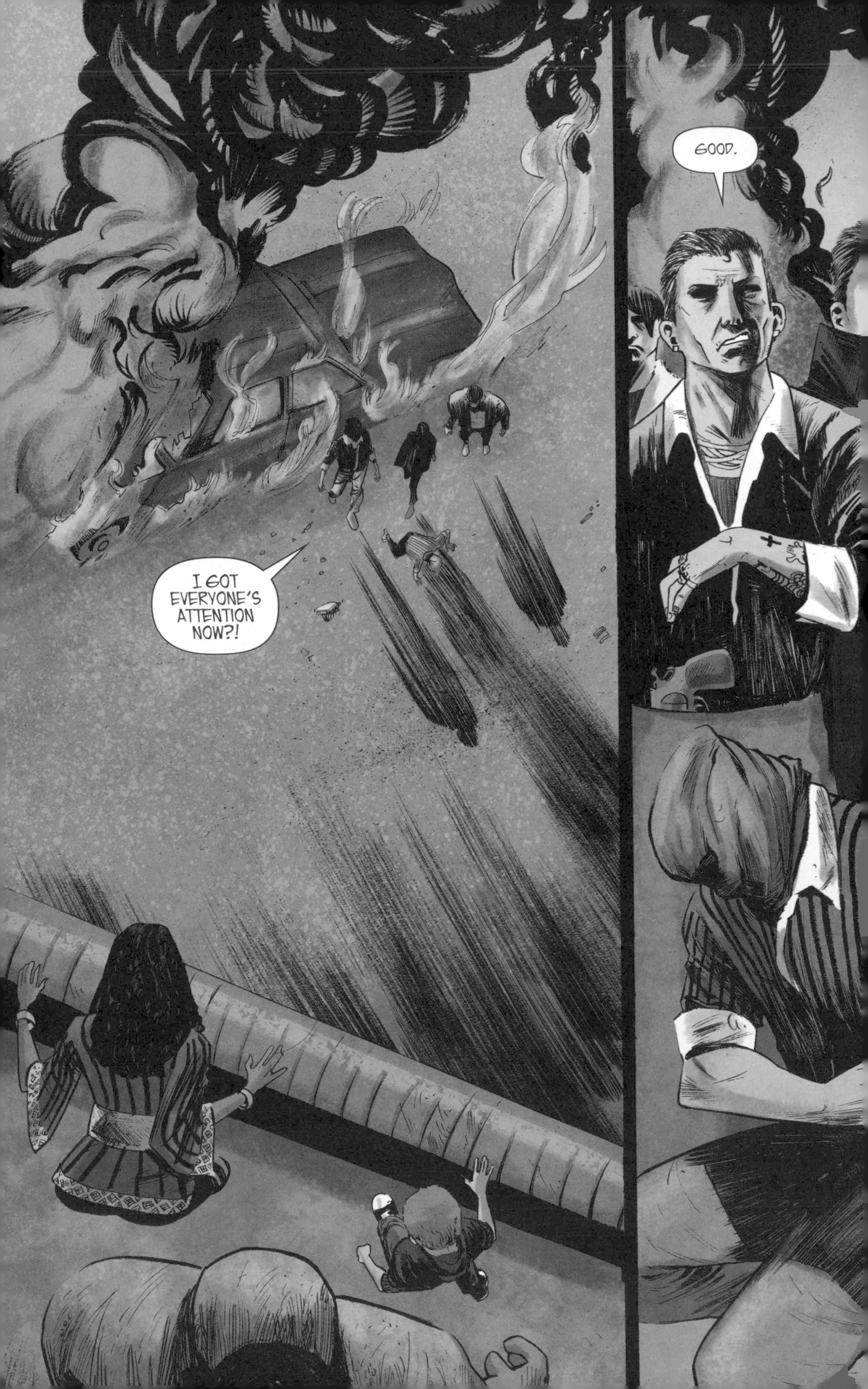
I GOT EVERYONE'S ATTENTION NOW?!
GOOD.

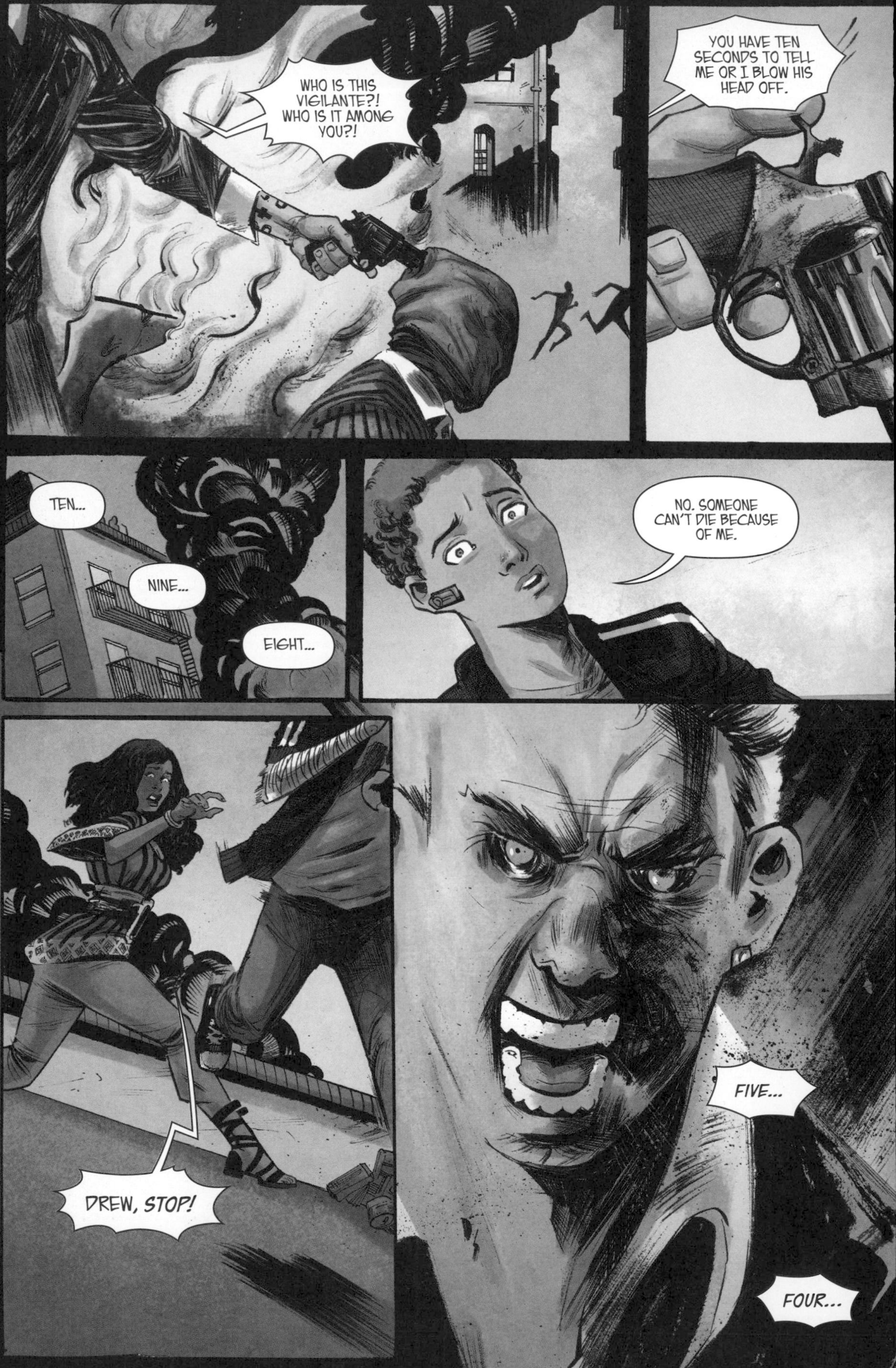
WHO IS THIS VIGILANTE?! WHO IS IT AMONG YOU?!
YOU HAVE TEN SECONDS TO TELL ME OR I BLOW HIS HEAD OFF.
TEN...
NINE...
EIGHT...
NO. SOMEONE CAN'T DIE BECAUSE OF ME.
DREW, STOP!
FIVE...
FOUR...

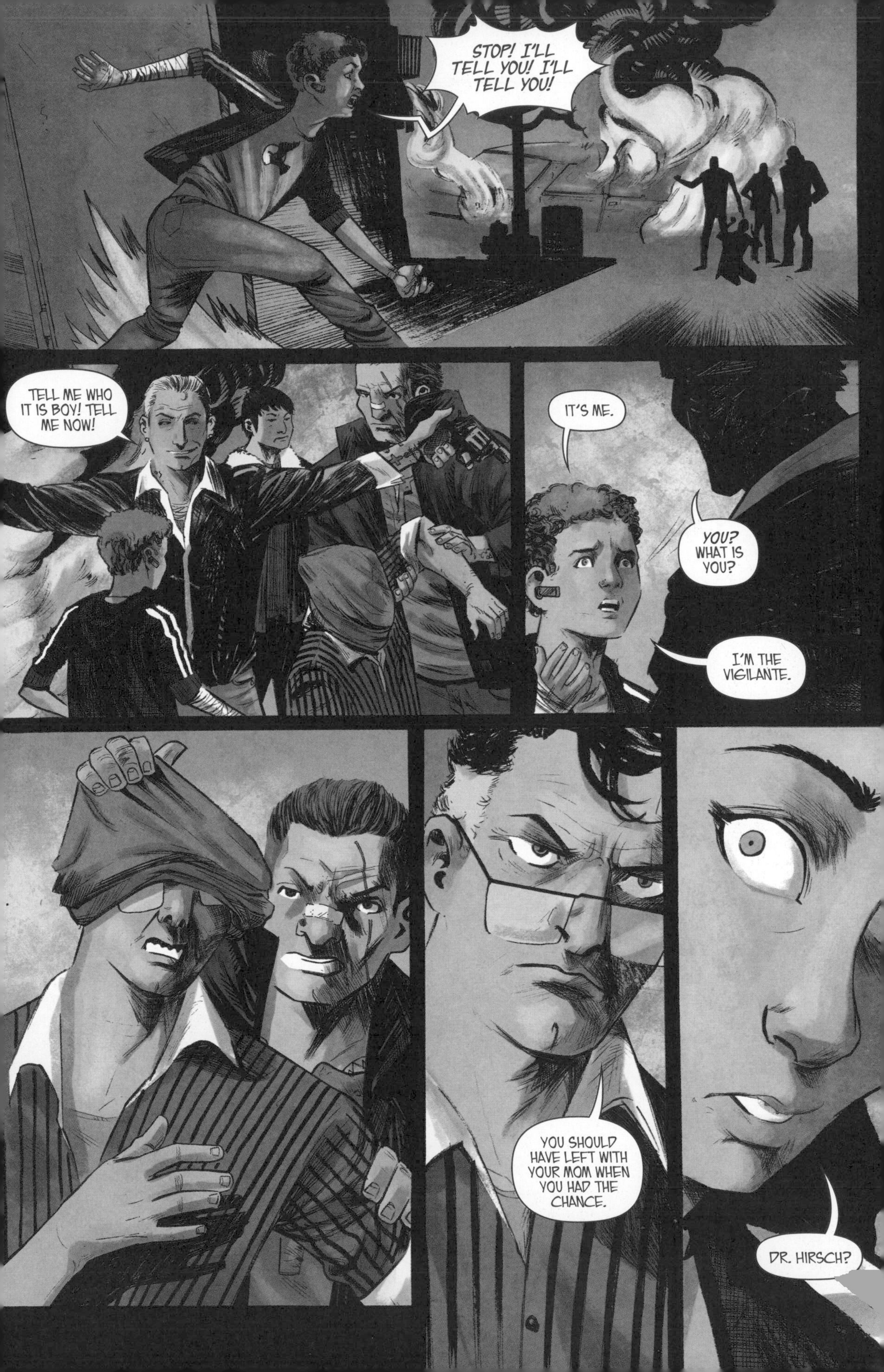
STOP! I'LL TELL YOU! I'LL TELL YOU!
TELL ME WHO IT IS BOY! TELL ME NOW!
IT'S ME.
YOU? WHAT IS YOU?
I'M THE VIGILANTE.
YOU SHOULD HAVE LEFT WITH YOUR MOM WHEN YOU HAD THE CHANCE.
DR. HIRSCH?

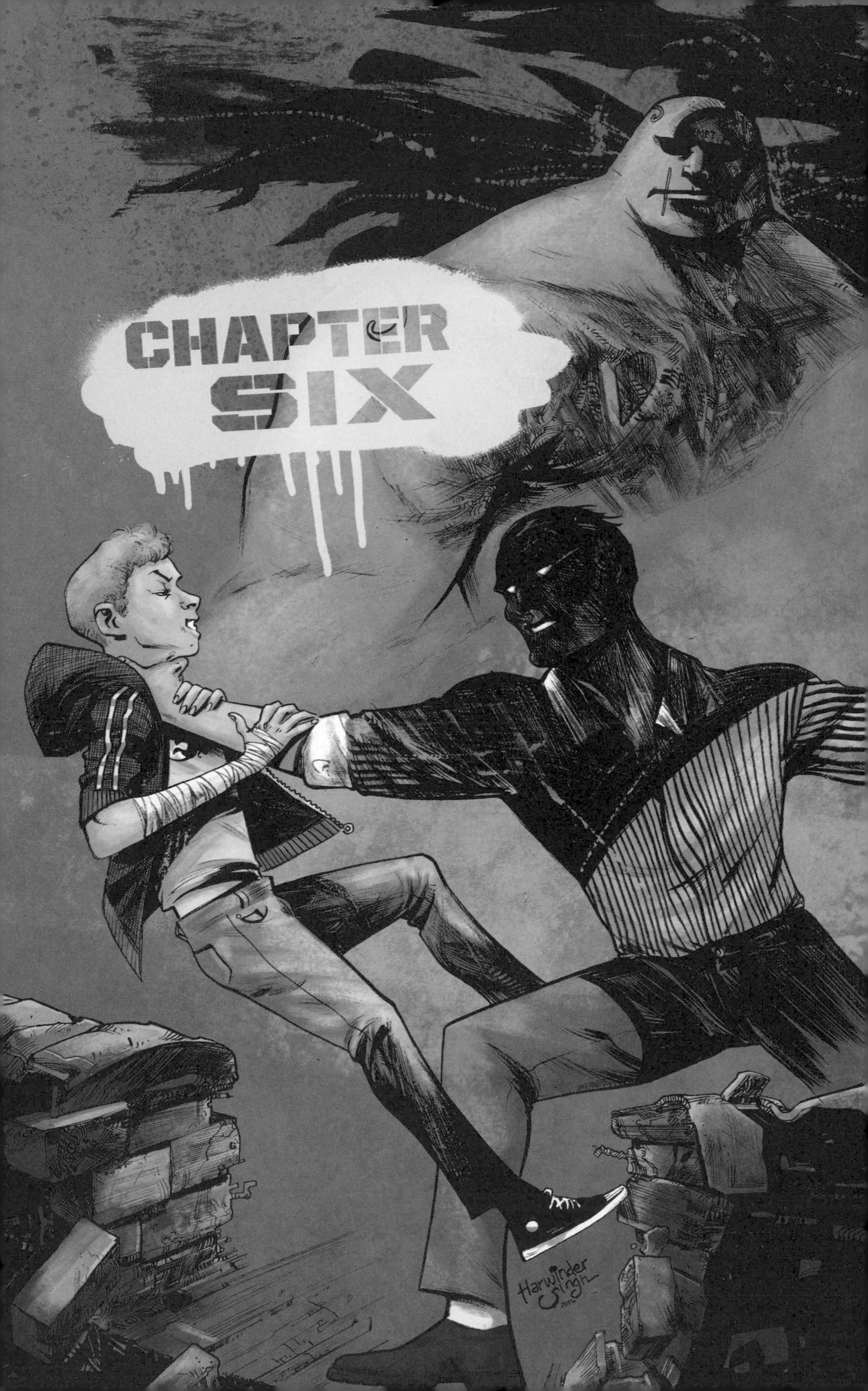
CHAPTER
SIX
Harwinder Singh

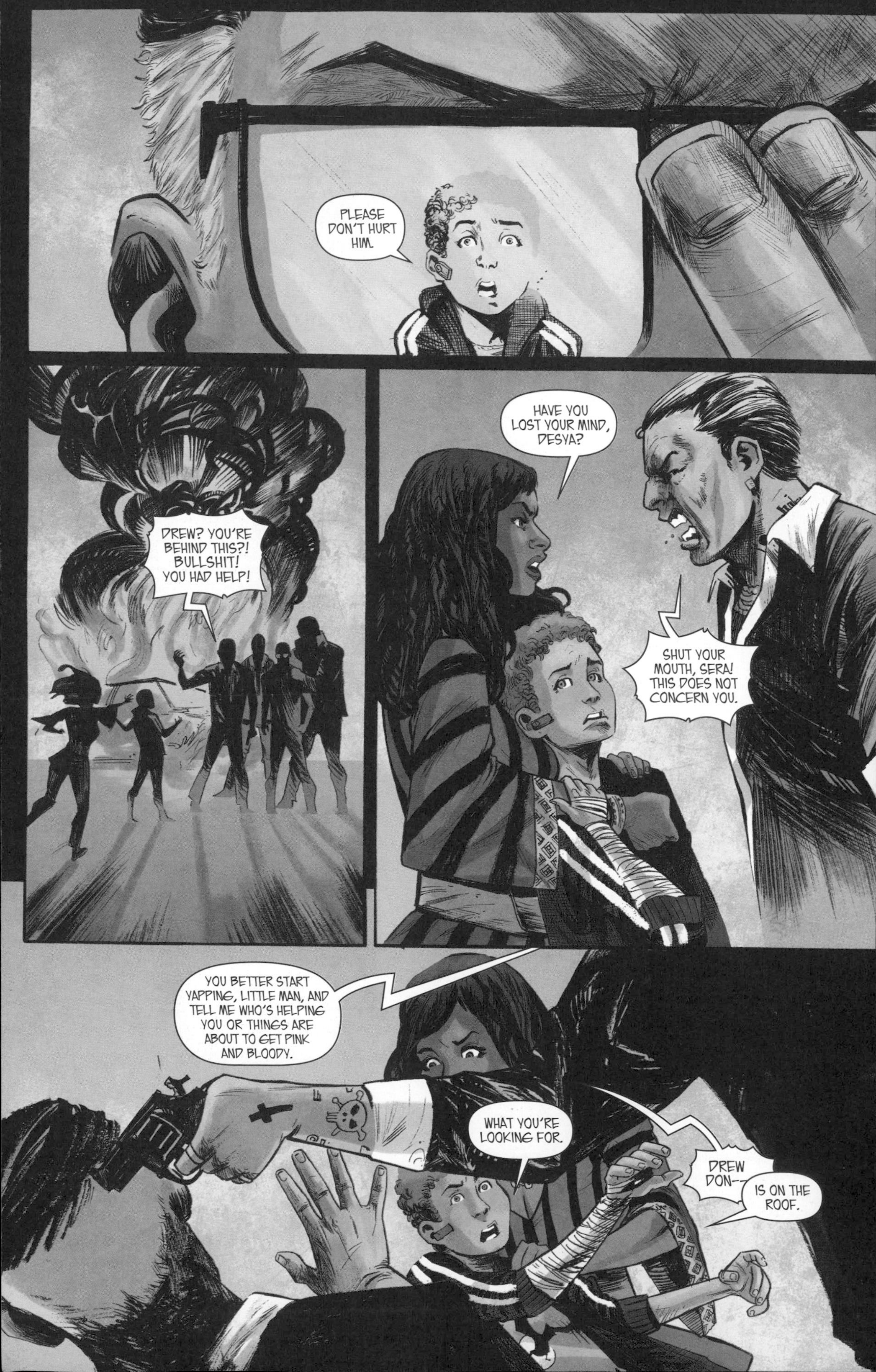
PLEASE DON'T HURT HIM.
DREW? YOU'RE BEHIND THIS?! BULLSHIT! YOU HAD HELP!
HAVE YOU LOST YOUR MIND, DESYA?
SHUT YOUR MOUTH, SERA! THIS DOES NOT CONCERN YOU.
YOU BETTER START YAPPING, LITTLE MAN, AND TELL ME WHO'S HELPING YOU OR THINGS ARE ABOUT TO GET PINK AND BLOODY.
WHAT YOU'RE LOOKING FOR.
DREW DON--
IS ON THE ROOF.

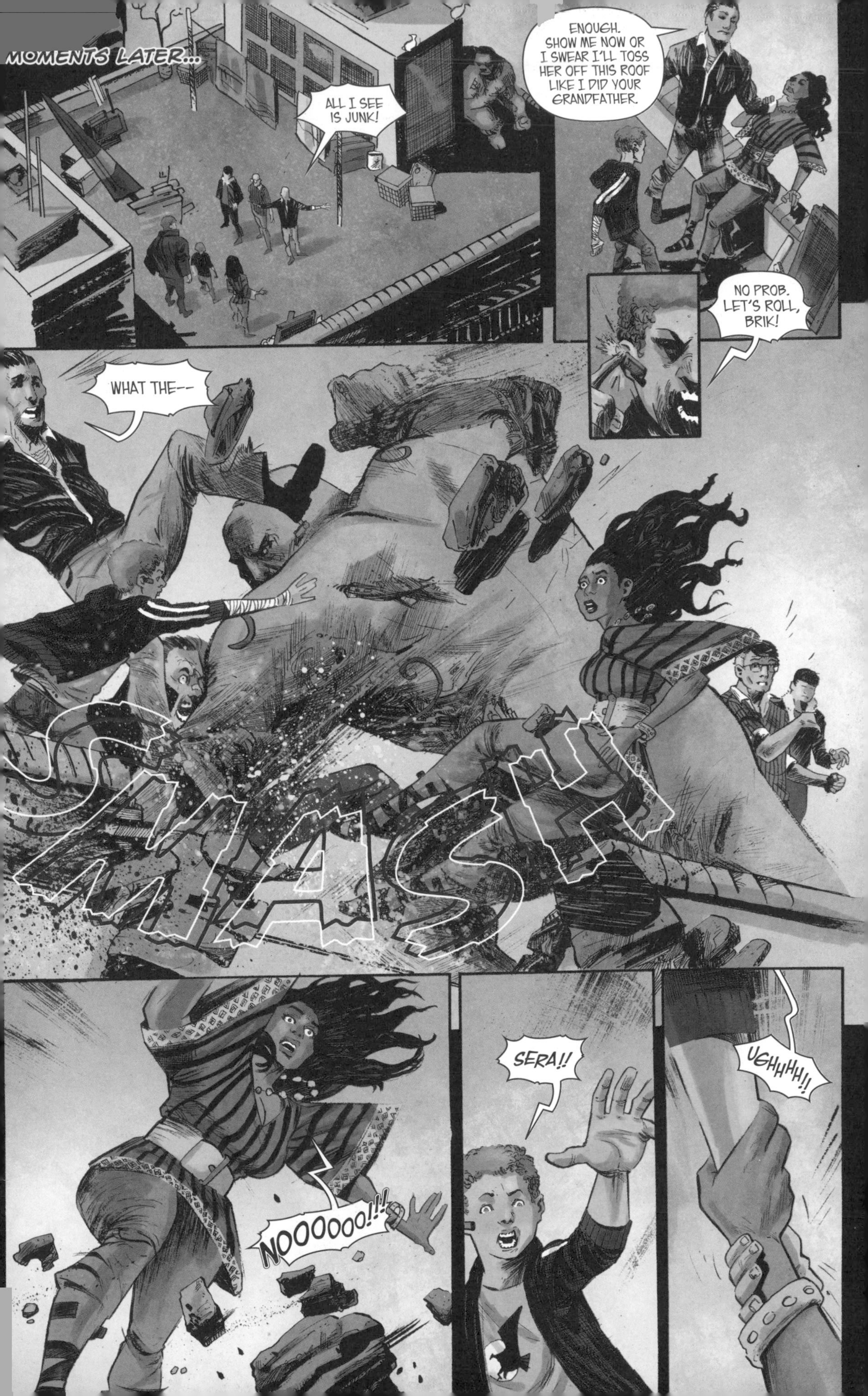
MOMENTS LATER...
ALL I SEE IS JUNK!
ENOUGH. SHOW ME NOW OR I SWEAR I'LL TOSS HER OFF THIS ROOF LIKE I DID YOUR GRANDFATHER.
NO PROB. LET'S ROLL, BRIK!
WHAT THE--
SMASH
NOOOOOO!!!
SERA!!
UGHHHH!!

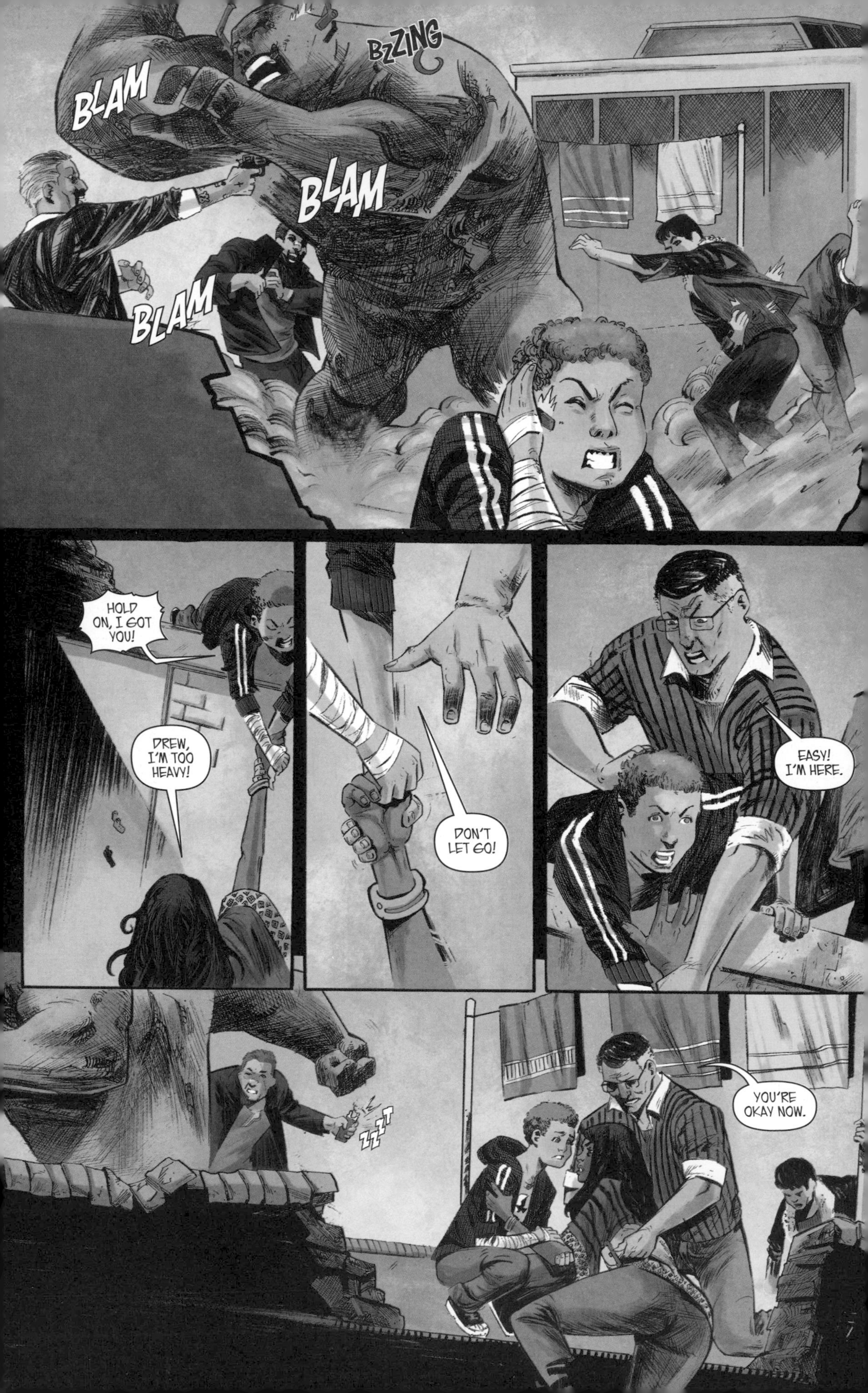
BZZING
BLAM
BLAM
BLAM
HOLD ON, I GOT YOU!
DREW, I'M TOO HEAVY!
DON'T LET GO!
EASY! I'M HERE.
ZZZT
YOU'RE OKAY NOW.

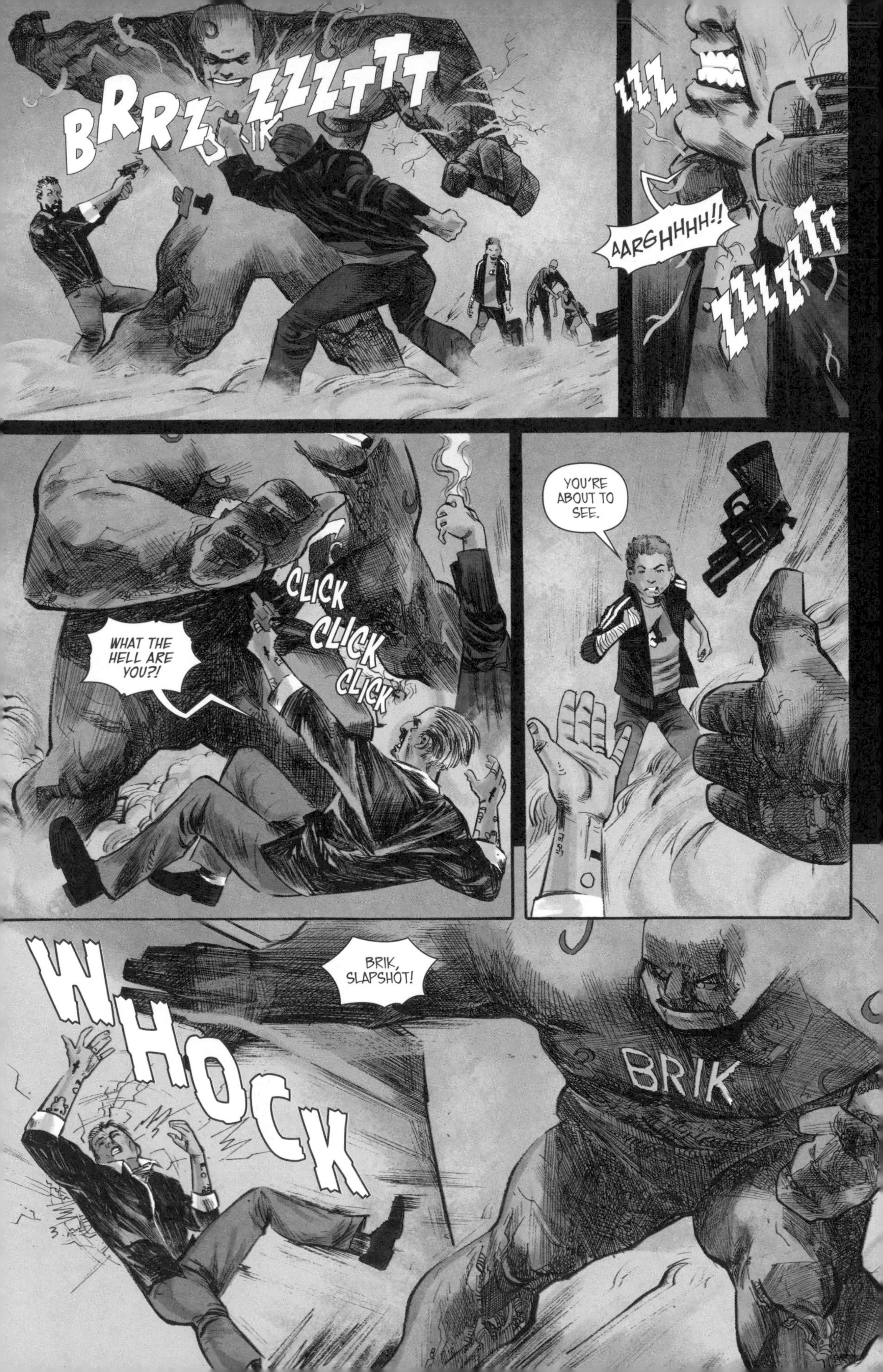
BRRZ ZZZZTTT
ZZZ
AARGHHHH!!
ZZZZZZTTT
CLICK
CLICK
CLICK
WHAT THE HELL ARE YOU?!
YOU'RE ABOUT TO SEE.
BRIK, SLAPSHOT!
WHOCK
BRIK

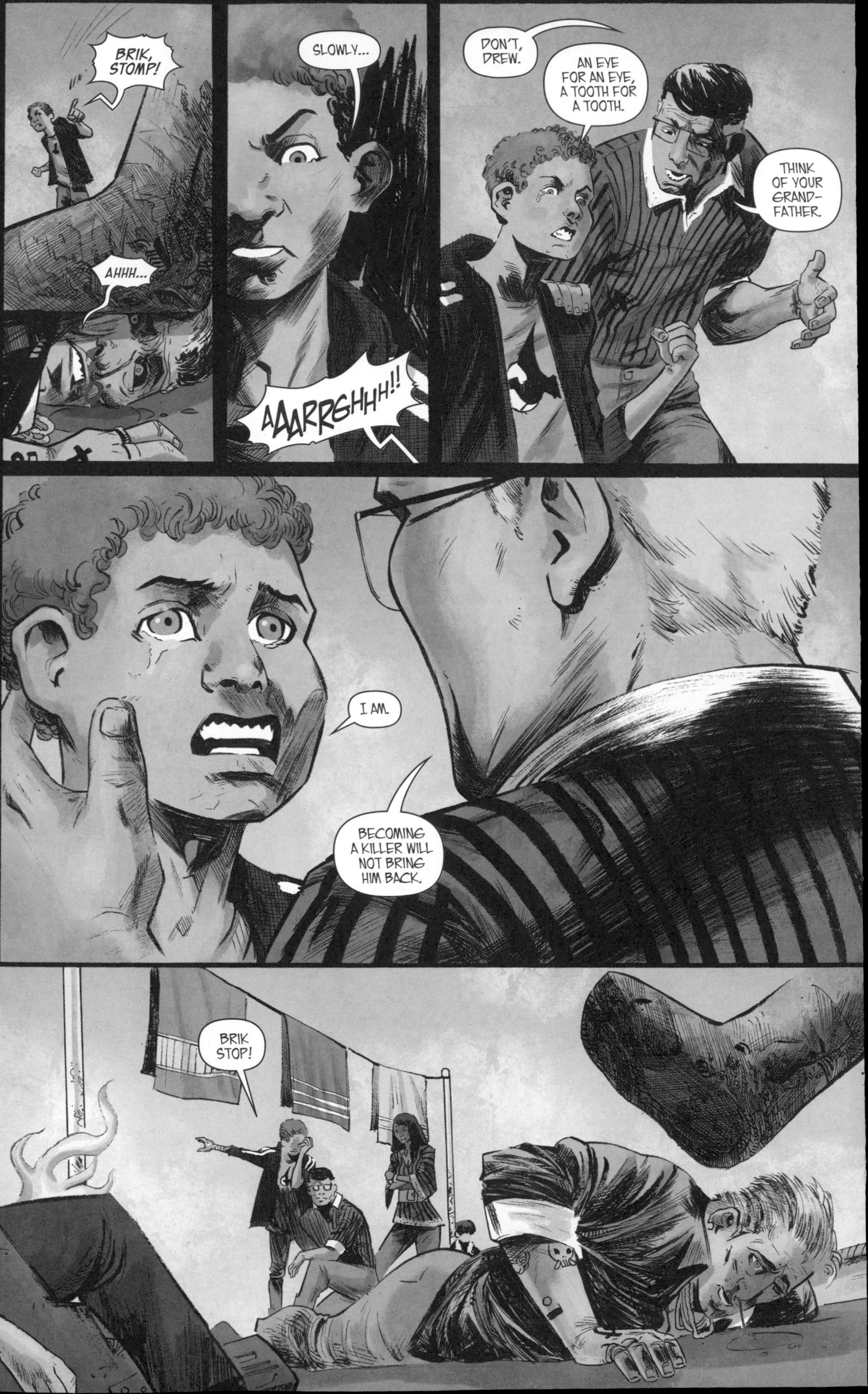
BRIK, STOMP!
AHHH...
SLOWLY...
AAARRGHHH!!
DON'T, DREW.
AN EYE FOR AN EYE, A TOOTH FOR A TOOTH.
THINK OF YOUR GRAND-FATHER.
I AM.
BECOMING A KILLER WILL NOT BRING HIM BACK.
BRIK STOP!

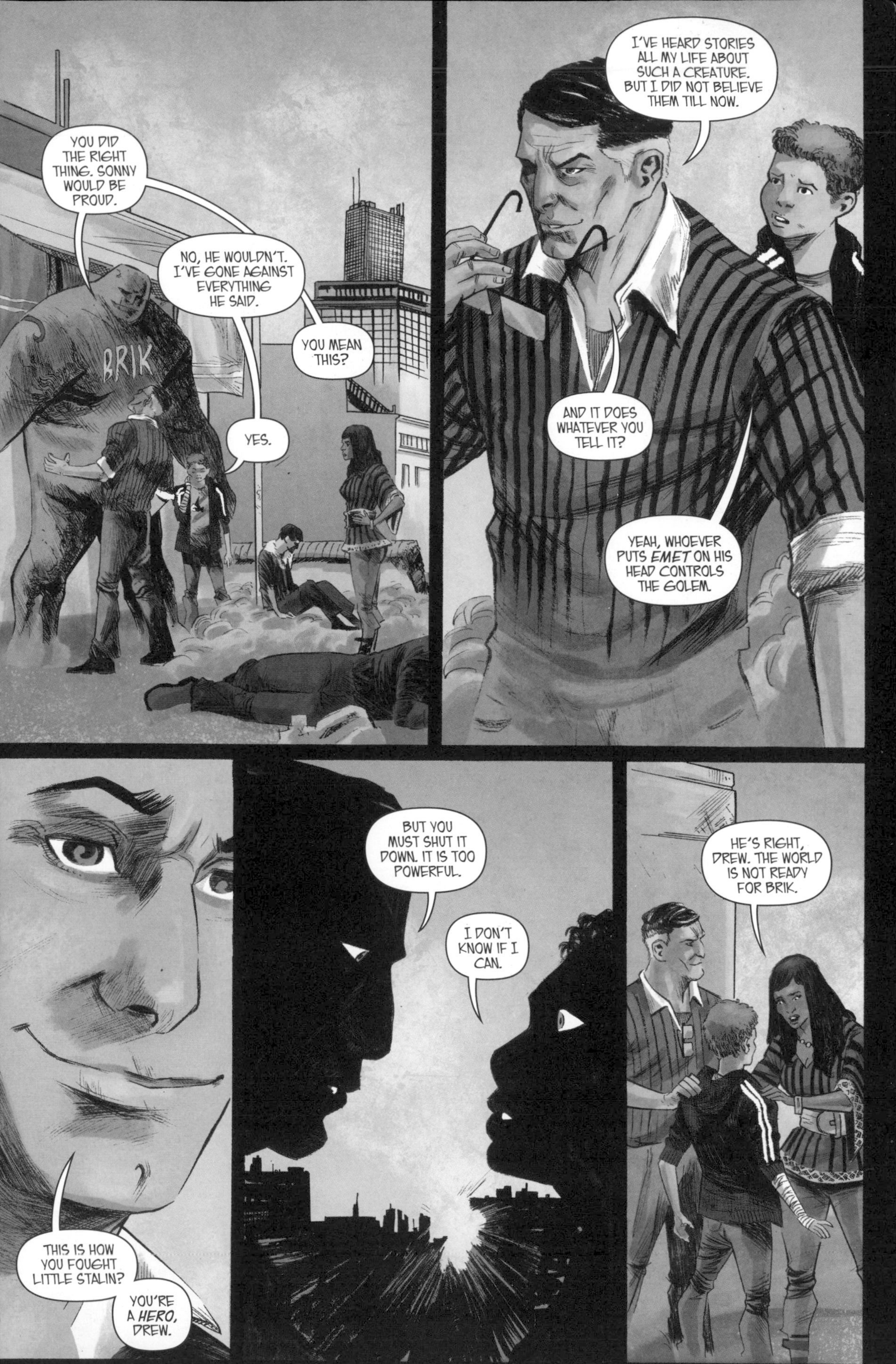
YOU DID THE RIGHT THING. SONNY WOULD BE PROUD.
NO, HE WOULDN'T. I'VE GONE AGAINST EVERYTHING HE SAID.
YOU MEAN THIS?
YES.
BRIK
I'VE HEARD STORIES ALL MY LIFE ABOUT SUCH A CREATURE. BUT I DID NOT BELIEVE THEM TILL NOW.
AND IT DOES WHATEVER YOU TELL IT?
YEAH, WHOEVER PUTS *EMET* ON HIS HEAD CONTROLS THE GOLEM.
THIS IS HOW YOU FOUGHT LITTLE STALIN?
YOU'RE A *HERO*, DREW.
BUT YOU MUST SHUT IT DOWN. IT IS TOO POWERFUL.
I DON'T KNOW IF I CAN.
HE'S RIGHT, DREW. THE WORLD IS NOT READY FOR BRIK.

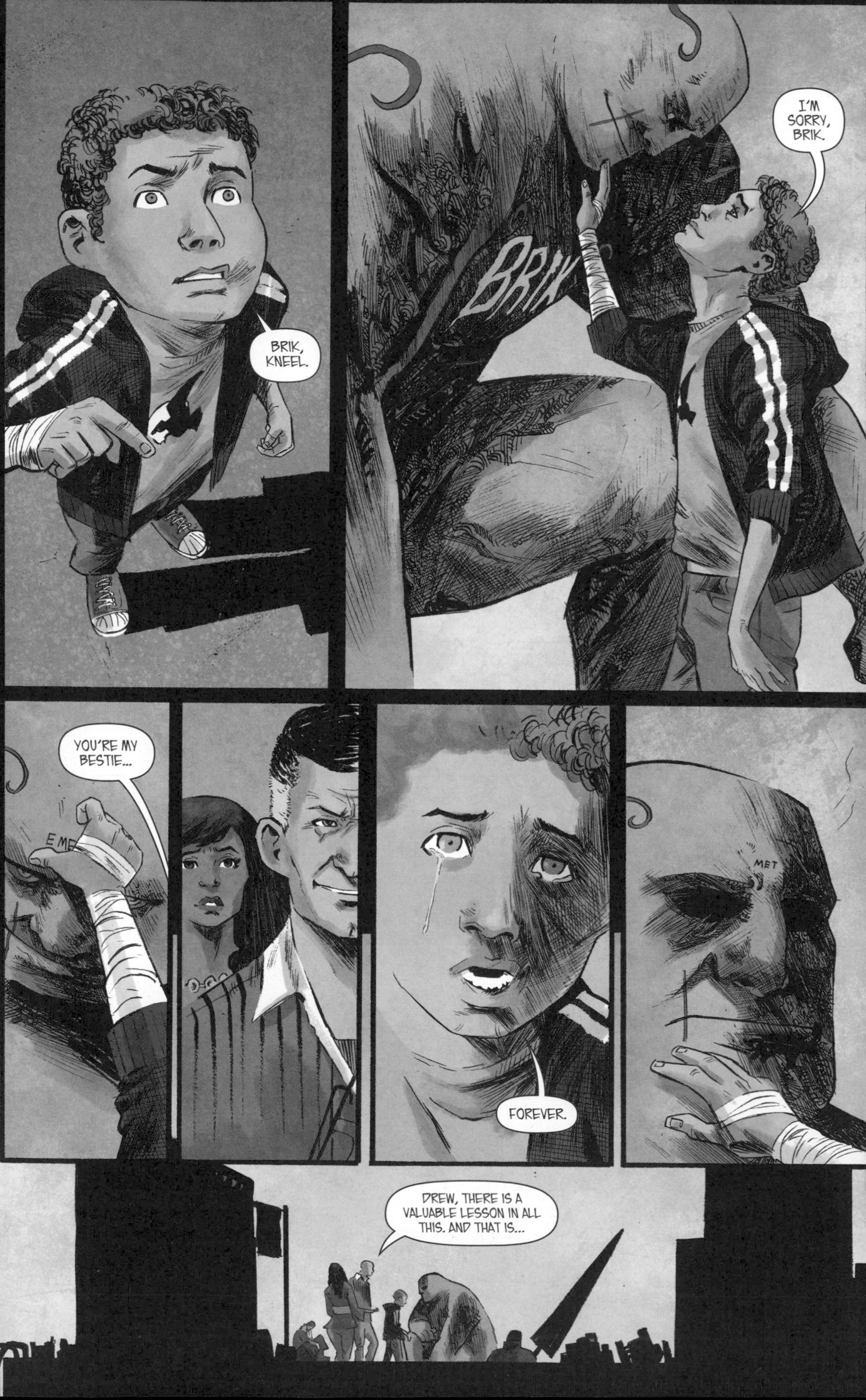
BRIK, KNEEL.
I'M SORRY, BRIK.
BRIK
YOU'RE MY BESTIE...
FOREVER.
DREW, THERE IS A VALUABLE LESSON IN ALL THIS. AND THAT IS...

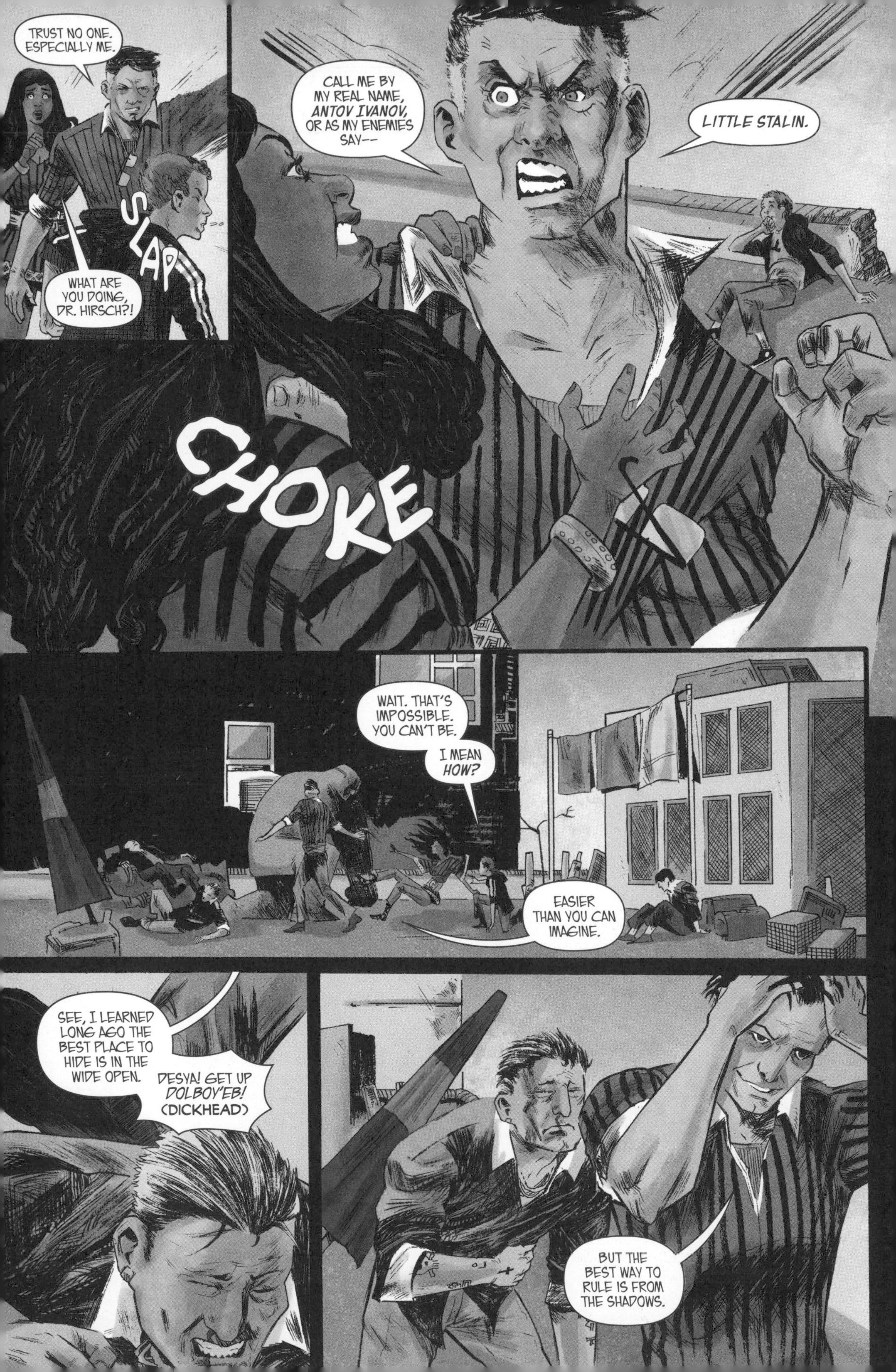
TRUST NO ONE. ESPECIALLY ME.
SLAP
WHAT ARE YOU DOING, DR. HIRSCH?!
CALL ME BY MY REAL NAME, ANTOV IVANOV, OR AS MY ENEMIES SAY--
LITTLE STALIN.
CHOKE
WAIT. THAT'S IMPOSSIBLE. YOU CAN'T BE.
I MEAN HOW?
EASIER THAN YOU CAN IMAGINE.
SEE, I LEARNED LONG AGO THE BEST PLACE TO HIDE IS IN THE WIDE OPEN.
DESYA! GET UP DOLBOY'EB! (DICKHEAD)
BUT THE BEST WAY TO RULE IS FROM THE SHADOWS.

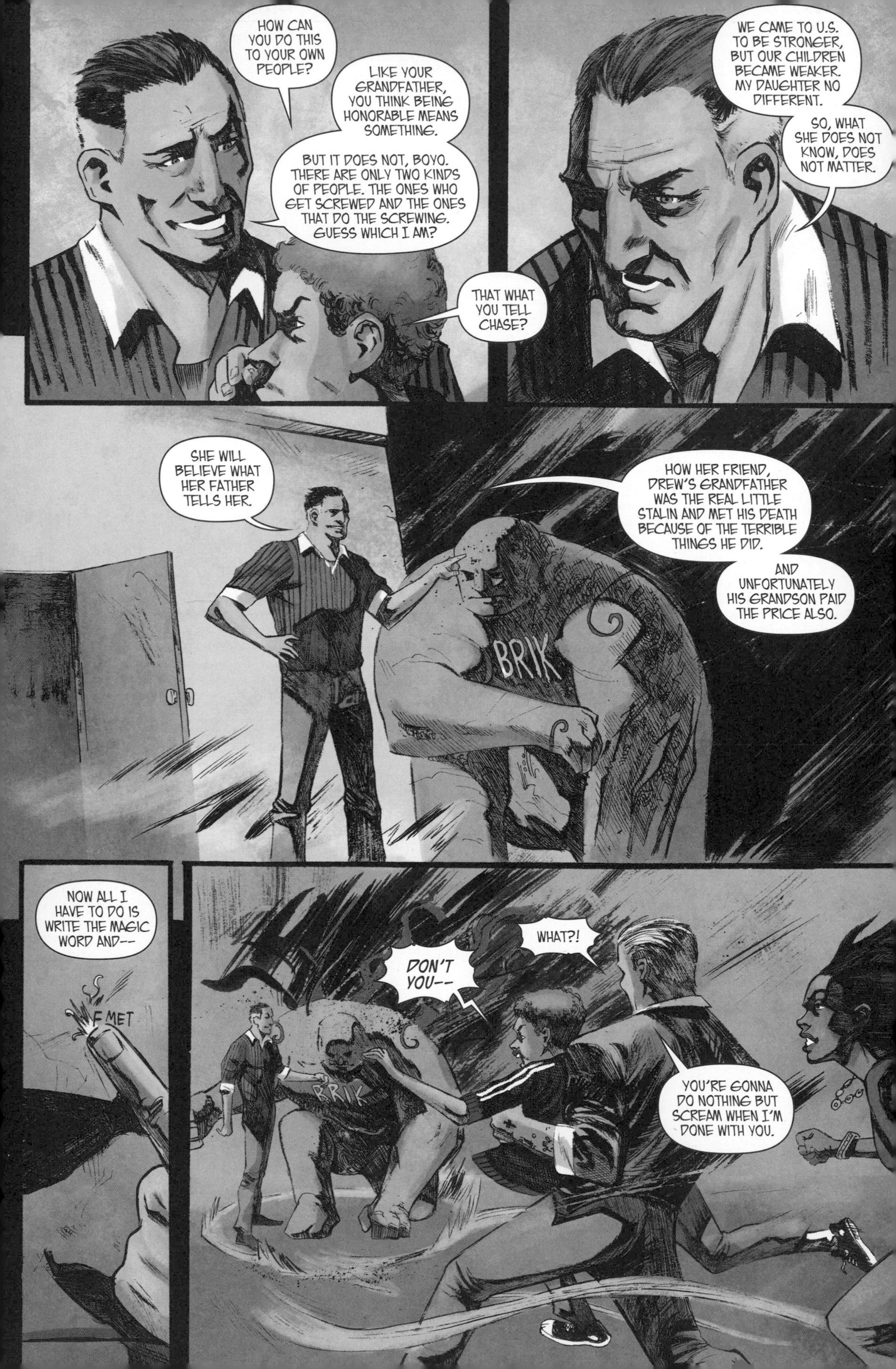

HOW CAN YOU DO THIS TO YOUR OWN PEOPLE?
LIKE YOUR GRANDFATHER, YOU THINK BEING HONORABLE MEANS SOMETHING.
BUT IT DOES NOT, BOYO. THERE ARE ONLY TWO KINDS OF PEOPLE. THE ONES WHO GET SCREWED AND THE ONES THAT DO THE SCREWING. GUESS WHICH I AM?
THAT WHAT YOU TELL CHASE?
WE CAME TO U.S. TO BE STRONGER, BUT OUR CHILDREN BECAME WEAKER. MY DAUGHTER NO DIFFERENT.
SO, WHAT SHE DOES NOT KNOW, DOES NOT MATTER.
SHE WILL BELIEVE WHAT HER FATHER TELLS HER.
HOW HER FRIEND, DREW'S GRANDFATHER WAS THE REAL LITTLE STALIN AND MET HIS DEATH BECAUSE OF THE TERRIBLE THINGS HE DID.
AND UNFORTUNATELY HIS GRANDSON PAID THE PRICE ALSO.
BRIK
NOW ALL I HAVE TO DO IS WRITE THE MAGIC WORD AND--
E MET
WHAT?!
DON'T YOU--
YOU'RE GONNA DO NOTHING BUT SCREAM WHEN I'M DONE WITH YOU.
BRIK

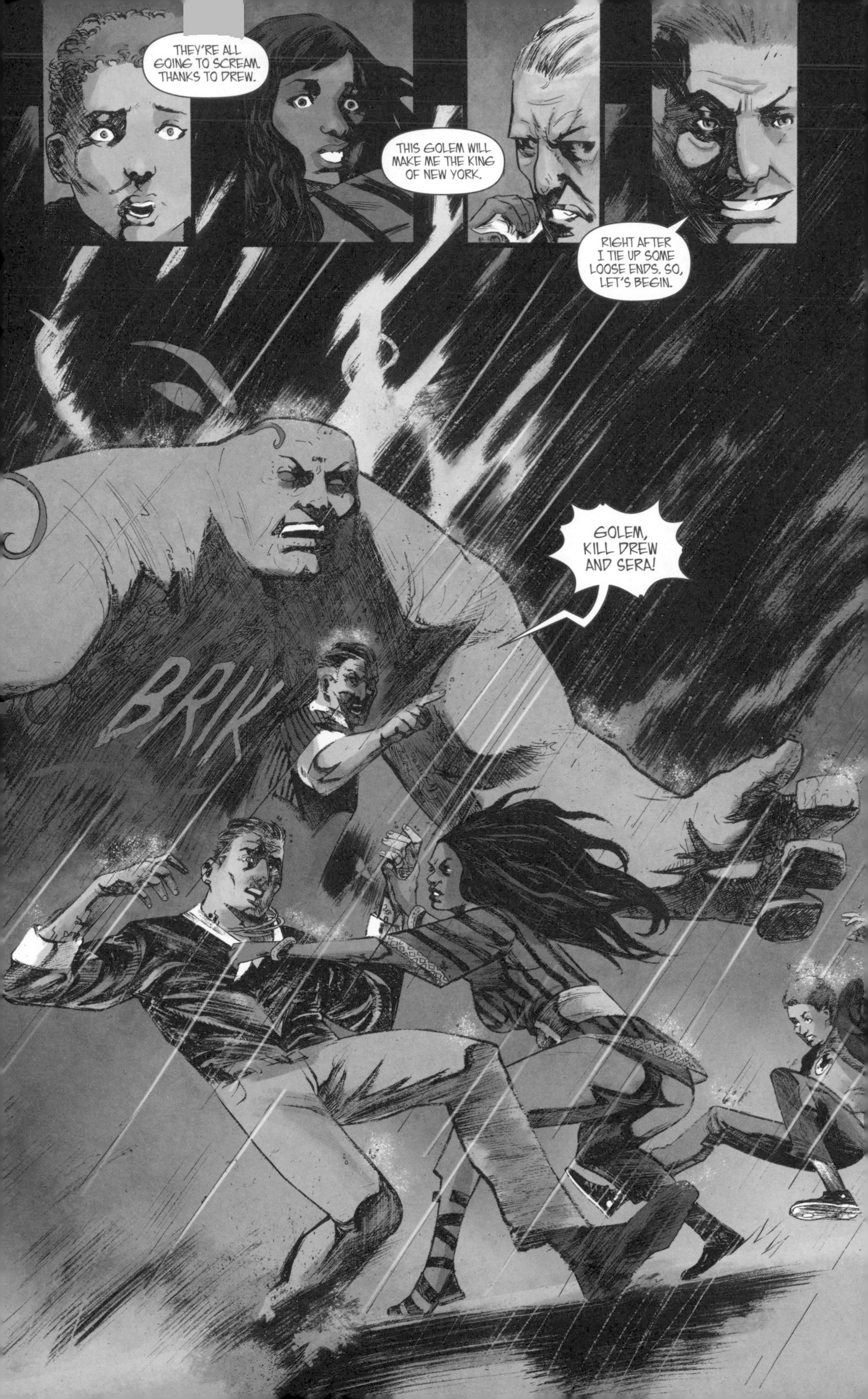
THEY'RE ALL GOING TO SCREAM THANKS TO DREW.
THIS GOLEM WILL MAKE ME THE KING OF NEW YORK.
RIGHT AFTER I TIE UP SOME LOOSE ENDS. SO, LET'S BEGIN.
GOLEM, KILL DREW AND SERA!
BRIK

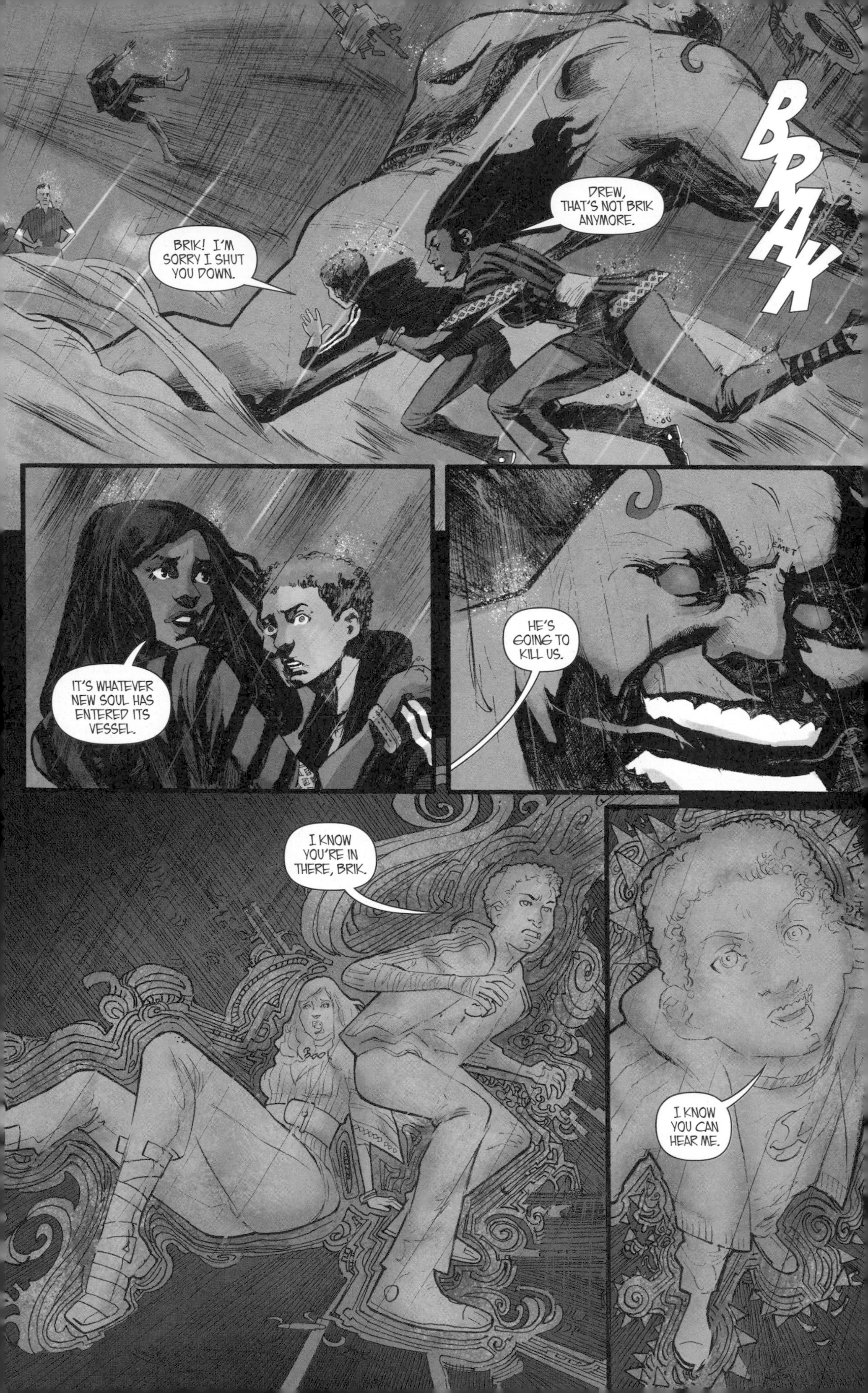
BRAK
DREW, THAT'S NOT BRIK ANYMORE.
BRIK! I'M SORRY I SHUT YOU DOWN.
IT'S WHATEVER NEW SOUL HAS ENTERED ITS VESSEL.
HE'S GOING TO KILL US.
I KNOW YOU'RE IN THERE, BRIK.
I KNOW YOU CAN HEAR ME.

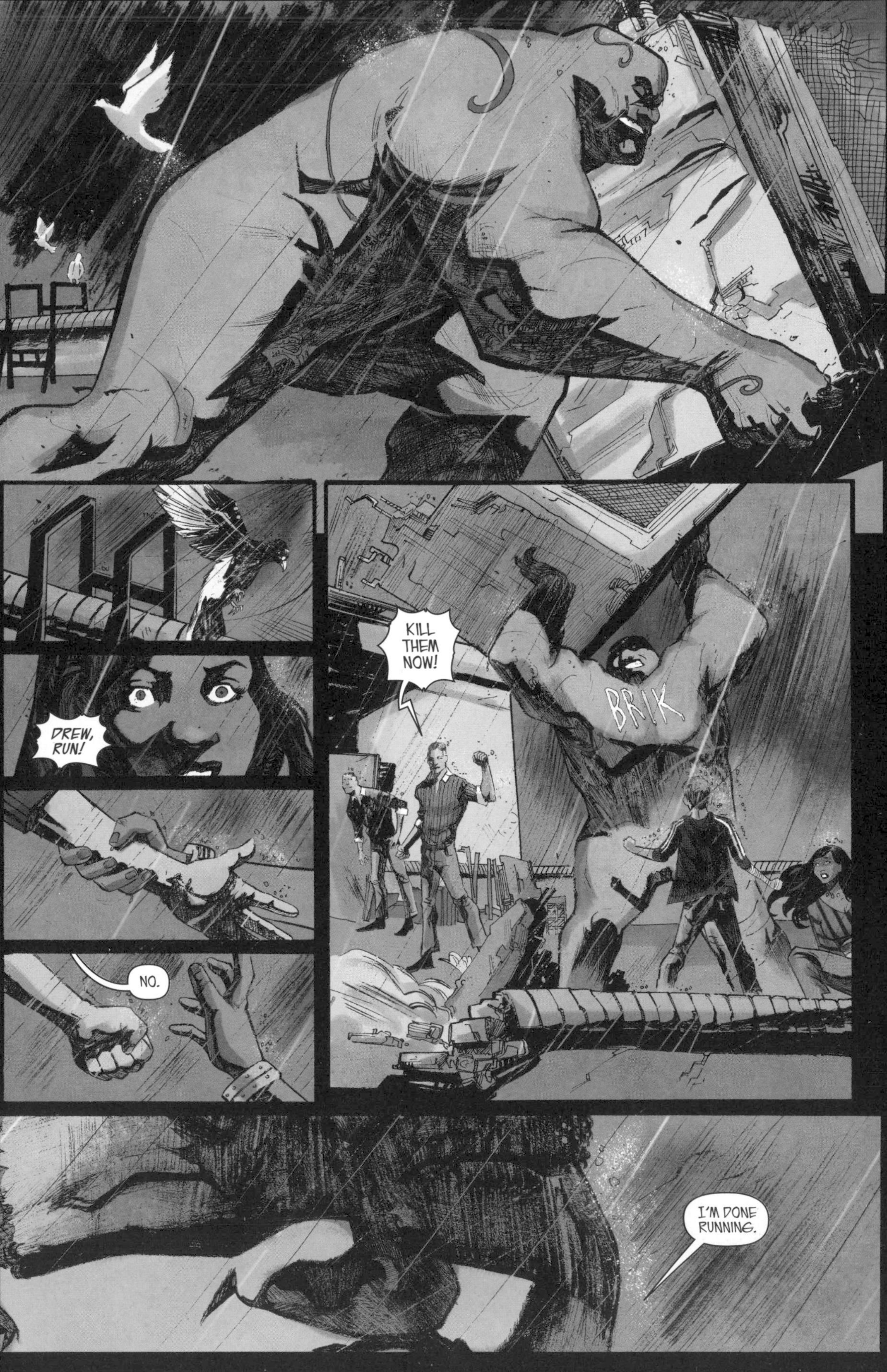
DREW, RUN!
NO.
KILL THEM NOW!
BRIK
I'M DONE RUNNING.

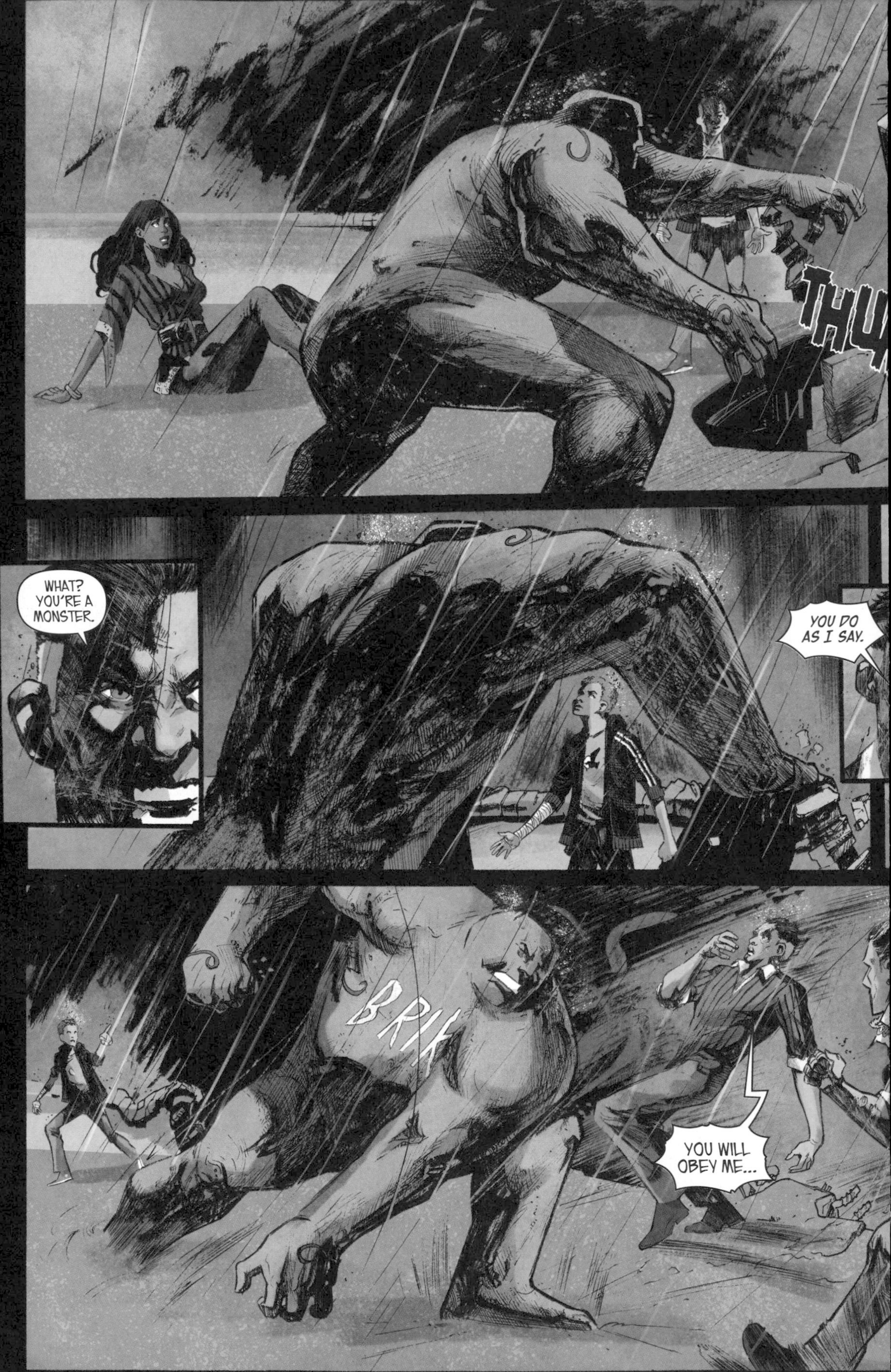
THU
WHAT? YOU'RE A MONSTER.
YOU DO AS I SAY.
BRIK
YOU WILL OBEY ME...

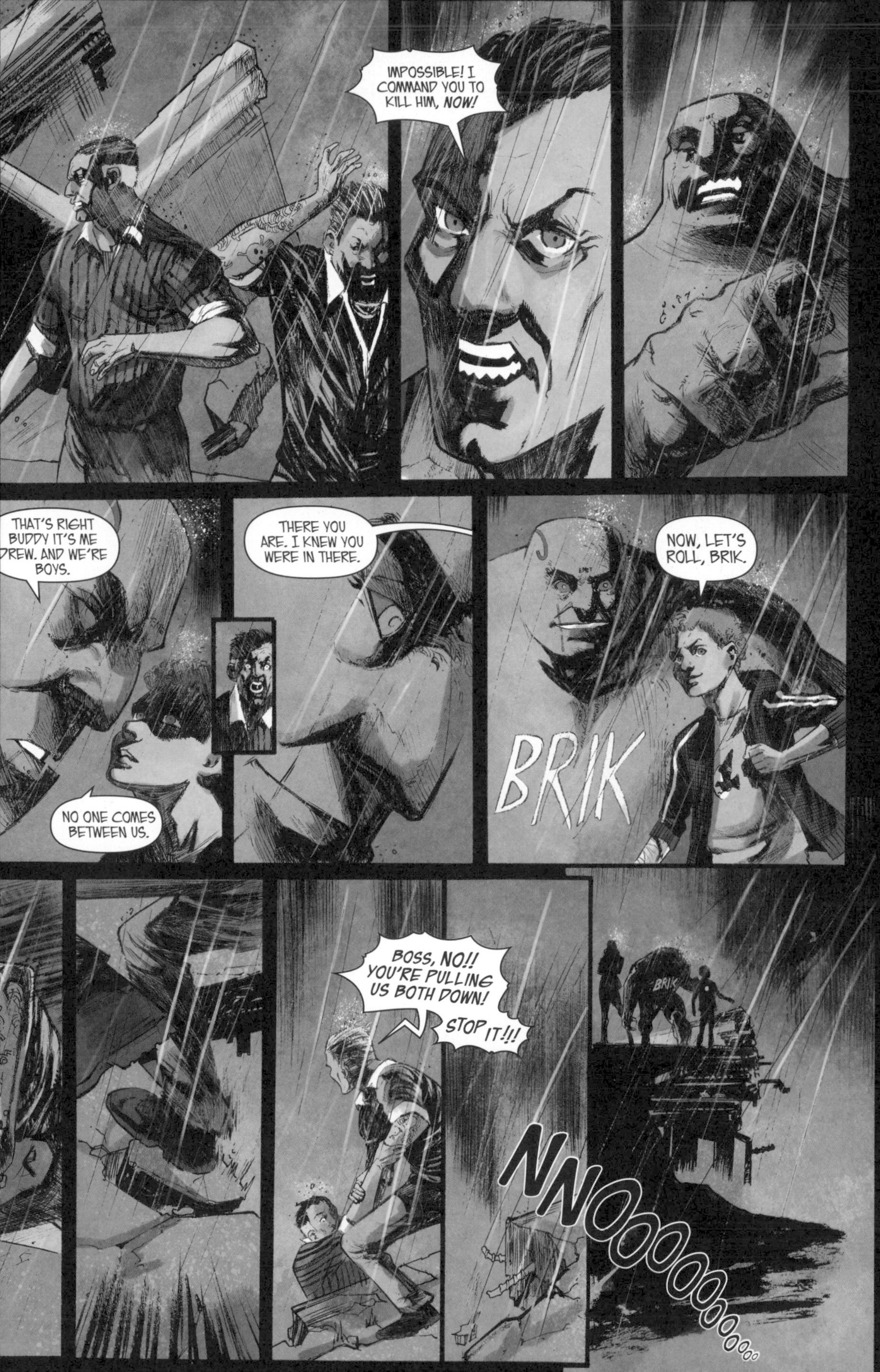
IMPOSSIBLE! I COMMAND YOU TO KILL HIM, NOW!
THAT'S RIGHT BUDDY IT'S ME DREW. AND WE'RE BOYS.
NO ONE COMES BETWEEN US.
THERE YOU ARE. I KNEW YOU WERE IN THERE.
NOW, LET'S ROLL, BRIK.
BRIK
BOSS, NO!! YOU'RE PULLING US BOTH DOWN!
STOP IT!!!
BRIK
NNOOOOOOoooo

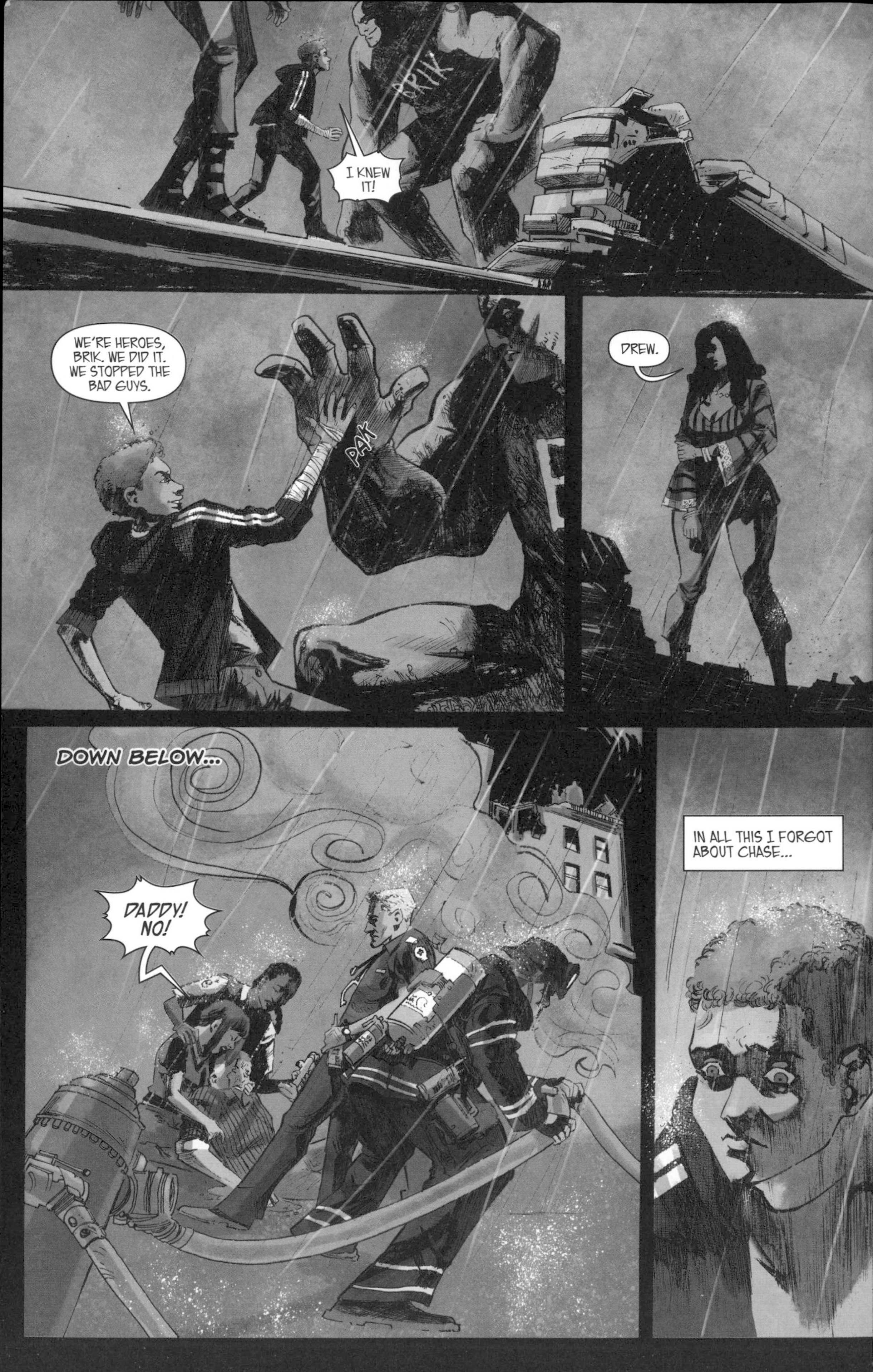
I KNEW IT!
WE'RE HEROES, BRIK. WE DID IT. WE STOPPED THE BAD GUYS.
PAK
DREW.
DOWN BELOW...
DADDY! NO!
IN ALL THIS I FORGOT ABOUT CHASE...

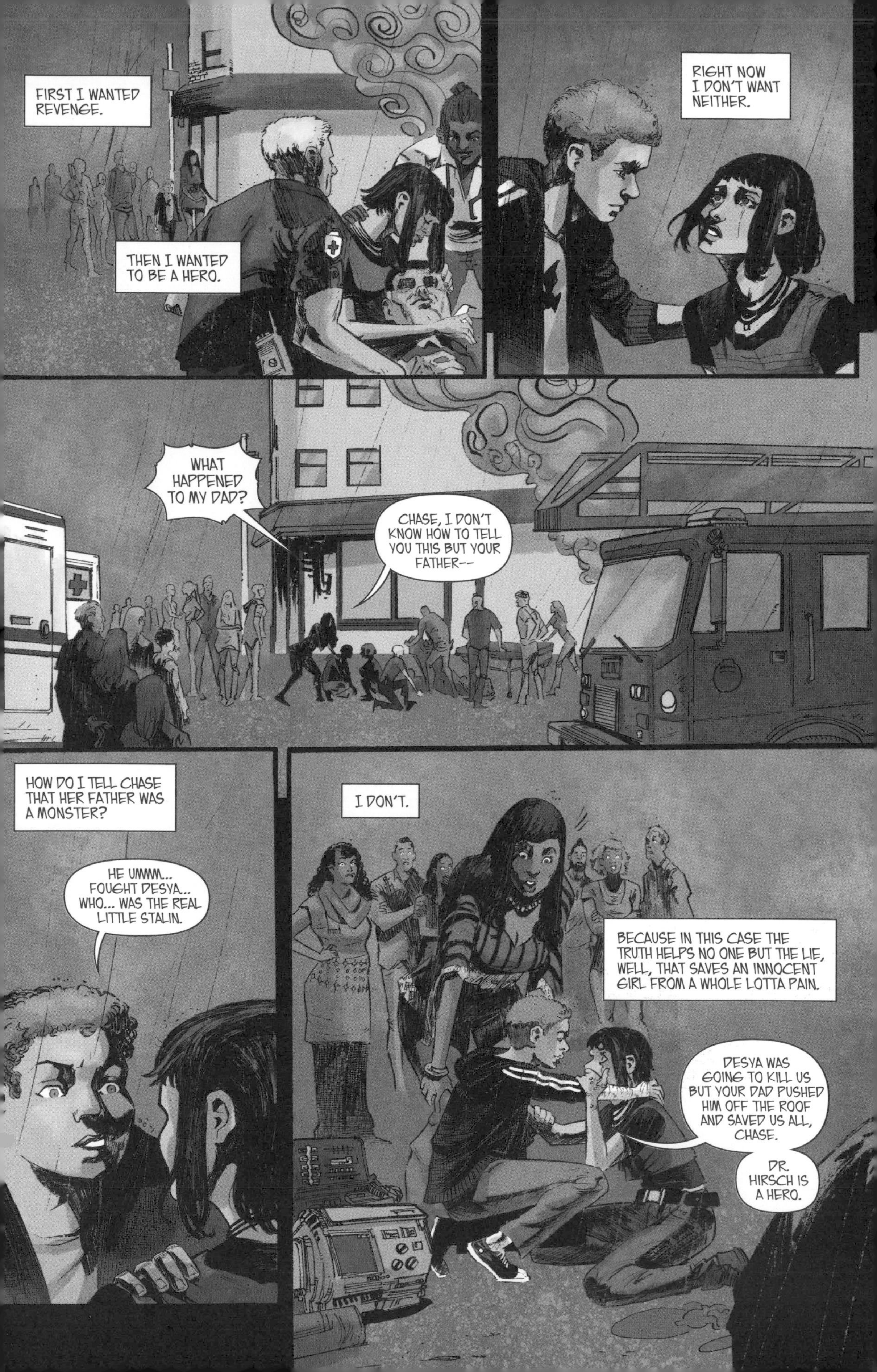
FIRST I WANTED REVENGE.
THEN I WANTED TO BE A HERO.
RIGHT NOW I DON'T WANT NEITHER.
WHAT HAPPENED TO MY DAD?
CHASE, I DON'T KNOW HOW TO TELL YOU THIS BUT YOUR FATHER--
HOW DO I TELL CHASE THAT HER FATHER WAS A MONSTER?
HE UMMM... FOUGHT DESYA... WHO... WAS THE REAL LITTLE STALIN.
I DON'T.
BECAUSE IN THIS CASE THE TRUTH HELPS NO ONE BUT THE LIE, WELL, THAT SAVES AN INNOCENT GIRL FROM A WHOLE LOTTA PAIN.
DESYA WAS GOING TO KILL US BUT YOUR DAD PUSHED HIM OFF THE ROOF AND SAVED US ALL, CHASE.
DR. HIRSCH IS A HERO.

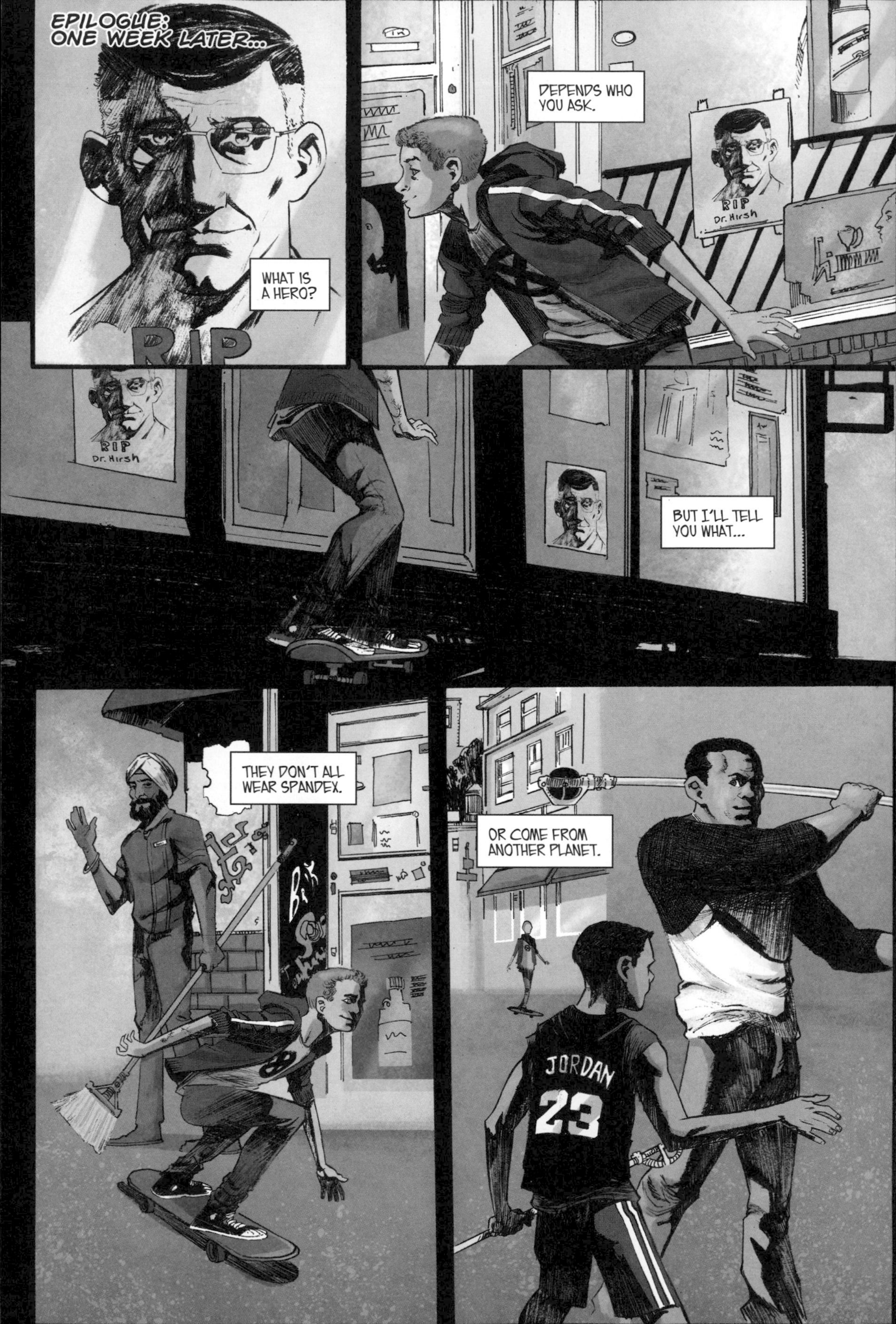
EPILOGUE: ONE WEEK LATER...
RIP
WHAT IS A HERO?
DEPENDS WHO YOU ASK.
RIP
Dr. Hirsh
RIP
Dr. Hirsh
BUT I'LL TELL YOU WHAT...
THEY DON'T ALL WEAR SPANDEX.
OR COME FROM ANOTHER PLANET.
JORDAN
23

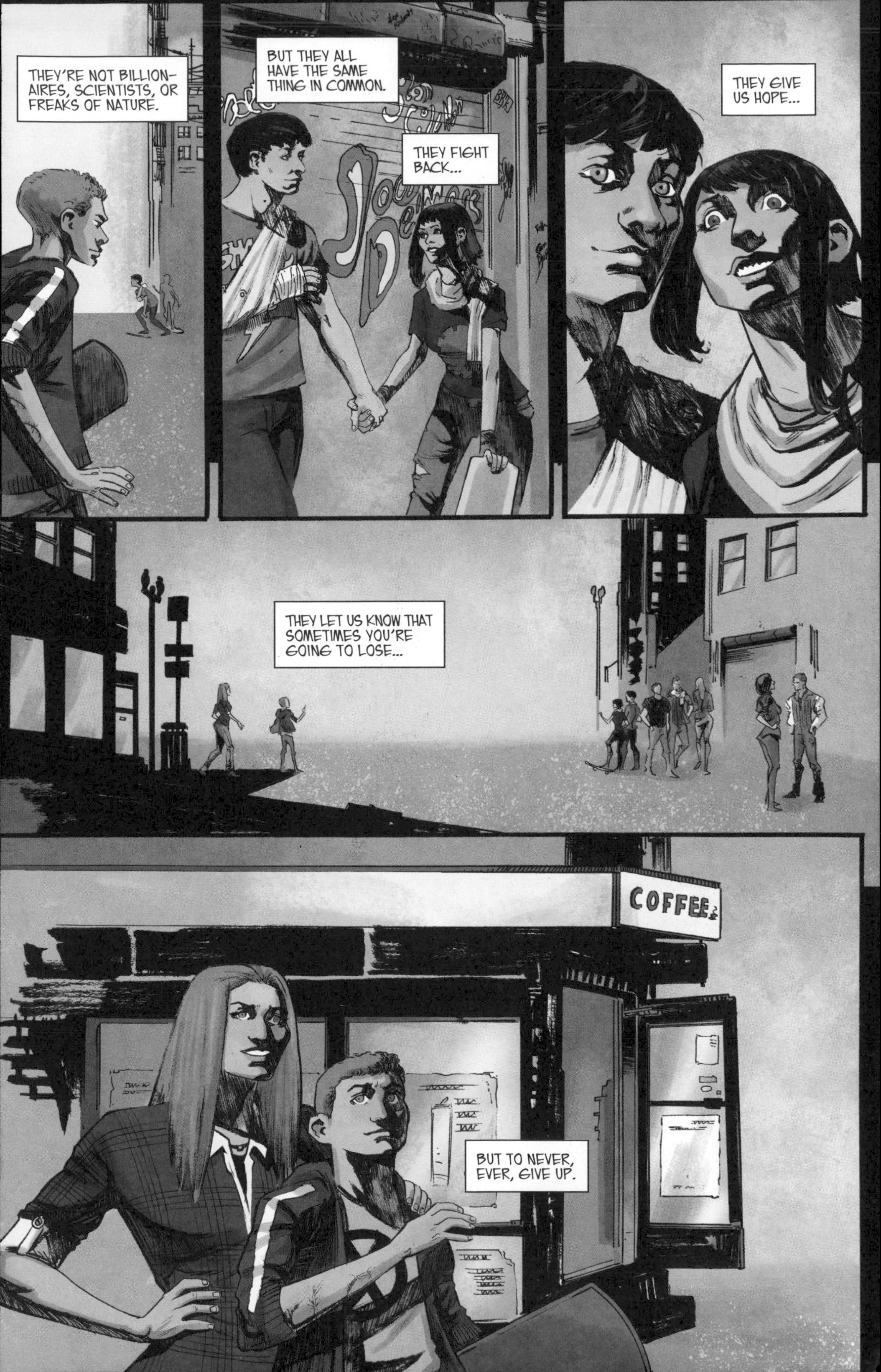
THEY'RE NOT BILLIONAIRES, SCIENTISTS, OR FREAKS OF NATURE.
BUT THEY ALL HAVE THE SAME THING IN COMMON.
THEY FIGHT BACK...
THEY GIVE US HOPE...
THEY LET US KNOW THAT SOMETIMES YOU'RE GOING TO LOSE...
COFFEE
BUT TO NEVER, EVER, GIVE UP.

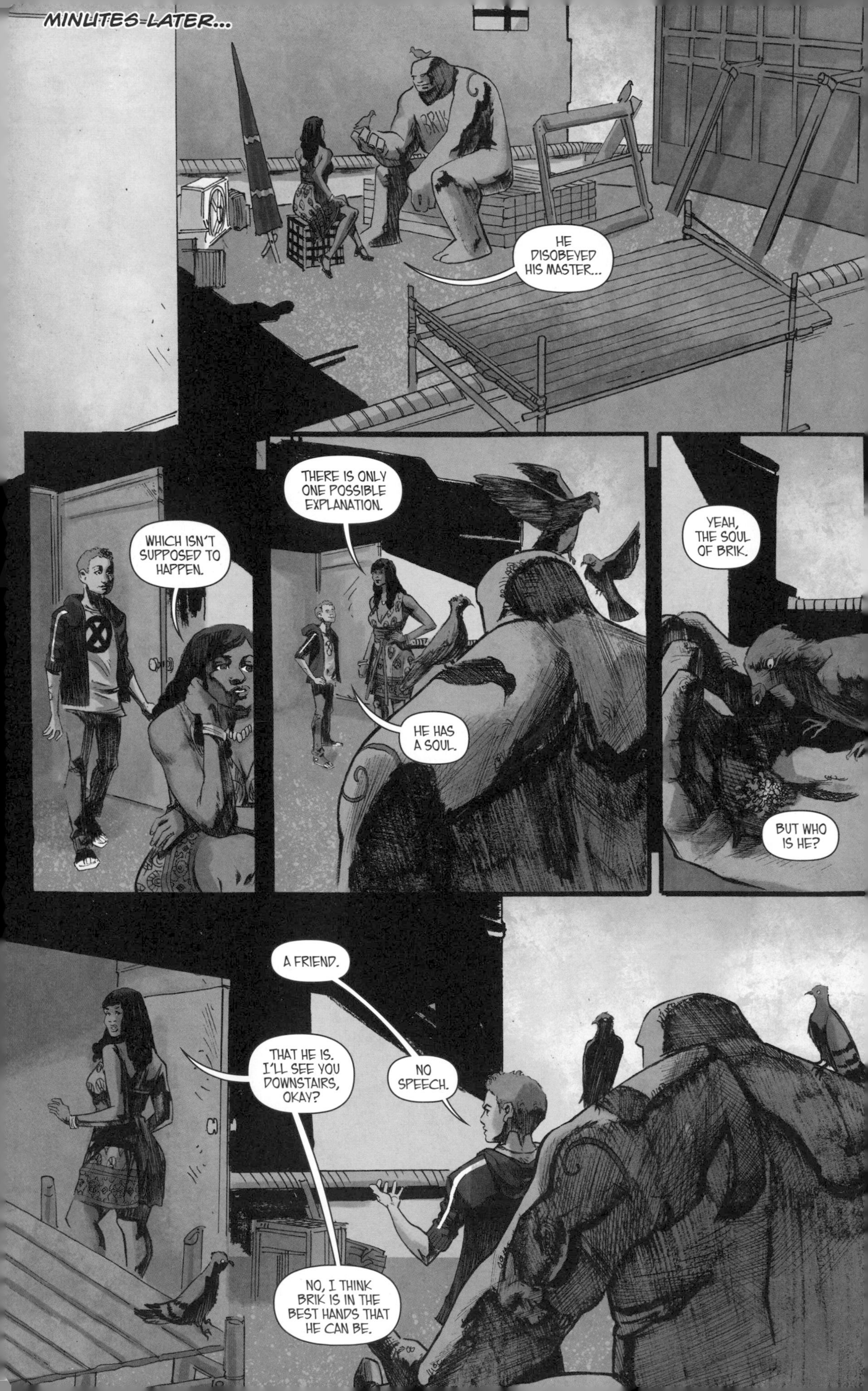
MINUTES LATER...
HE DISOBEYED HIS MASTER...
WHICH ISN'T SUPPOSED TO HAPPEN.
THERE IS ONLY ONE POSSIBLE EXPLANATION.
HE HAS A SOUL.
YEAH, THE SOUL OF BRIK.
BUT WHO IS HE?
A FRIEND.
NO SPEECH.
THAT HE IS. I'LL SEE YOU DOWNSTAIRS, OKAY?
NO, I THINK BRIK IS IN THE BEST HANDS THAT HE CAN BE.

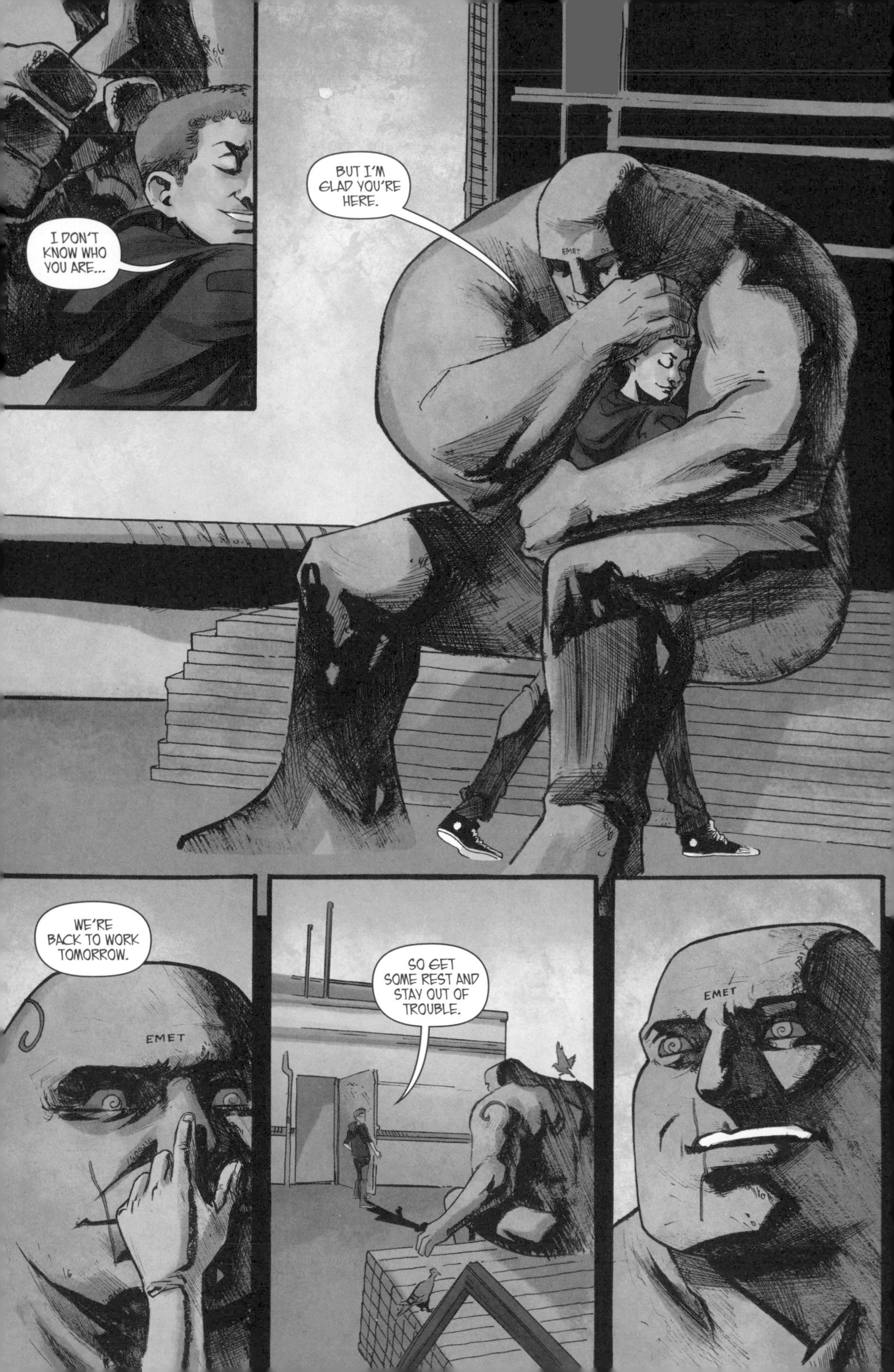
I DON'T KNOW WHO YOU ARE...
BUT I'M GLAD YOU'RE HERE.
EMET
WE'RE BACK TO WORK TOMORROW.
EMET
SO GET SOME REST AND STAY OUT OF TROUBLE.
EMET

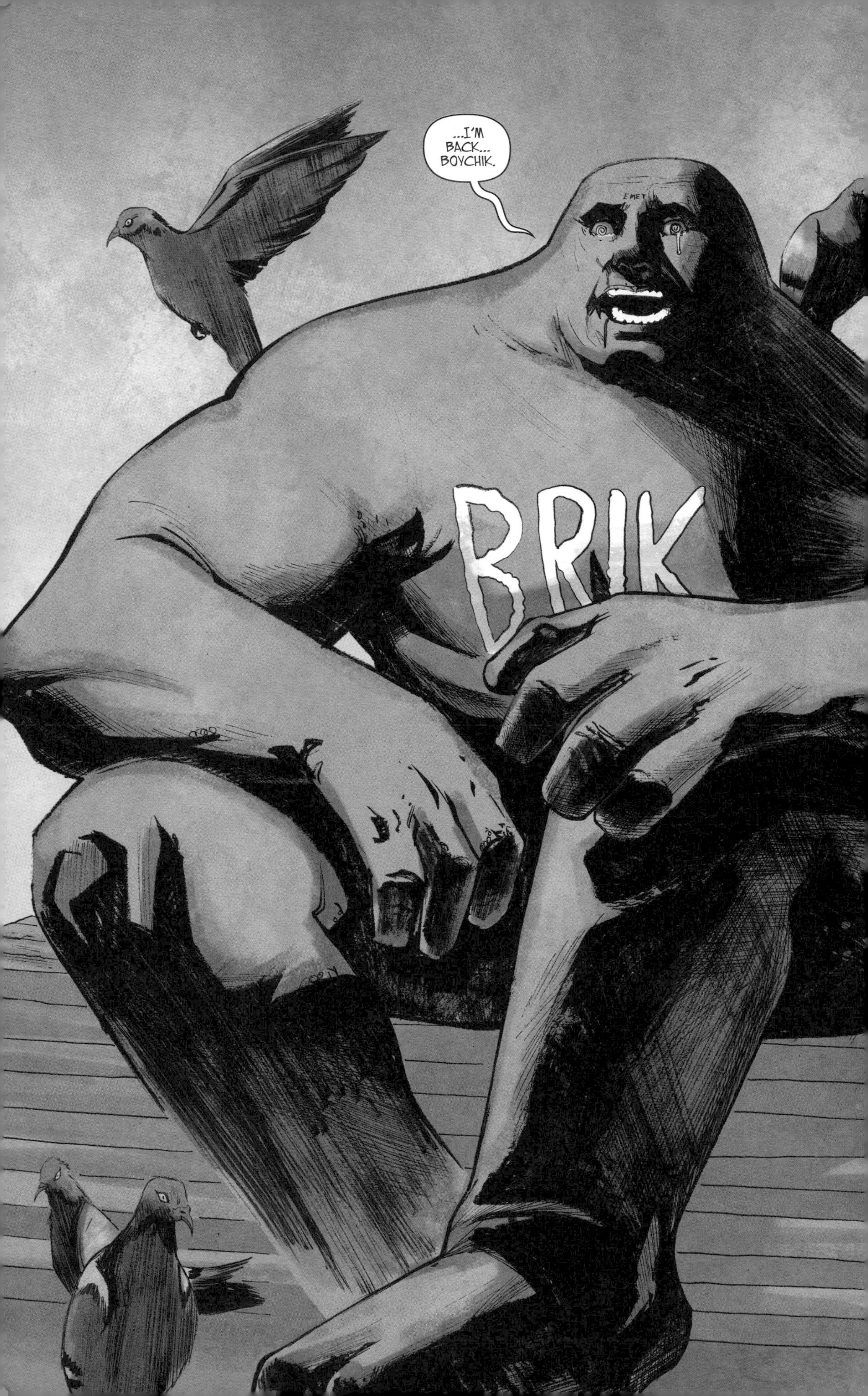
...I'M BACK... BOYCHIK.
EMET
BRIK

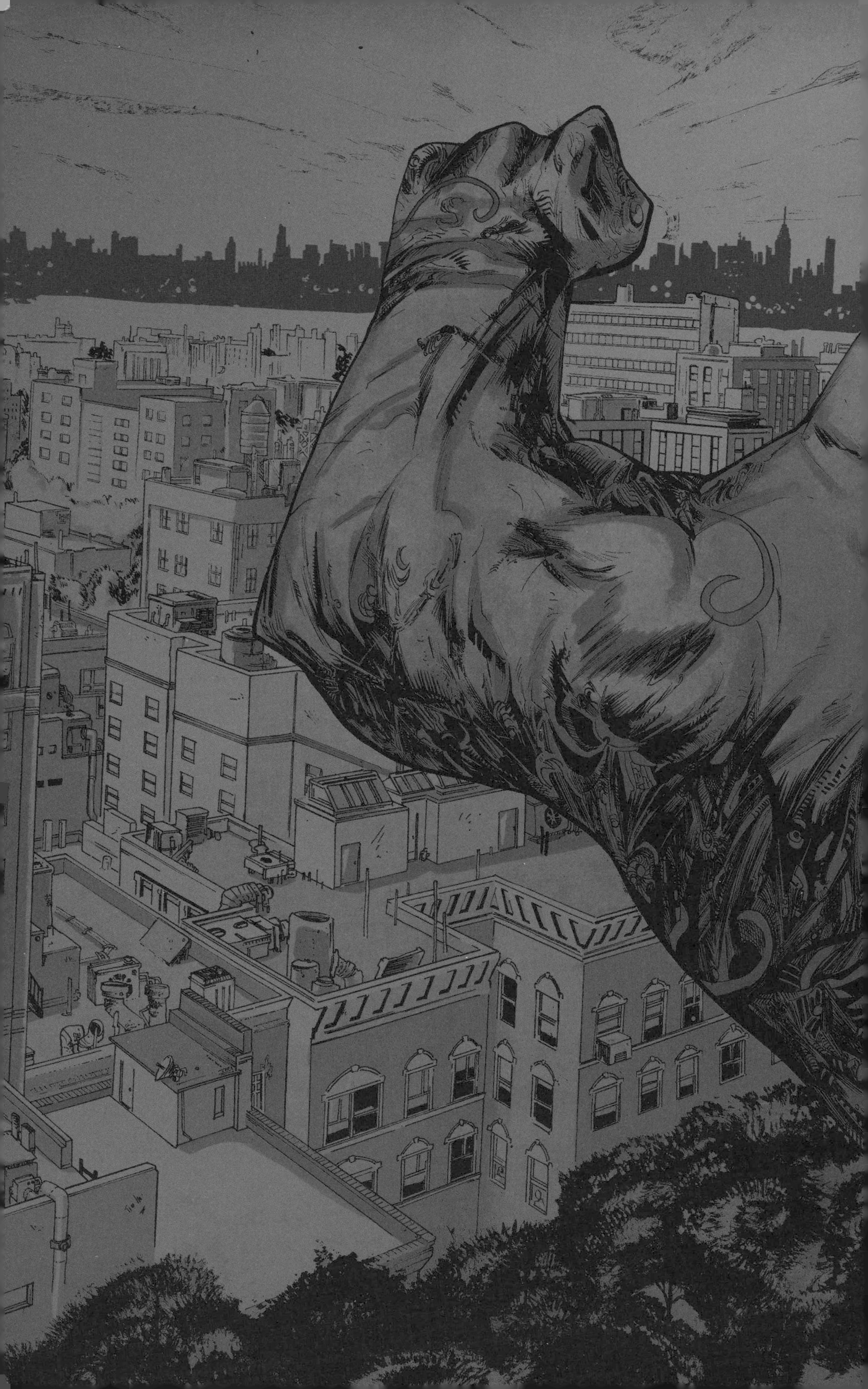

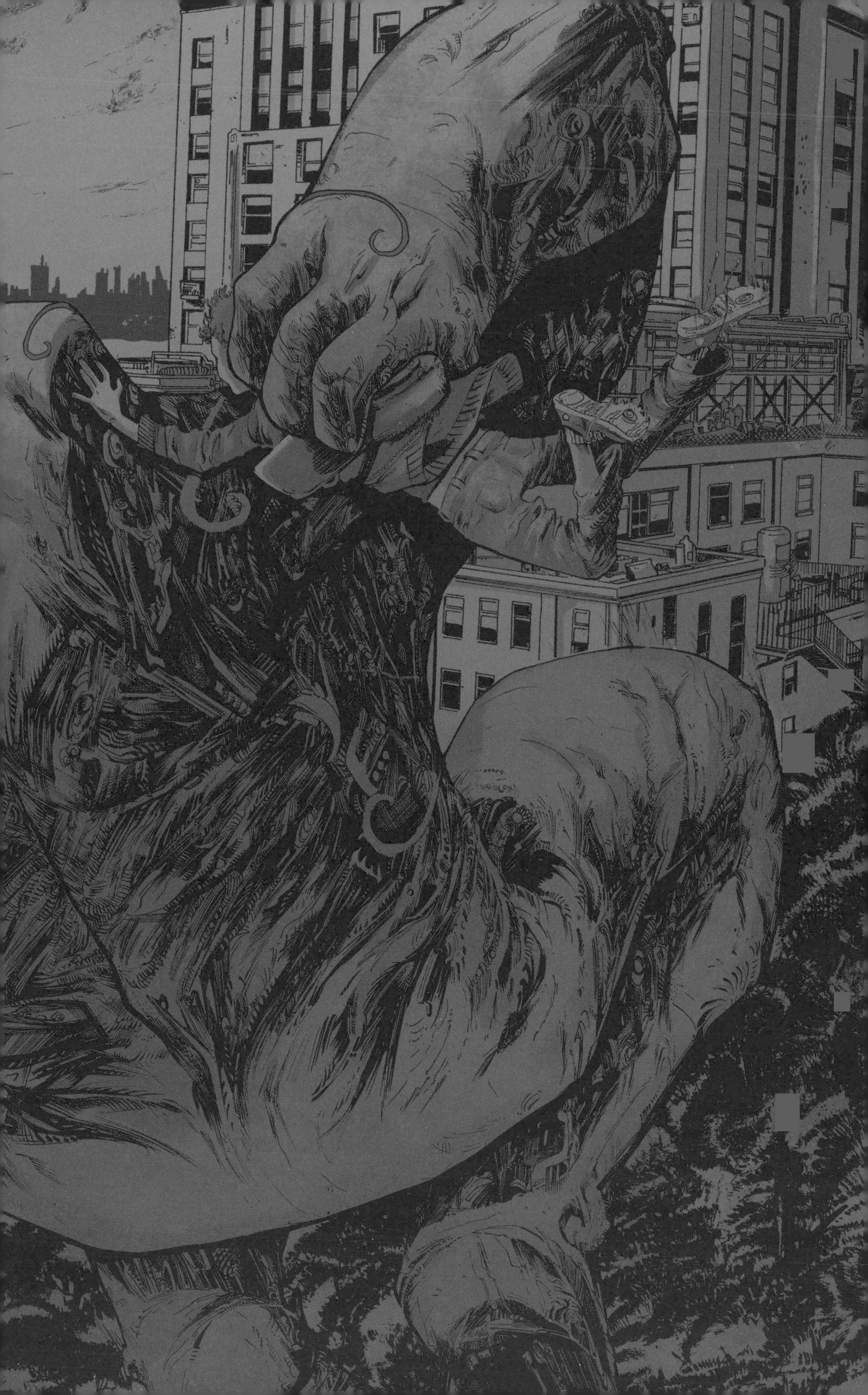

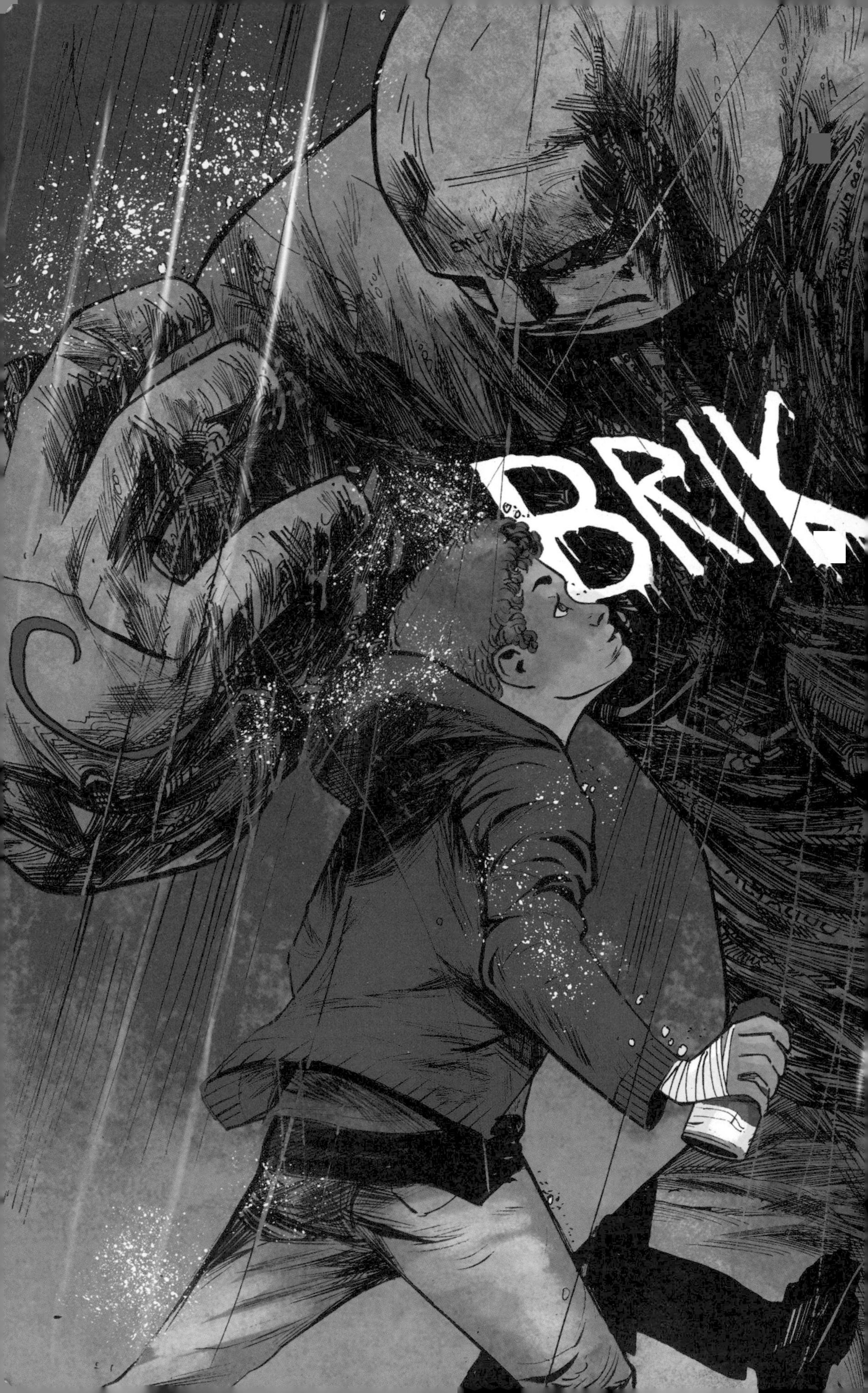
BRIK

ABOUT THE AUTHORS

ADAM GLASS

Though NYC will always be home, Adam Glass resides in Los Angeles and is a TV Writer/Executive Producer of such shows as **SUPERNATURAL**, **COLD CASE** and now is the co-show runner of **CRIMINAL MINDS: BEYOND BORDERS** on CBS. When Adam is not writing for TV or films, he's writing graphic novels. Marvel Comics', **DEADPOOL: SUICIDE KINGS** and DC Comics', **SUICIDE SQUAD** were all NY Times Best Sellers. Other books Adam has written or co-written for Marvel Comics are, **DEADPOOL: PULP**, **LUKE CAGE: NOIR**, **DEADPOOL TEAM-UP** and **LUKE CAGE: ORIGINS**; and for DC, **JLA ANNUAL** and the Flashpoint Series, **LEGION OF DOOM**. Adam also wrote **ROUGH RIDERS** for Aftershock Comics, which is a reimagining of Teddy Roosevelt's involvement in the Spanish-American War.

MIKE BENSON

Mike Benson started his career in TV. He has been a writer and show-runner on a number of Emmy-nominated shows including **THE BERNIE MAC SHOW** and **ENTOURAGE**. When Benson is not writing for TV, he's writing for Marvel and DC, home of the colorful characters that he loved so much as a kid. Mike's first project was scribing a Frank Castle story in **PUNISHER MAX ANNUAL #1**, and writing three Moon Knight arcs which was a major step in his comic writing career. Benson also proved his comic writing chops with **DEADPOOL: SUICIDE KINGS**, which made the NY Times Best Seller List and **LUKE CAGE: NOIR**, which won the prestigious Glyph Award for best book of the year. He lives in Los Angeles with his wife, twin boys and English Bulldog.

HARWINDER SINGH

Harwinder Singh is a professional illustrator, painter, and comic artist working out of Ellicott City, Maryland. Singh was born in Punjab, India and at the age of nine, immigrated to the United States of America where he quickly formed a love for comics, cartoons and video games. Harwinder's love of drawing eventually led to art school, and the rest is history. **BRIK**, which he co-created with Adam Glass & Mike Benson, is his first comic book series.

GONZALO DUARTE

Gonzalo Duarte was born in Buenos Aires, Argentina, in 1986. After a couple of years working in the animation industry he made the jump to comic books, his lifelong passion. He's been working since 2009 as a writer in the Argentine comics scene on magazines such as **TERMINUS** and **PROXIMA**, and as a colorist on titles such as Boom! Studios' **BIG TROUBLE IN LITTLE CHINA** and Oni Press' **HELLBREAK** and **BRIK**.

READ MORE FROM ONI PRESS!

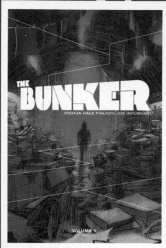

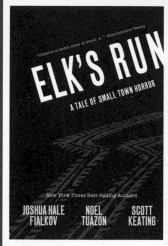